Recording Great Audio Tracks

in a Small Studio

The S.M.A.R.T. guide to

Bill Gibson

THOMSON
COURSE TECHNOLOGY
Professional ■ Trade ■ Reference

The S.M.A.R.T. Guide to Recording Great Audio Tracks in a Small Studio
by Bill Gibson

Front cover image of the C100 mixer is courtesy of Solid State Logic. Front cover images of Taye drums, Gibson CL-40 acoustic guitar, and body text photos taken by Bill Gibson except front cover Martin headstock provided by Steve Ramirez.

Publisher and GM of Course PTR: Stacy L. Hiquet
Associate Director of Marketing: Sarah O'Donnell
Marketing Manager: Kristin Eisenzopf
Manager of Editorial Services: Heather Talbot
Executive Editor: Mike Lawson
Senior Editor: Mark Garvey
Marketing Coordinator: Jordan Casey
PTR Editorial Services Coordinator: Elizabeth Furbish
Interior Layout Tech: Bill Gibson
Cover Designer: Stephen Ramirez
DVD Producer: Bill Gibson
Indexer: Kelly Talbot
Proofreader: Cathleen D. Snyder

ISBN: 1-59200-695-7
Library of Congress Catalog Card Number: 2005921046
Printed in the United States of America
05 06 07 08 09 BU 10 9 8 7 6 5 4 3 2 1

THOMSON
COURSE TECHNOLOGY
Professional ■ Trade ■ Reference

Thomson Course Technology PTR, a division of Thomson Course Technology
25 Thomson Place
Boston, MA 02210
http://www.courseptr.com

Dedication

This book is dedicated to my daughter, Kristi. You have been a source of constant joy in my life—you are true blessing. A father could not be more proud of a daughter than I am of you. I love you.

Acknowledgements

To all the folks who have helped support the development and integrity of these books.
Thank you for your continued support and interest in providing great tools for us all to use.

Acoustic Sciences, Inc.
Antares
Gibson Guitars
Mackie
Mike Kay at Ted Brown Music in Tacoma, WA
Monster Cable
MOTU
Primacoustic Studio Acoustics
Radial Engineering
Sabian Cymbals
Shure
Spectrasonics
Taye Drums
Universal Audio
WAVES Plugins

About the Author

Bill Gibson, president of Northwest Music and Recording, has spent the last 25 years writing, recording, producing, and teaching music and has become well-known for his production, performance, and teaching skills. As an instructor at Green River College in Auburn, Washington, holding various degrees in composition, arranging, education, and recording, he developed a practical and accessible teaching style which provided the basis for what was to come—15 books, a DVD, and a VHS video for MixBooks/ArtistPro, along with a dozen online courses for members of ArtistPro.com. Gibson's writings are acclaimed for their straightforward and understandable explanations of recording concepts and applications.

Introduction

This is *The S.M.A.R.T. Guide to Recording Great Audio Tracks in a Small Studio*. The title stands for Serious Music and Audio Recording Techniques, and everything contained in this series is designed to help you learn to capture seriously great sound and music. These books are written by a producer/engineer with a degree in composition and arranging, not in electronics. All explanations are straightforward and pragmatic. If you're a regular person who loves music and wants to produce recordings that hold their own in the marketplace, these books are definitely written just for you. If you're a student of the recording process, the explanations contained in these books could be some of the most enlightening and easy to understand that you'll find. In addition, the audio and video examples on the accompanying DVD were produced in a direct and simple manner. Each of these examples delivers content that's rich with meaning, accessible, and very pertinent to the process of learning to record great-sounding audio.

Table of Contents

Chapter 2 - Recording Great Electric Guitar Tracks 31

Chapter 3 - Recording Great Acoustic Guitar Tracks.................71

Chapter 4 - Recording Great Drum and Percussion Tracks 97

Chapter 7 - Recording Great Piano and Rhodes Tracks..............245

Audio and Video Examples

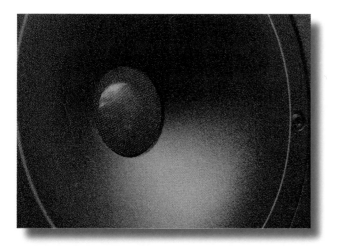

Preface

Welcome to the second book in the *S.M.A.R.T. Guide* series from Thomson Course PTR. This edition is designed to show you the ins and outs of recording great tracks, focusing on the vocals and the basic rhythm section instruments: piano, guitars, bass, and drums.

The explanations and examples in this book will help you get great sounds, whether you're operating in your home studio or in a professional recording facility. However, if you're creating music in a small studio or at home, this book has hundreds of great time-tested techniques designed to specifically help you. The most important factor involved in getting great sounds anywhere is what you know, not where you are.

Be sure to listen to and watch the enclosed DVD. The audio examples demonstrate many of the concepts that are explained in the text and accompanying illustrations. The video examples show you specifically how to optimize your recordings in crucial musical situations. Instructionally, they are very powerful. These video clips are produced with your education in mind, You won't find a lot of rapid-motion, highly stylized shots; you will find easy-to-understand instructional video that is edited for optimal instruction and learning.

Audio Examples are indicated like this.

Video Examples are indicated like this.

In this era of ever-changing technology, some information is classic and timeless. Much of the material in this book fits that category. Great audio is consistent—it has common ingredients across most genres. The set of guidelines and techniques contained in this book will help you get great-sounding tracks. Use your creativity to shape and mold each technique to your taste, style, and musical needs. Learn the basics, then stretch out. Find your sound with assurance that you know your technical tools and how they fit into your musical world.

Acoustic Considerations

No matter what high-tech gear you've combined with classic vintage gear, if certain acoustic considerations haven't been addressed, you're going to have a rough time getting world-class sounds. Vocals recorded in an empty bedroom are brutally damaged by standing waves and unwanted reflections. Once they're on tape or disc, they can't be made to sound as smooth and warm as they could have if they'd been recorded in a properly treated acoustic environment.

Somehow, your studio must be broken up acoustically. At home, most of us operate in a bedroom-sized recording room that acts as a studio, control room, machine room, storage room, maintenance room, office, and possibly bedroom. The disadvantage to this setup is that you can't spread out into areas that are optimized for a specific purpose. The advantage is that you probably have a lot of stuff in your studio—stuff that absorbs, reflects, and diffuses sound waves.

Though you might have a lot of furniture and gear in your studio, additional help should be considered. Shaping the space around your recording microphones is clearly advantageous, especially in a room that is acoustically live. A room that is acoustically *live* contains a lot of hard flat surfaces that reflect sound waves efficiently, causing substantial ambient reverberation. A room that is acoustically *dead* contains a lot of soft surfaces that absorb most of the reflections. Live acoustics are good when they've been designed to enhance the acoustic properties of a voice or an instrument. However, uncontrolled acoustical reflections are potentially destructive and must be managed.

Dealing with Acoustics

For your recording setup, you might be using a converted bedroom, or you might have the luxury of building a new studio-—each scenario offers unique challenges. The majority of home studios begin in an existing room, but no matter what your acoustic situation, there are effective methods to help you develop an environment that is conducive to creativity. There are many acoustic principles and treatment products that you can apply to your situation. Let's take a look at some factors that affect the way your music sounds when it's recorded in an acoustic environment.

The Room

It is possible to build a room that sounds great without much acoustic hocus-pocus at all. The way sound waves interact as they reflect between major surfaces and as they're diffused around the room is very much influenced by the dimensions of the room as well as by absorption and material density.

If you begin your construction phase with dimensional relationships that work together to create an even and consistent frequency response and coverage in each space, you'll be way ahead in your quest to create a functional and trustworthy studio.

Reflections

This diagram shows just a few of the more predominant reflections in a simple acoustic space. Even with these basic reflections, the picture quickly becomes complex. Imagine the reality of omnidirectional sound generation and the thousands of active echoes in a live acoustical environment. Though it seems very overwhelming to consider the incredible number of possible reflections, it's better for our purposes to have many random, yet controlled, reflections. It's when a pattern forms and repeats itself that we start to realize problematic acoustics. These problematic patterns typically occur between the side walls, the end walls, and the ceiling and floor.

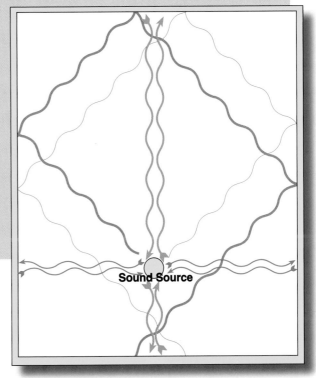

It is ideal in a recording studio to avoid parallel surfaces. A rectangular room, although cost effective to build and most common, provides us with three sets of parallel opposing surfaces: two sets of side walls and the ceiling and floor.

Typically, more randomness is better in an acoustical environment, at least for our recording purposes. Designing rooms with non-parallel opposing walls often accomplishes this in the construction phase. Study any excellent studio. You'll notice interesting angles and unique shapes. These are designed to randomize the reflections of sound waves in the room.

Diffusion and Absorption

As well as manipulating room dimensions and/or angles, we must consider the importance of diffusion and absorption. Diffusing a waveform causes it to career off its otherwise sonically destructive path. Absorption diminishes the waveform's ability to reflect—it decreases the acoustic energy, often to the extent of completely eliminating reflection. The amount of absorption accomplished is dependent on the frequency of the waveform, the amplitude, and the absorption properties of the reflecting surface.

It's really not all that great for our purposes to operate in a highly absorptive environment. Although it calms the reflections down, too much absorption also robs the sound of life and sparkle. We're typically much better off if the ambient sound is controlled through a combination of minimal absorption and well-designed diffusion.

Mode/Standing Wave/Resonance

Modes are simply reflections that set up a pattern between surfaces in an acoustic space. The problems that modes create are destructive to the reliability of the sound heard in the room. Modes are also called *standing waves*. This term provides an accurate mental image of this acoustical problem. If a sound wave reflects back along the same path from which it came, it will reflect again once it reaches its originating surface, then back again, and so on. In essence the sound wave forms a pattern that, if you could see it with your eyes, would seem to stand still in the room as it reflects back and forth. Such a standing wave poses multiple potential problems.

+ If the sound wave follows the identical path on its reflection, increasing the size of the crest and trough of the affected frequency, a resonance (an increase in energy from that frequency) occurs.

Standing Waves/Modes

The waveform that fits evenly between two opposing surfaces will create a pattern as it reflects back and forth between the walls. This illustration demonstrates a complete waveform between two surfaces; however, half of this waveform also fits between these surfaces (one crest or one trough). In addition, whole-number multiples of that crest or trough also fit evenly between those same surfaces and, likewise, create a standing pattern.

These standing waves, also called modes, are what determine the "sound" of a room. Any room which lets the same frequency stand between multiple surfaces (side walls, front and back walls, and ceiling and floor) will typically need acoustical treatment to enable reliable and musical recordings.

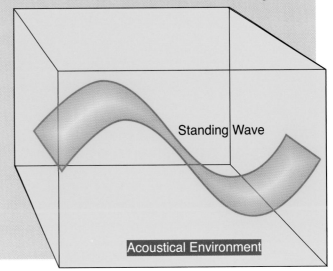

Standing Wave

Acoustical Environment

+ If the sound wave reflects out of phase with the original sound wave, cancellation occurs.

+ If the same modes occur between multiple surfaces, they work together to increase the overall anomaly within the space.

There are three types of standing waves that we must consider: axial, tangential, and oblique.

Calculating the Frequency of Standing Waves in a Room

A study of sound waves reveals that they exhibit physical, as well as aural, characteristics. One of those characteristics is wavelength, abbreviated by the symbol Lambda (λ). Since we easily calculate the wavelength of a specific frequency, using the equation Wavelength (λ)=Speed (1120 feet/sec.) ÷ Frequency (Hertz), it's a simple matter of cross multiplication to deduce the equation to calculate the frequency of a specific wavelength: Frequency (Hz) = Speed (1120 feet/sec.) ÷ Wavelength.

Consider any set of room dimensions. We can easily calculate the possible standing waves between any two opposing surfaces, since waves create modes only when they fit evenly between two surfaces. Whereas the equation Hz = 1120 ÷ λ provides the frequency of the complete sound wave that fits between the two surfaces, our actual first possible problem frequency is twice as large as the distance between the opposing surfaces—180 degrees into the wave cycle also fits evenly between the surfaces, offering the potential to create a standing pattern. The equation for the first standing frequency is, therefore, Hz = 1120 ÷ 2 λ.

Once we've calculated the first standing frequency, we simply multiply that frequency by consecutive whole numbers to develop a list of the other frequencies that fit evenly between the surfaces.

Axial Standing Waves

Axial standing waves (axial modes) stand between two surfaces: opposing walls as well as the floor and ceiling. These modes cause the most acoustical damage. When a sound wave reflects back and forth between two surfaces there is ample opportunity for energies to accumulate and cancel. This simple reflection must be diffused in order to be eliminated as a problem.

The basic calculations for determining potential acoustical anomalies consider axial modes below 300 Hz. Frequencies above 300 Hz are easier to deal with, using absorption and diffusion, than those below 300 Hz. Frequencies below 300 Hz contain enough energy that they're minimally affected by absorption and even some minor non-parallel construction techniques. In acoustic design, the goal is to minimize the number of problematic standing waves; however, complete elimination is unrealistic in most studios, especially in the home studio, where existing rooms are the norm.

Because we know standing waves are an issue in most home studios and because most home recording setups exist in fairly simple room designs, we can only expect to predict potential problems. We then must choose to select treatments to minimize those problems or, given the knowledge of their existence, electronically compensate.

Tangential

Whereas axial modes stand between two surfaces, tangential modes reflect off four surfaces in a consistent pattern. For instance, a sound wave that reflects off all of the walls travels around the room as a tangential standing wave. Once an axial mode is turned into a tangential mode, it is no longer considered a problem because there is little likelihood that the pattern will stand in the room. Substantially more

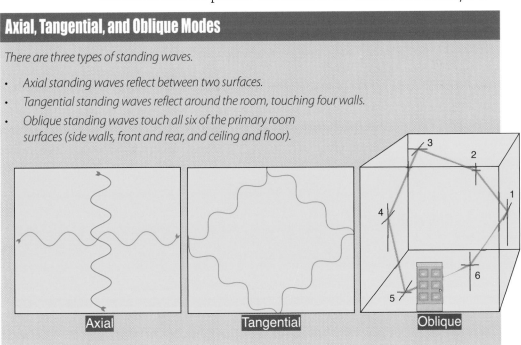

Axial, Tangential, and Oblique Modes

There are three types of standing waves.

- *Axial standing waves reflect between two surfaces.*
- *Tangential standing waves reflect around the room, touching four walls.*
- *Oblique standing waves touch all six of the primary room surfaces (side walls, front and rear, and ceiling and floor).*

Axial

Tangential

Oblique

energy is required to enable a waveform to repeat its pattern when reflecting off four surfaces.

Oblique

An oblique standing wave must touch six surfaces—for example, all four side walls as well as the ceiling and the floor. Oblique standing waves offer few problems in acoustic design because of the increased amount of energy required to repeat the pattern throughout all six reflections and the unlikely chance that the pattern will actually stand.

In acoustic design, it is beneficial to, through construction and diffusion techniques, transform axial modes into tangential or oblique modes.

Calculating Problematic Modes

Our study of acoustics is relatively simple and is designed for your understanding of basic concepts. In the real world, the science of acoustics is very complex. Accurate prediction and compensation techniques typically involve many complex calculations, along with the use of acoustical analysis tools, which help the acoustician determine the proper course of action for a given acoustical space.

We can, however, develop a solid understanding of the basics of this complex science through the analysis of simple acoustical environments. In a home studio, the extra bedroom typically ends up as the control room. For our understanding and educational use, a room like this offers an excellent starting point for acoustical calculations.

Consider All Opposing Surfaces

We use the equation previously mentioned ($Hz = 1120 \div 2\lambda$) to determine the first mode in any dimension. First, consider the first mode in all three dimensions (length, width, height). Multiply the first mode

Calculating Axial Standing Waves

Using an equation to calculate modes is efficient, but it's more efficient to use a spreadsheet with all calculations built in. This way you can easily see the impact of a slight dimensional change.

Room Dimensions		Ratio
Height	8	1.00
Width	12	1.50
Length	16	2.00

Plug in values and
then the run macro
"Create Sorted List"

Notice the coincident mode between all three surfaces at 140 and 280 Hz, both isolated by 35 Hz on the high and low sides. This room has problems and needs some well-thought-out treatment.

Height Modes	Width Modes	Length Modes		Height Modes	Spacings
70.00	46.67	35.00		35.00	-11.67
140.00	93.33	70.00		46.67	-23.33
210.00	140.00	105.00		70.00	0.00
280.00	186.67	140.00		70.00	-23.33
350.00	233.33	175.00		93.33	-11.67
	280.00	210.00		105.00	-35.00
	326.67	245.00		140.00	0.00
	373.33	280.00		140.00	0.00
	420.00	315.00		140.00	-35.00
		350.00		175.00	-11.67
		385.00		186.67	-23.33
				210.00	0.00
				210.00	-23.33
				233.33	-11.67
				245.00	-35.00
				280.00	0.00
				280.00	0.00
				280.00	-35.00
				315.00	-11.67
				326.67	-23.33
				350.00	-23.33
				373.33	
				385.00	
				420.00	
				420.00	

Equation for modes Hz=1120÷2λ

by consecutive whole numbers (1, 2, 3, 4, etc.) up to 300 Hz. Make a list of the results of these calculations for each dimension.

For example, consider one room with a length of 14 feet. Calculate the first mode by plugging 14 into the equation (Hz = 1120 ÷ 2λ). Hz = 1120 ÷ 28 = 40 Hz. Once you have calculated the first mode, create a list of whole-number multiples up to 300 Hz (40, 80, 120, 160, 200, 240, 280).

Now perform this calculation for width and height. Next, combine all three lists into one sequential list that contains all results from each dimension in ascending numerical order.

Red Flags

Once the list is created, we are looking for coincident standing frequencies (frequencies that occur in more than one dimension). When the same frequency occurs in more than one dimension, there's an increased likelihood that the modes will accumulate, resulting in a resonant frequency.

When we studied the basics of equalization in *The S.M.A.R.T. Guide to Mixers, Signal Processors, Microphones, and More*, we discovered that cutting a specific frequency range exposed the adjacent frequency bands. If the mids are cut, it often sounds like the highs and lows are boosted. That same principle applies to our study of acoustics. Once we've listed all possible modes, in addition to noting coincident frequencies, we must also note frequencies that are isolated on either side by more than 25 Hz. In other words, on our sequential numeric list of modes, we must take note of increments of 25 Hz or greater.

Obviously, any room with two or three dimensions the same provides multiple opportunities for coincident modes and isolations.

Flutter Echo

Flutter echoes can be heard after the sound source ceases. They sound like a ringing or hissing sound. As mid frequencies stand, especially between sidewalls, they resonate after the source is through. Try clapping your hands in an empty room with a lot of hard surfaces. The ringing after you clap is probably flutter echo.

Flutter echoes are easily controlled using absorption of diffusion. Simply note hard, flat surfaces on opposing surfaces. Something needs to break up the natural reflection back and forth between parallel walls.

Your Location in the Room Matters

As you notice problem frequencies, you must be cognizant of potential problems in those frequencies. Because these problem frequencies are standing between surfaces, the effect is dependent on where the listener is in relation to the cumulative energy of the standing wave.

A node is the point where the crest turns into the trough. At this node, there is decreased acoustic energy for the specific frequency. If you are located at a node point, you'll hear little of that frequency. However, if you move a few feet closer to or farther from the source, you might realize a huge increase in the amplitude of that same frequency. Your physical position in the acoustical environment determines the frequency content of the sound you hear.

Everything Else in the Room Matters

Sound waves are reflected and absorbed, to some degree, by each piece of furniture or equipment in the room. The number of people and their dispersion throughout the room affects the sonic characteristics. For reasons like this, acoustics and the prediction of sound interaction with the acoustic space become very complicated.

It is true, however, that a sound will only be effectively isolated by an object larger than the wavelength. In our calculations of potential problem frequencies, we consider that frequencies above 300 Hz can be controlled through absorption and diffusion—we concentrate on frequencies below 300 Hz. These lower frequencies contain more energy potential because of their size and the amount of air they move. In addition, as we consider the length of a 300-Hz sound wave (3.73 feet), and as we look around most rooms, there aren't many objects between opposing surfaces that are that large or larger—there just aren't many common physical objects that will control those frequencies.

The Rectangle

The reality is, most studios built in existing spaces, whether in a commercial location or at home, end up in a rectangular room, simply because that is the most affordable way to build a room. Unfortunately, in its basic state, a rectangular room is ineffective for creating reliable audio recordings. Flutter echo and standing waves combine with the direct sound in a way that decreases intimacy, reliability, and sonic integrity. So, we must use knowledge and creativity to create an adequate working environment.

The Goal

What are we really trying to accomplish in controlling the sonic character of a recording space?

- In their simplest form, we want to randomize patterns of energy within the environment. Sound waves that reflect, forming a pattern in the room, cause problems—we want to avoid them.

- We must also realize that standing waves happen, especially in a regular home studio setting. Our goal is to manipulate the environment in such a way that there are as few coincident axial modes as possible when we consider all dimensions.

- We must do what we can to avoid isolation of specific frequencies via larger than acceptable spacings between axial modes (greater than 25 Hz).

Solutions to Acoustical Problems

Dimensional Proportions

If you're fortunate enough to construct your own studio, there are a few suggested proportional equations when considering basic room dimensions. These ratios act as guidelines for determining dimensions resulting in acoustic environments with minimal peaks and nodes.

The "Golden Section" or "Golden Ratio" (1:1.6:2.33) is often referenced as a ratio between length, width, and height that produces a room with minimum anomalies. Once you determine the ceiling height, this ratio determines the other dimensions. If the ceiling height is 8 feet, the width and length are 12.8 feet (8 x 1.6) and 18.64 feet (8 x 2.33).

There are several other suggested dimensional ratios that result in the minimum number of resonances and nodes:

1.0:1.9:1.4
1.00:1.9:1.3
1.00:1.5:2.1
1.00:1.5:2.2
1.00:1.2:1.5
1.00:1.4:2.1

Adjusting Angles

As we noted before, axial modes hold the most potential for problematic acoustical phenomena. One of the reasons studio designers avoid parallel surfaces is to minimize axial modes. This technique alone is not enough to control sound reflections in an acoustical environment.

It takes a fairly extreme angle to deflect an axial mode into a tangential or oblique mode. The typical room can't afford the decrease in square footage required to skew walls enough to make a huge difference.

We must keep in mind that for every flat surface, there are two corners—one at each end—plus, there are angles at the floor and ceiling. As walls, ceilings, and floors meet, they form one of two different types of angles: concave and convex. Concave angles come to a point, or bend, away from you. Convex angles come to a point, or bend, toward you.

Concave Angles

A concave angle, like a typical corner in a room, focuses reflections in a particular direction. Since most of the flat surfaces in any acoustical environment form concave angles at the connection points with other surfaces, there's no way we can avoid concave angles. However, we must realize the effect they have on room acoustics and adjust our setup accordingly.

Concave Angles

Concave angles focus sound waves at a specific point. In the recording studio, contrary to the effect of the concave angle, we traditionally make an effort to randomize and confuse audio sound wave focus for our acoustic purposes.

Whereas we must avoid focusing and providing the opportunity for sonic patterns to accumulate, the large concave design is the basis of the amphitheater. In a concert setting, musicians positioned in the "bowl" enjoy the fact that their performance is focused on the audience.

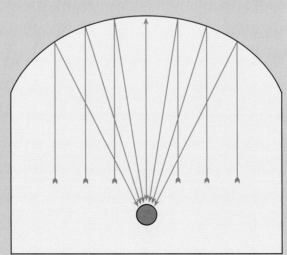

Concave angles can be used for positive purposes. The front wall of many control rooms is slightly concave in order to control and focus the stereo or multi-channel image at the mixing location. In this scenario, however, the rear and side walls are typically treated and designed to minimize strong reflections.

Convex Angles

Convex angles diffuse reflections. A convex angle comes to a point or bends toward you, leaving only one point where the sound wave can bounce directly back in the direction from which it came. All other points on the convex angle deflect the sound wave. In construction, convex angles offer an excellent means to transform axial modes into tangential or oblique modes.

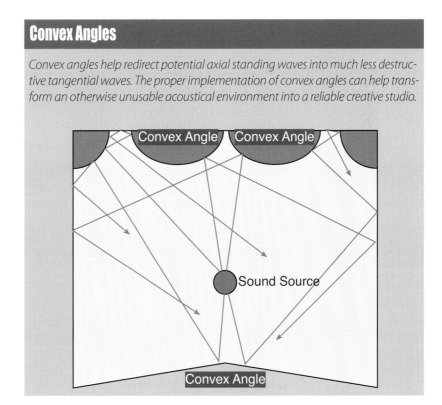

Convex Angles

Convex angles help redirect potential axial standing waves into much less destructive tangential waves. The proper implementation of convex angles can help transform an otherwise unusable acoustical environment into a reliable creative studio.

Convex Angle   Convex Angle

Sound Source

Convex Angle

Treating Surfaces

Most studio designs incorporate a blend of hard and soft surfaces, controlling reflections rather than eliminating them. This provides a very comfortable and creative environment. A recording studio that has been overly deadened, using lots of very absorptive surfaces, lacks life—it is a very unnatural listening environment and typically produces mixes that are inaccurate and unreliable.

Many studios utilize a principle that includes one live end (reflective surface) and one very controlled dead end (absorptive surfaces). A room like this maintains some of the acoustically ambient life in the room, while controlling detracting reflections and echoes.

Absorption Coefficient (Absorbers)

As we implement absorptive material, we must be aware that each material has a unique ability to absorb specific frequency bands with varying efficiency. The quantification of this absorptive trait is called the *absorption coefficient*. This reaction to sound waves is typically rated at a specified frequency and is noted in terms of absorption effectiveness.

A window is the typical image representing 100% absorption because all sound enters and none returns. We think in terms of percentage and speak in terms of two decimals. A material that absorbs half of the energy at the specified frequency is said to have an absorption coefficient of .50. The window is said to have an absorption coefficient of 1.00.

All materials exhibit an absorption coefficient: wood, fabric, glass, marble, etc. As we consider, for example, our list of standing waves, if we notice coincident modes at 240 Hz, isolated by 35 Hz from adjacent modes, it might do us a lot of good to include materials in the design that exhibit a high absorption coefficient at about 240 Hz. In this way, we can use the existing space effectively, controlling the problematic tendencies rather than simply dealing with the problems. This very simple example is the basis for much of what designers consider when they select dimensions and materials.

The absorption coefficient is specified at six frequencies: 125 Hz, 250 Hz, 500 Hz, 1 kHz, 2 kHz, and 4 kHz. Remember, the closer the absorption coefficient is to 1.00, the greater the absorption. Notice, on the following chart, the difference in absorption between lower and higher frequencies. Many soft surfaces, which one might guess would

Absorption Coefficients

This chart indicates the reflective properties of various types of materials. Remember, an absorption coefficient of 1.00 is ultimately capable of absorbing sound waves.

Material	125 Hz	250 Hz	500 Hz	1 kHz	2 kHz	4 kHz
Window	.35	.25	.18	.12	.07	.04
Concrete Block	.10	.05	.06	.07	.09	.08
Gypsum Board on 16" o.c. 2 x 4s	.29	.10	.05	.04	.07	.09
Heavy Carpet on Concrete	.02	.06	.14	.37	.60	.65
¾" Acoustical Tile	.09	.28	.78	.84	.73	.64
Concrete Floor	.01	.01	.015	.02	.02	.02
Wood Floor	.15	.11	.10	.07	.06	.07
Linoleum on Concrete	.02	.03	.03	.03	.03	.02

be very absorptive (carpet, acoustical tile, etc.) exhibit little to no absorption at 125 Hz.

Diffusers

In a small room, such a bedroom studio, it's often most desirable to control interfering reflections using diffusion instead of absorption. Diffusers confuse and randomize reflections rather than absorbing them. This tool provides control without robbing all ambient life from the room.

There are several different designs used to construct diffusers. Some are constructed of wood and some use synthetic materials; however, the purpose is the same, regardless of the physical characteristics. Diffusion panels are placed at any position in the studio that requires reflection control.

Diffusion Panels

Diffusion panels randomize reflections. Their physical design, in a seemingly random pattern, effectively disperses otherwise focused waveforms.

The Ceiling

Ceiling design is a critical factor in studio design. Standing waves between the ceiling and floor provide ample opportunity for tonal coloration and destructive sonic interaction. It is common practice to form a convex angle across the width or length of the ceiling, with the surface angling down to a point toward the floor.

Along with the convex angle there is often treatment in the corners where the walls meet the ceiling. All of these treatments are implemented in an effort to randomize reflections while avoiding modes and other tonal colorations.

Convex Ceiling Angle

This simple diagram illustrates the benefit of incorporating a convex angle in the ceiling design of a recording studio. This is just one technique that helps randomize reflections, avoiding standing patterns. Notice the corner treatments and how they help minimize the focus of any corner toward the center of the room.

The reflections indicated here are just a few examples to illustrate the process of redirecting otherwise damaging reflections. In reality, sound radiates omnidirectionally. Therefore, there are thousands of reflections working together to create the ambient tone of every acoustical environment.

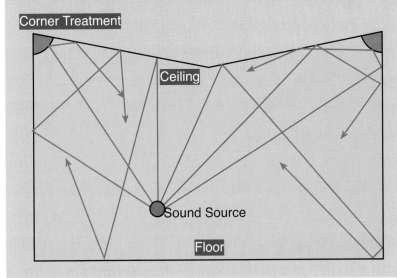

Corner Treatment

Ceiling

Sound Source

Floor

The Bass Trap

By now, it's probably pretty clear to you that low frequencies pose the most looming problem in our quest for perfect sound. When listening to his mixdown played back outside the studio, an inexperienced recordist performing a mixdown typically finds the greatest disappointment in how his mixes sound in the low frequencies.

If the resonances and nodes are controlled in any acoustic environment, the mixes performed therein become much more reliable, especially when played back on other systems outside the studio. The bass trap is designed to address these issues.

There are basically three types of bass traps:

+   The Helmholtz resonator

+   The panel trap/membrane resonator

+   The broadband bass absorber

The Helmholtz resonator is simply a large, tuned box with a hole in it that resonates at a specific frequency. Much like a flute, pan flute, or pop bottle, this resonator responds to one frequency. The fact that it resonates at a predetermined frequency, which ideally corresponds to a problem acoustical frequency, helps minimize that frequency in the ambient room sound. Because it takes energy to resonate the box, that energy is diminished in the room. The Helmholtz resonator can be designed for one specific frequency or for a broad band of frequencies. They work well, but they're difficult to construct accurately and they're not very space-efficient.

The panel trap is essentially a wood frame with a thin plywood (or similar material) front panel. Fiberglass insulation is often placed in the panel to help increase absorption. The frequencies affected by the panel trap are dependent on size and material density. It's typical to incorporate panels that absorb frequency bands centered at 100 and 200 Hz. This is an efficient way to control modes in the trouble frequency range below 300 Hz.

The broadband bass absorber utilizes a rigid fiberglass material that is about four times more dense than fiberglass insulation. It is often placed behind a wall or other structure. I have used an effective design that incorporates an angled back wall made from varying sizes of wood boards spaced at somewhat random distances from each other (between .5 and 1.5 inches). In this design, the boards act as random resonators, the heavy fiberglass (often Rockwool) absorbs very efficiently, and the slatted design allows low frequencies to enter the void behind the boards.

Broadband Bass Absorber

This broadband bass absorber design includes deflection, absorption, and trapping. The angled wall constructed of wood boards provides reflection control, the dense fiberglass provides absorption, and the slots between the boards let sound in without providing a direct path for reflection to re-enter the room.

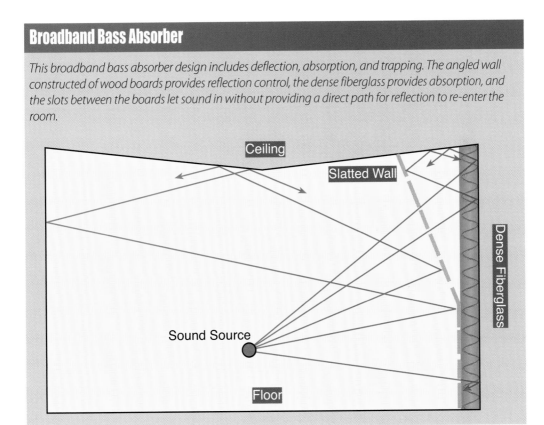

Change the Position of the Key Factors

The characteristic of room modality is dependent on room dimensions; however, it also dependent on the distance between the speakers and the back wall. Moving the speakers any number of inches changes the EQ characteristic of the room. If you don't like the room sound, try moving your monitors a little, then reassess the situation.

The other moveable ingredient is you—the engineer. Different positions in the room realize varied peaks and nulls. If you move back or forward by a foot, you might hear an amazing difference in the room sound. The difference of a couple feet could mean the difference between a thin, weak sound and a full, powerful sound. Test your mixes on other systems outside the studio. If they sound boomy in the low end, you might be better off mixing from the position that sounds fuller in the studio. If your mixes sound thin outside the studio, try mixing from the position that sounds thinner in the studio—this forces you to include more low-frequency content to get the sound you like in the studio.

Implement the Plan

Now that you understand some of the factors involved in designing trustworthy acoustical environments, draw a diagram of your recording space—control room and studio. Consider obvious reflections from the source (speakers or instrument) and how they accumulate at the major listening and recording positions (mix engineer or microphone). Basically, sound reflects like a billiard ball struck straight and clean—if it contacts a reflective surface from 60 degrees, it leaves at 60 degrees across the axis. The angle of attack equals the angle of retreat.

It's pretty easy to see where reflective accumulations develop once you create a rough drawing. Next, determine where treatment should be implemented and choose whether absorption or diffusion is appropriate. Most simple acoustical treatments affect a broad band of frequencies. True acoustic design considers room analysis, which exposes the reflective qualities of multiple frequency bands. Armed with this type of data, the acoustician considers absorption coefficients to select treatments that address anomalies at troublesome bands, molding the room response into a reliable recording and listening space.

Live End Dead End

One of the most common acoustic control designs is referred to simply as *Live End Dead End*. This is just what it sounds like—one end uses a lot of absorption materials and the other allows controlled reflections. This design typically provides a reliable recording space.

In any design there must be the proper balance between reflection and absorption. A room that is too live sounds bright, causing the recordist to compensate by adding too little high-frequency

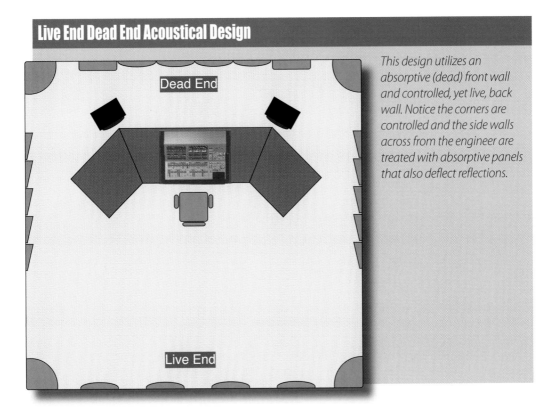

Live End Dead End Acoustical Design

Dead End

Live End

This design utilizes an absorptive (dead) front wall and controlled, yet live, back wall. Notice the corners are controlled and the side walls across from the engineer are treated with absorptive panels that also deflect reflections.

Live End Dead End Application

1. This is the wall behind the mixer in my home studio, manufactured by Primacoustic Studio Acoustics. Notice the materials on the wall, structured to provide frequency-specific absorption, combined with the bass traps where the ceiling and wall meet.

2. This is the wall opposing the dead end. It utilizes foam for a type of diffusion without completely deadening the back wall.

information. Recordings mixed in a very live space usually sound dull when played outside the studio. A room that is too dead sounds dull, causing the recordist to compensate by adding too much high-frequency information. Recordings mixed in a very dead space usually sound too bright when played outside the studio.

Typically, the front of the room is deadened and the back of the room (behind the mix engineer) is controlled but not completely deadened. There is also usually treatment on the side walls to minimize flutter echo at the mix position.

Portable Acoustical Treatments

Tube Traps

Physical structures within the acoustic space provide the best diffusion of otherwise detrimental waves. Though soft surfaces dampen high frequencies, the low mids, which can be most damaging to sound, must be diffused or reflected to ensure a smooth, even frequency response. Listen to Audio Examples 1-1. The first part demonstrates the intense room sound on a vocal mic in my family room. The second part demonstrates the same setup with the addition of a tool called a Studio Trap from Acoustic Sciences Corporation.

Audio Example 1-1

Voice Recorded with and without Studio Traps

Acoustic Control with Tube Traps

Tools like these compensate for all kinds of acoustic problems. Even in a controlled studio, these devices help shape the ambient intimacy of virtually any vocal or instrumental recording. Surround the microphone in a tight pattern for a more intimate sound. For a more open, yet controlled, live sound, simply move the Studio Traps out away from the mic until the desired effect is achieved.

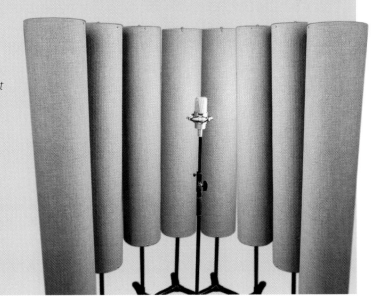

When absorption panels are hung on the studio walls and tools like the Studio Trap or baffles are used to confuse standing waves, the sounds you record are easier to mix. Suddenly, your recordings sound more like the hits you hear on professional recordings. To overlook these considerations is to create a troublesome situation for your recording and mixing sessions. Whether tracking or mixing, address these issues so your music can have the best possible chance of impacting the listener with the power and emotion you know it deserves.

Audio Examples 1-2 and 1-3 demonstrate more settings that benefit from acoustical treatment.

Audio Example 1-2

Acoustic Guitar with and without Studio Traps

Audio Example 1-3

Distant Voice and Guitar with and without Tube Traps

Monitoring: Turn It Down

The louder your system is, the more opportunity there is for destructive acoustic interaction. The sheer amount of energy in any acoustical environment determines how strong the modes and nodes are. If you monitor at a minimal listening volume, the effect of your room is minimized.

Of course, as indicated by the Fletcher-Munson curve, we hear the most accurate balance of high and low frequencies when we listen at about 85 – 90 dB. However, this takes into consideration that the listener is in a well-controlled and acoustically trustworthy room.

Many highly experienced and successful mix engineers monitor at a minimal volume for most of the mixdown process, turning the system up to 90+ dB only occasionally to check the low-frequency

Acoustic Designs in Action

This series of photos demonstrates many of the design principles discussed in this chapter. Studio X in Seattle is a world-class facility designed by Studio Bouton and equipped with an excellent array of modern and vintage equipment. Check it out at www.studioxinc.com.

Look for each of the principles laid out in this chapter: reflections, diffusion, absorption, etc.

content. Turning the monitors down during mixdown accomplishes a few important things:

Acoustic Treatments at Home

The previous illustration demonstrated what can happen when a studio is designed from the ground up. Most home studios are developed over time in a spare bedroom. I, personally, never wanted a "studio" in my house. I have been chief engineer at large facilities, and I get to rent some of the nicest places on the planet. However, equipment has gotten so powerful and affordable in recent years that I've ended up doing much of my work at home—you absolutely can't beat the commute.

The more serious you are about your music, the more you'll want to ensure that your home studio is accurate and reliable—acoustic treatment is fundamental to that goal. These photos demonstrate a small room that works very well for many applications. The acoustic treatment is an excellent and reasonably priced product from Primacoustic Studio Acoustics. I mounted their side wall flutter control systems on hardboard—they hang in place in the control room or I can take them into other rooms for additional flexibility and control.

- It takes the room virtually out of play. The decreased acoustic energy dissipates rapidly—the quieter it is, quicker it dissipates, so there's less chance of noticeable standing waves.

- It is much easier on your ears. Over the years, loud music takes a toll on your ears. Save them while you can. The difficult part about monitors at high volumes is that your ears get fatigued after a while, causing you to turn the volume up more to feel the same impact. Before you know it, you're happy as a clam and someone else comes into the room with fresh ears and can't take the volume! You become oblivious to how loud it really is.

- It increases the potential length of your workday. You can literally mix nonstop for days at low volume levels with no ear fatigue or damage.

- It ensures that when you play your music for the big record executive and he puts it in his office system and plays it way too softly to get the full impact, it still sounds good.

- It makes it bearable when you show your music off to your parents and other family and friends—they rarely understand the joy of feeling the music.

- If your music sounds great at quiet levels, it usually sounds awesome once you turn it up! At low listening levels, our ears are least efficient in the low frequencies (below about 400 Hz) and in the high frequencies (above about 4 – 5 kHz), so it's necessary to listen at high volumes occasionally, specifically to check the accuracy of those frequency ranges. What you'll usually find is that once you turn it up, your minimalist volume during mixdown results in a mix that sounds bright and clear in the high end and full and deep in the low end.

I have found that as I monitor at modest volume levels, over the course of the day I keep turning the volume down further—it seems that my ears become more sensitive. You might ask for quantification of "quiet" levels. It really depends on the acoustics in your room, the amount of ambient noise, the size of the room, etc. The most important factor is that you just turn it down. If someone walks in during a mixdown, you should be able to easily hear them. Most of the time I start mixing with the level at about 65 dB.

Conclusion

This chapter is not designed to turn you into a master acoustician. It is, however, written with the heartfelt desire that you gain an understanding of the basics of acoustics, so you're equipped to make some design decisions and informed enough to realize the importance of professional help in this complex science.

Recording Great Electric Guitar Tracks

There is so much more to a guitar sound than there has ever been! It's really quite amazing. Creative options abound and excess is abundant. From very low and ominous heavy rock and metal sounds to sweet jazz tones and pop, guitar is fundamental in the establishment and authenticity of a sound.

Anyone who has been around music for a while will testify to the cyclical nature of trends in guitar sounds. As the era of electronics in music grows, we can expect that the sounds we love today will become dated or irrelevant tomorrow. With equal certainty, as we continue to move forward, history will repeat itself. Someone will rediscover the beauty of an era gone by, revive it, and reclaim it. The bottom line is: save your toys. They will be cool again!

Let's jump in. The guitar is a great instrument and offers definitive sounds that crystallize the stylistic feel of the song.

Guitar Fundamentals

A guitar isn't really a full-range instrument. Although it offers a full sound, which can seem ear-piercing, it's musical and sonic strength lies in the efficiency of its range rather than its breadth.

The frequency range of the fundamental pitches in the guitar is fairly narrow. The fundamental frequency of the lowest guitar note is E2 (82 Hz). The fundamental frequency of the highest note on a standard 22-fret six-string guitar is D6 (1.174 kHz).

Standard tuning for the six-string guitar is E2 (82 Hz), A2 (110 Hz), D3 (147 Hz), G3 (196 Hz), B3 (247 Hz), and E4 (330 Hz). It's interesting that most of the frequencies we accentuate in a guitar

Keep Your Toys

Now that we're in the electronic era, trends in guitar sounds are cyclical. What was cool then is probably cool now, and what is cool now will probably be cool in the future, once it's been uncool for a while. The moral to this story is, keep your toys!

recording are well above the majority of its fundamental frequency range. It's typical procedure to roll off the frequencies below about 100 Hz; fullness is usually around 250 Hz, and boosting a frequency range between 3 and 5 kHz adds clarity.

We should deduce from these facts that the harmonic content of the guitar is what we really find most appealing about its sound.

Tone and Timbre

Physical Properties

Tone and *timbre* are terms that are often used interchangeably; however, closer inspection of the guitar and its tonal characteristics leads us into a study of the subtle differences between these two terms. Whereas the tone controls on the electric guitar decrease high frequencies or low frequencies, in actuality timbre has more to do with the instrument's harmonic content.

Individual guitars sound different for various reasons. The type of wood used is a factor, especially in the instrument's sustain. More dense materials tend to produce instruments with a greater capacity for natural sustain. Softer woods tend to provide a greater sonic warmth, often at the expense of sustain.

The physical composition of each instrument influences its harmonic content or, in other words, its timbre.

Pickup Placement

The position of each pickup on an electric guitar is very important to the sound of the instrument. The reason why the bridge pickup sounds thinner than the neck pickup is explained by the harmonic content at each location.

For a simple illustration of this concept, let's consider the neck pickup on a standard Stratocaster. Sonically, this pickup provides a deep, warm, and somewhat hollow sound—much warmer than the other pickups. If we look at the physical position of the pickup, we'll see that it is exactly one-quarter of the distance from the bridge to the nut.

Most guitarists know about harmonics on the guitar neck, especially at the twelfth fret, where lightly touching the string while plucking divides the string into two halves, producing a harmonic one octave above the fundamental. If we were to position a pickup at the twelfth fret we would not hear much of the harmonic because the string is essentially still at that location—we've stopped the fundamental and allowed the first harmonic to ring freely in the two halves of the string. This point at which there is no vibration is called a *node*.

Pickup Placement Determines Timbre

The neck pickup on a Stratocaster is positioned precisely at the node position of a harmonic—exactly one-quarter of the distance from the bridge to the nut. The fact that this harmonic is missing creates the hollow and round sound that is so characteristic of the neck position setting (forward position on the five-way pickup selector).

Notice the position of the other two pickups. They receive different harmonic information; therefore, they provide a different timbre.

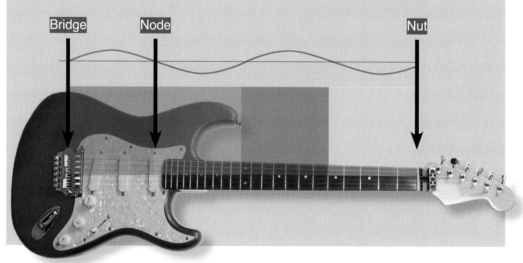

There are also natural harmonics at other locations on the neck. One of these is at the fifth fret, which is the point where the string is divided into four segments. This harmonic produces three nodes between the bridge and nut—one at each quarter of the length of the string. A standard Stratocaster neck position pickup is positioned directly below this node, explaining its hollow and deep tone. Whereas this pickup hears next to nothing from this harmonic, it receives a strong fundamental and first harmonic. In fact, the first harmonic (stopped at the twelfth fret) is strongest at this point. Like equalization, in which reducing one frequency band accentuates the bands on either side, the same concept applies to harmonic content. The virtual elimination of this midrange harmonic results in a sound that is full in lows and rich in highs.

This simplified illustration of harmonic content provides a clear delineation between tone and timbre. Timbre consists of the sound created by the relative levels of harmonics. In this Strat neck position, no amount of tone control—frequency boost or cut—can add back in what is harmonically missing because it simply isn't an available timbral ingredient.

In actuality, there is a constantly varying balance of timbre as the guitarist moves up and down the neck. As the length of the string changes during the fretting process, the balance of harmonics changes at each pickup position. This becomes part of the inherent sound of the instrument, which provides musical inspiration for the virtuoso and, at times, frustration for the novice. Each song provides a new opportunity for sonic inspiration as the key changes and the relative typical string length controls the available textures at each pickup position.

Tone Controls

Most guitars offer passive filters for tonal control. When the bass or treble controls are all the way up they are providing 100% of what the pickup has to offer for that range. Backing off the treble control simply trims off the frequencies above a certain point—functioning as a variable low-pass filter. Backing off the bass control trims off frequencies below a certain point—functioning as a variable high-pass filter.

Guitars with active circuitry typically contain amplification circuitry that provides boosted treble or bass frequencies.

Frequency Content

Most guitars and guitar amplifiers exhibit a fairly modest high-end rolling off above 5 or 6 kHz.

An electric guitar can be adjusted to include massive amounts of low-frequency content. This might sound great when you're alone in your bedroom, but in the context of a band, it will probably sound muddy. In order to fit the guitar perfectly into a mix, you must decide which frequency range supports the song best, then adjust the tone accordingly.

Recording the Electric Guitar

When recording an electric guitar, we have the option of:

+ Using a microphone at the speaker
+ Running directly into the mixer
+ Combining both of these approaches
+ Using software plug-ins applied to the direct guitar sounds

Each technique offers advantages and disadvantages. Running directly into the mixer produces ultimate separation. If you process the direct guitar sound, you don't risk altering the sound of another instrument because no other instrument has had the opportunity to bleed into a microphone.

Miking the guitarist's speaker cabinet, although it allows for leakage of another instrument into the guitar mic, typically produces the best sound. Using a microphone on the electric guitarist's cabinet captures the essence of the sound the guitarist designed for the part he is playing. Because sound plays such an important role in what and how a guitarist plays, miking the cabinet is often the only way to capture the guitar part in a musically authentic way.

It's pretty simple to record the miked signal while recording the direct sound from the guitar. This direct sound is useful for selecting or augmenting effects after the fact and offers creative options that simply can't be duplicated without rerecording the part.

Software plug-ins offer creative freedom during mixdown. During tracking, most plug-ins easily function in real time so the musical inspiration is not lost. However, the affected sound might never be printed to a recorder track. It might simply exist as an effect, incorporated during mixdown like reverberation of delay effects.

Direct Electric

For the sake of understanding some of the more fundamental variables involved in recording the electric guitar, we'll first plug directly into the mixer. When running a guitar directly into the mic input of a mixer, plug the guitar into a direct box first, then plug the direct box into the mixer. The signal going into the direct box can come straight from the guitar or from any effect or group of effects that the guitar is plugged into. The quality of the DI plays an important role in the sound of the instrument. Direct boxes are available in both passive and active circuitry, and the sound quality from device to device varies greatly. If you're a

Patching the Electric Guitar Directly into the Mixer

The procedure used to patch the electric guitar directly into a mixer depends on the input type. There are two basic scenarios:

1.   If you have access to the mixer line inputs, it's usually good to plug the guitar straight into the mixer, without a direct box (DI). This works well most of the time, but success and signal quality are dependent on pickup signal strength and impedance of the mixer line input. Most modern guitars and mixers get along quite well.

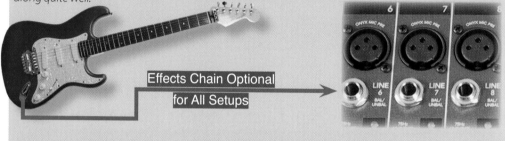

Effects Chain Optional for All Setups

2.   If you're plugging into a mic input, you must use a DI to match impedance and to optimize levels.

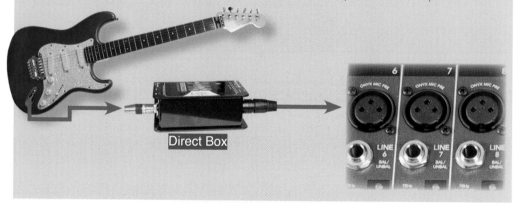

Direct Box

guitarist, find the direct box that gives your guitar the sound you like, buy it, then carry it with you to each recording situation.

As an alternative, simply plug the guitar straight into the line input of the mixer. This works very well on most modern mixers.

Some guitar amps have a line output, which can be plugged directly into the line input of the mixer. This technique lets you capture some of the amplifier's characteristic sound while still keeping the advantages of running directly into the mixer.

Using the Amplifier Line Output and Speaker Output

Some amplifiers have a line output that can be plugged into the mixer line input. This technique helps maintain some of the character of the amplifier electronics.

Caution! Do not plug the guitar amplifier's speaker output directly into the mixer line input.

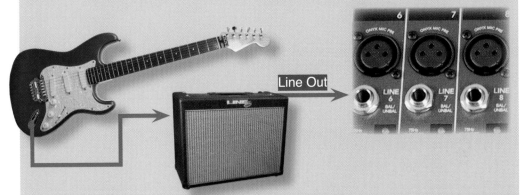

Line Out

Be careful! Never plug the powered speaker output from your amplifier directly into any device that you're not completely certain is designed to accept it.

Some DIs provide a switched input, letting you select INSTRUMENT or AMPLIFIER as the signal source. This technique can work very well. It adds the characteristic sound of the amplifier EQ and effects along with the tone of the amplifying circuitry.

Speaker Output

Always be sure the DI is selected to accept an input from the speaker output when using this technique.

Try using a direct box that will receive a powered signal straight out of the speaker output of the guitar amp. This will give you the most guitar amp sound you can get without using a mic. Be careful! Never plug a speaker output into any input until you've been assured by someone whose opinion you trust implicitly that the input is designed to accept a powered output!

Advantages of Running Direct

There are four main advantages to running directly into the mixer.

1. It's easy. Just plug and play.
2. There's no leakage from other instruments recorded at the same time.
3. It can sound great. With the advent of new guitar effects, the sound can actually be pretty amazing.
4. You can record at home as late as you want without waking the your family, the neighbors, or the police.

Though there's still nothing quite like the sound of a great guitar through a great amp, there are many situations in which running direct is more than acceptable.

Miking the Speaker Cabinet

Turn the amp up to a fairly strong level. This doesn't have to be screaming loud, but most amps sound fuller if they're turned up a bit.

Next, place a moving-coil mic about one foot away from the speaker. Most guitar amps will have one or two full-range speakers. These speakers are typically 8 to 12 inches in diameter. Moving-coil mics are the preferred choice for close-miking amplifiers because they can handle plenty of volume before they distort the sound. Also, the tone coloration of a moving-coil mic in the higher frequencies can add bite and clarity to the guitar sound.

If the amp you are miking has more than one identical speaker, point the mic at one of the speakers. Point the mic at the center of the speaker

Aiming the Microphone at the Speaker

Pointing the microphone at the center of the speaker produces a tone that is edgy and contains more high-frequency content than other mic locations.

Pointing the microphone away from the center and toward the outer edge of the speaker cone produces a warmer, smoother tone with less high-frequency content than other mic locations.

Before using equalization and other processing, use mic choice and placement to define the desired sound. There is a broad range of sound available at this initial phase of recording.

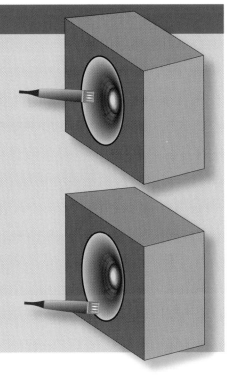

to get a sound with more bite and edge. Point the mic more toward the outer rim of the speaker to capture a warmer, smoother sound.

If you're miking a speaker enclosure with separate tweeter, midrange and bass speakers, you'll need to move the mic back two or three feet just to get the overall sound of the cabinet. This gets us into a situation in which the room sound becomes an important part of the sound that goes onto the tape.

Audio Example 2-1 demonstrates the sound of an amp with the mic placed six inches from the speaker and pointed directly at the center of the speaker.

Audio Example 2-1

Mic at the Center of the Speaker

Audio Example 2-2 demonstrates the sound of the same amp, same guitar and same musical part as Audio Example 2-1. Now the mic is aimed about one inch in from the outside rim of the speaker, while maintaining the distance of six inches from the speaker.

Audio Example 2-2

Mic at the Outer Edge of the Speaker

Video Example 2-1

Changing Mic Position on the Speaker Cabinet

When the mic is within a foot of the speaker, the room sound has a minimal effect on the sound that goes to tape, especially if the amp volume is fairly strong. If the guitarist hasn't already included reverb and delay in his selection of effects, this approach will give you consistently close-sounding tracks that you can add distance (ambience) to by adding reverb or delay in the mix.

Powerful guitar sounds often include the sound of the immediate space (the room) that the amp is in. This can be accomplished with reverb, but natural ambience can add an unusual and distinct quality to a recording. Try including the sound of the room with the sound of the guitar. This technique often breathes life into an otherwise dull sound.

As we move the mic back more than a couple of feet from any amp, we're using distant miking. The room sound becomes part of the overall sound. We can get great guitar sounds if we put one mic within a foot of the amp and one mic back in the room several feet away from the amp. Using this technique, we can blend the sound of the mic closest to the amp with ambient sound captured by the mic that is farther away. We can combine these two sounds to one track as we record, or if tracks permit, we can print each mic to a separate track and save the blending or panning for mixdown. The effectiveness of this approach is dependent on whether the sound of the room is musically appropriate.

Use a condenser mic to record the most accurate sound of the room. Condensers have a fuller sound from a distance than moving-coil or ribbon mics, and they capture the subtleties of the room sound in more detail. In Audio Example 2-3, I've placed a condenser mic about seven feet away from the amp.

Audio Example 2-3

Condenser Mic Seven Feet from the Amp

Audio Example 2-4 demonstrates the amp in Audio Example 8 through a close mic.

Audio Example 2-4

Close-Miking the Amp

In Audio Example 2-5, I blended the sound of the close mic with the sound of the distant mic and then panned the two apart.

Audio Example 2-5

Combining the Close and Distant Mics

Audio Example 2-6

Multiple-Room Miking

It's often difficult to get that perfectly blended electric guitar sound. Experimentation with microphone techniques can really help solve some problems. The key factors involved in shaping guitar sounds are the raw sound from the instrument, choice of effects, and acoustical interaction of the sounds in the room. There's much room for creativity here. Start practicing and building your own arsenal of techniques that you like. With the rapid development of affordable technology right now, you'll

Accentuating the Room Sound

If you're looking for a unique guitar sound, try including more of the room sound by simply moving the microphone farther away from the amp. If you'd like to increase the apparent room size, try this technique. Aim the amp at a wall, then aim the microphone at the same wall, pointing away from the amp. This effectively increases the distance from the amp.

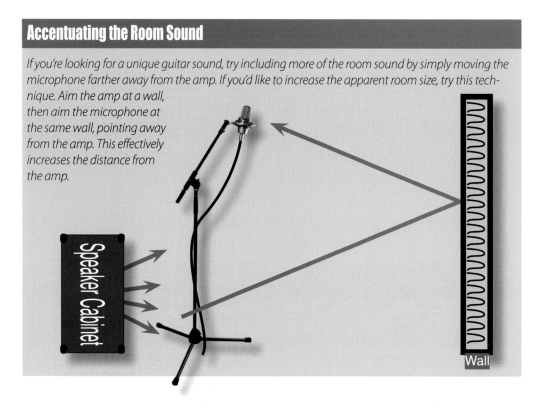

need to use all available resources to create a new and unique sound that can rise above the masses.

Combining the Miked and Direct Signals

It's possible and common to blend the miked amplifier signal with the direct signal. Plug the guitar into the direct box, then plug into an amplifier from the DIs Out to Amp jack. Once this is completed, proceed with miking the amp. From the direct box you can also patch the low-impedance XLR output into the mic input of your mixer. With this setup the direct signal is coming in one channel, and the microphone signal is coming in another channel.

Listen to Audio Example 2-7. I'll turn up the direct signal alone, then I'll turn the miked signal up alone, and finally I'll blend the two sounds and pan them apart.

Audio Example 2-7

Combining Miked and Direct Signals

Combining the Direct and Miked Sounds

This technique lets you blend the direct and miked sounds, including the intimacy of the direct sound with the warmth of the miked sound. Blend both of these sounds onto one mono track or record them to two separate tracks—saving the blend for mixdown.

1. *Plug the guitar into the effects (optional), then into the 1/4" DI input.*

2. *Plug the THRU (Out to Amp) jack on the DI into the amplifier input.*

3. *Patch the DI XLR output into the mixer XLR input.*

4. *Mike the speaker, connecting the mic to a separate mixer input.*

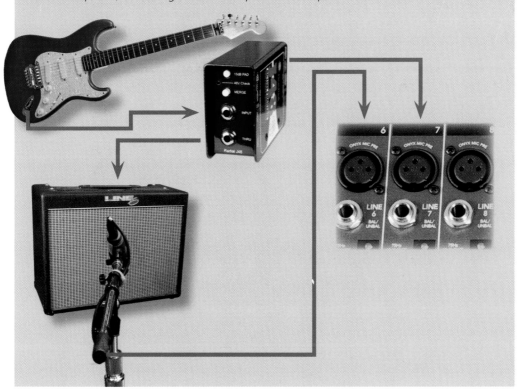

Miking the Strings and the Amp or DI

Try miking the acoustic sound of the strings and blending that with the DI or amplified sound. Sometimes the sound of the string transient adds an interesting and unique character to the electric sound.

Audio Example 2-8

Miking the Strings and the Amp

Making the Most of Your Home Studio Space

There are a few ways to make your recording environment sound bigger than it really is. Try this technique. It yields a very impressive and large stereo image without having a large or impressive acoustic space in which to record.

1. *Turn the amplifier up. You'll need enough volume to fill rooms A and B.*

2. *Connect all three mics to different mixer channels.*

3. *Mic 1 picks up the close sound; it should be panned to the center position.*

4. *Pan mic 2 left and mic 3 right. This results in a very big acoustic sound. The farther the amp is from rooms A and B, the larger the sound.*

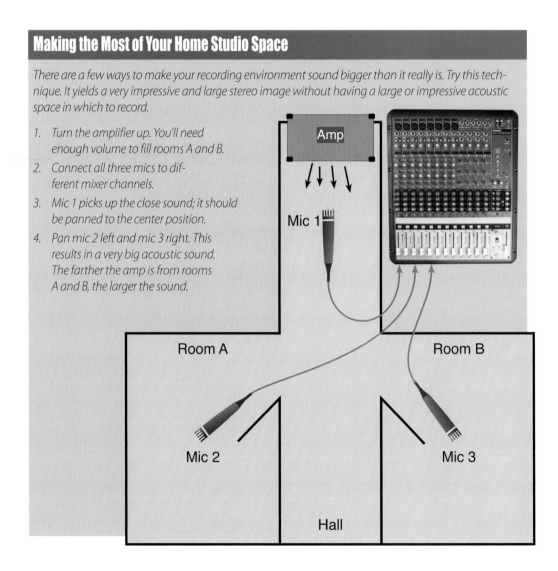

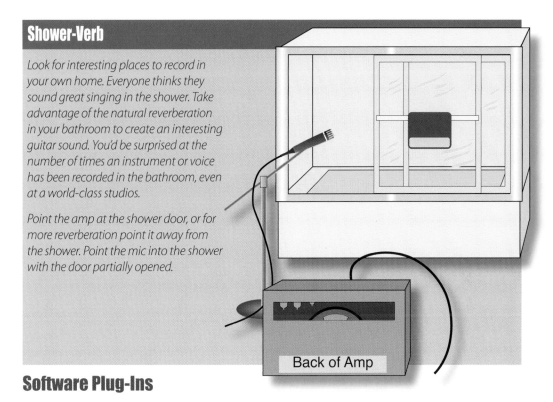

Shower-Verb

Look for interesting places to record in your own home. Everyone thinks they sound great singing in the shower. Take advantage of the natural reverberation in your bathroom to create an interesting guitar sound. You'd be surprised at the number of times an instrument or voice has been recorded in the bathroom, even at a world-class studios.

Point the amp at the shower door, or for more reverberation point it away from the shower. Point the mic into the shower with the door partially opened.

Back of Amp

Software Plug-Ins

Everything you need to shape an interesting guitar sound is available in software, as well as hardware. Whether you want distortion, amp modeling, compression, EQ, or effects, you can create the sound in the computer. Simply plug the guitar straight into the audio interface and create.

This approach has an up side and a down side:

+ The up side is that you don't have to have a lot of pedals and amplifiers to get a decent guitar sound. You can even record the guitar directly, without effects, and build the sound as the song develops.

+ The down side is that you might be sacrificing sound quality for convenience. In addition, guitarists are typically inspired to perform according to the sound they hear when they play. Tracking with a dry or inferior sound might limit creativity.

There are certainly many great plug-ins that work well on guitar. I still prefer, as most artists do, getting the basic guitar sound, including amplifier, dynamics, and overdrive, recorded first. Once that is taken care of, use effects like reverberation, delay, and EQ to shape the size and depth of the sound to fit the mix.

Recording Levels

Analog Levels

When we record guitars, the VU meter should usually read 0 VU at the peaks. There can be a couple of exceptions to this rule.

Distorted guitar sounds are often recorded very hot to tape (in the neighborhood of +3 to +5 on the VU meter). Some engineers believe that this adds a little more edge to the part and that the tape being oversaturated has the effect of compressing the sound. This compression helps keep the part in a tighter dynamic range so it can be heard more consistently.

Be careful when recording hot to tape. The signal could become too distorted. You might print so much signal on tape that it begins to spill onto the adjacent tracks as well as onto the track on which you're trying to record. The tape recorder and size of tape determine whether you can successfully print stronger-than-normal signals to tape.

Digital Levels

There is no advantage to pushing levels on a digital recording system such as your computer workstation, hard disk recorder, or MDR. The goal is to simply record the peak level of the track close to or at full digital level. Recording any instrument at unreasonably low digital levels can produce substandard tracks that sound grainy, inaccurate, or even noisy.

Transients

If the strings of a guitar are plucked with a hard pick, there are transients in their sound. The extent of the transient depends on the specific instrument, type of guitar pick, and the strings. Some acoustic guitar parts contain exaggerated transients because of the way they've been compressed. Digital meters do a reasonable job of indicating these transients. However, these parts need to be recorded with especially conservative VU levels to compensate for the increased transient attack. Transients have an actual level that is up to 9 dB higher than the VU (average level) reading.

Pickups

Guitar pickups all work on the same essential principle. Their purpose is to convert the string vibrations into an electrical signal. This is performed by a combination of a magnet and copper wire coiled around the magnet. The string motion produces a variation in the magnetic field, resulting in an electrical image of the string vibration rate and intensity. The variations between pickups have become greater through experimentation with the amount of wire wrapped around the magnet and combinations of close-proximity pickup assemblies, but the fundamental structure is very consistent between pickups.

Increasing the amount of copper wire coiled around the magnet produces a stronger signal. In fact, some pickups create such a strong signal that they naturally overdrive the amplifier input. With super-high output pickups like this, the only way to get a clean sound is to reduce the instrument volume control. Some players prefer these stronger pickups because they provide an aggressive sound and feel. Some players prefer the natural clarity of a weaker pickup.

The main down side to extra-strength pickups is that they can reduce sustain. If the pickup configuration is too strong, the strings actually stop vibrating sooner than normal because of the magnet pull induced by the pickup.

Most players who experiment with pickups end up using a stronger pickup at the bridge position—since the signal is weaker at the bridge—along with a more natural-sounding, yet full, pickup in the neck position.

Pickup Position

Many people credit the pickup for the sound of the instrument. In actuality, that is partially true; however, the position of the pickup is often more influential on the sound of the instrument than the actual pickup design.

As I explained earlier in this chapter, the position of the pickup determines the harmonic content of the sound. If the pickup is placed at a node of one or two harmonics, it will sound vastly different than if it's placed at the precise point where all harmonics are working together optimally.

There is definitely an inherently different sound between single- and double-coil pickups, but their placement determines the essential sonic timbre.

Pickup Types

There are two basic types of guitars: single coil and double coil. Additionally, some modern pickups contain active circuitry.

Single-Coil

Single-coil pickups have a thin, clean, and transparent sound, but they can be noisy, picking up occasional radio interference. These pickups, typically found on a stock Fender Stratocaster, are usually about 3/4" wide and 2-1/2" long.

Audio Example 2-9

Single-Coil Pickup

Double-Coil Humbucking

Double-coil pickups have a thick, meaty sound and are the most noise-free of the pickup types. They get their name from the fact that they have two single coils working together as one pickup. These are wired together in a way that cancels the majority noise that is picked up. These

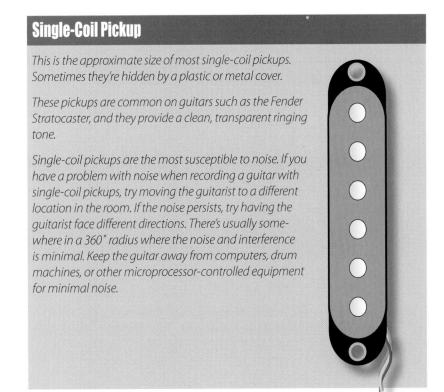

Single-Coil Pickup

This is the approximate size of most single-coil pickups. Sometimes they're hidden by a plastic or metal cover.

These pickups are common on guitars such as the Fender Stratocaster, and they provide a clean, transparent ringing tone.

Single-coil pickups are the most susceptible to noise. If you have a problem with noise when recording a guitar with single-coil pickups, try moving the guitarist to a different location in the room. If the noise persists, try having the guitarist face different directions. There's usually somewhere in a 360° radius where the noise and interference is minimal. Keep the guitar away from computers, drum machines, or other microprocessor-controlled equipment for minimal noise.

can also be called *humbucking pickups*. Double-coil pickups are common on most Gibson guitars, such as the Les Paul.

Audio Example 2-10

Double-Coil Pickup

Many guitars have a combination of single- and double-coil pickups. It's common for a double coil pickup to have a switch that will turn one of the coils off. This gives the player a choice between single- and double-coil.

Active

Active pickups contain amplifying circuitry to boost the pickup output level. Therefore, the active pickup typically uses fewer windings, resulting in decreased impedance and magnetic draw in the string vibration.

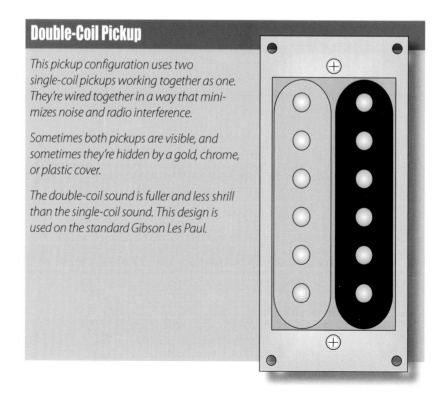

Double-Coil Pickup

This pickup configuration uses two single-coil pickups working together as one. They're wired together in a way that minimizes noise and radio interference.

Sometimes both pickups are visible, and sometimes they're hidden by a gold, chrome, or plastic cover.

The double-coil sound is fuller and less shrill than the single-coil sound. This design is used on the standard Gibson Les Paul.

Decreased impedance results in a signal that is less affected in the high frequencies by cable influences.

An active guitar pickup is typically capable of very clean sounds while also providing a strong signal for aggressive and characteristic distorted sounds.

Basic Types of Electric Guitars

There are several different types of guitars available, and each has a characteristic sound. Often, a guitarist will play one type of guitar but ask you to make it sound like another type of guitar. This can be very difficult but not always impossible. It's crucial that you're familiar with these basic guitar sounds.

Even within the basic electric guitar types, there are many different combinations of pickups and design configurations. The type of wood, style of body, and precision of assembly all play important parts in the sound of the instrument. All considerations aside, we can still break the electric guitar sounds into three recognizable categories:

+   Stratocaster: single coil
+   Les Paul: double coil
+   Hollow-body electric jazz guitar: double coil

Audio Examples 2-11 to 2-13 demonstrate the sounds of the three fundamental types of electric guitars. These are all recorded directly into the mixer so that you can hear the characteristic tone of each.

Audio Example 4-1 demonstrates the single-coil pickups on a Stratocaster. This guitar and its brother, the Telecaster, are very common in the rock, country, and pop fields.

Audio Example 2-11

Single-Coil Stratocaster

Audio Example 2-12 demonstrates the double-coil sound of the Les Paul. This warm, smooth, punchy sound is a favorite for rock, blues, pop and jazz.

Audio Example 2-12

Double-Coil Les Paul

Audio Example 2-13 demonstrates the double-coil sound of a large hollow-body jazz guitar. This instrument has a pure, rich sound. As a jazz instrument, it's traditionally treated with little or no effect. In fusion and some other jazz or rock styles, we can use any or all effects and techniques to shape the jazz guitar sound.

Audio Example 2-13

Hollow-Body Electric Jazz Guitar

These guitars have very different sounds and are suited for different types of music. Review these examples, and on a separate sheet of paper, write down as many descriptive adjectives as you can for each instrument. Use words such as thin, hollow, round, fat, beefy, or chunky. Have friends listen to these examples and list the terms they think describe each guitar sound. Putting a verbal tag on each sound will help you solidify your impression of these instruments. Verbalization will also help you communicate with other musicians about different guitar sounds.

Pickup Phase Relationship

Utilizing multiple pickups always provides an opportunity for negative phase interactions. Whether you're recording a Strat or Les Paul configuration, or any variation for that matter, whenever you select two or more pickups at once, the sound is completely dependent on the spacing between the pickups. Each pickup sees the string vibration at a different point in the phase cycle.

Some professionals who genuinely enjoy the sound of their bridge and neck position pickups rewire their guitar for stereo output. When each pickup feeds a separate amplifying system, the sound of each can be optimized and, when combined, can produce a much different feel and effect than simply combining them with the pickup selector switch.

Alternate Tunings

Some guitar sounds just seem undeniably huge. Many of the "larger than life" guitar sounds we hear on recordings are performed on guitars with alternate tunings. A change as simple as tuning the low E string down to a low D can drastically increase the size of the electric guitar sound.

Acoustic players have been utilizing alternate tunings for a long time. Now the electric guitar community has opened up to alternate tunings in a big way. It's common to tune the entire guitar down a half step, whole step, or more. Tuning down to a low C is not uncommon.

If you're serious about radical alternate tunings, adjust the individual string gauges to maintain a reasonably consistent tension on the neck and to avoid sloppy tonality.

Processing the Guitar Sound

Compressor/Limiter/Gate/Expander

It's very common to use a compressor on an electric guitar. Most guitars have a very wide dynamic range, and many instruments have uneven string volumes due to substandard adjustment of the pickups and string height. A compressor is what gives a guitar that smooth always-in-your-face sound. It puts all the notes and chords into a very narrow dynamic range so there might not be much (if any) volume difference between a lightly plucked single note and a full power chord.

An outboard compressor designed for studio use can do a good job on guitar, but it's normal for the boxes made especially for guitar to work well in a player's setup. Most guitarists use a compressor in their setup, so when recording their guitar sounds, you usually don't need to compress much, if at all. When the guitarist has his stuff together, your job as the recordist is pretty simple. Whether you're running directly in or miking the speaker cabinet, your job is to capture the existing sound accurately rather than creating and shaping a new sound. You can put a compressor on the signal that's coming into the mixer if you need to, but ideally, the guitarist will have a properly adjusted compressor in his kit.

In a guitar setup that uses several effects, the compressor should be the first effect in the chain. This will give the best-sounding results and will help guard the rest of the effects from strong signals that might overdrive their inputs.

With a healthy amount of compression, the guitar will sustain longer, plus each note will be audible (even if the guitarist has bad technique). Listen to the difference the compressor makes on the simple guitar sounds in Audio Examples 2-14 and 2-15. Audio Example 1 was performed and recorded with no compression.

Audio Example 2-14
No Compression

Audio Example 2-15 demonstrates the same part with a healthy amount of compression. I've used a ratio of 4:1 with about 10 dB of gain reduction.

Audio Example 2-15
With Compression

Distortion

Distortion is a prime ingredient in many guitar sounds. The type of distortion that's used defines the character of the part and often determines whether the part will blend well in the mix.

There are many different foot pedal distortion boxes for guitar, and they all have different sounds. Some are very buzzy and harsh. Some are very full and warm. Harsh and buzzy distortion sounds are usually best for special effects, but they typically don't work very well in a mix because their sound doesn't blend well in most mixes. The distortion sounds that do mix well in the final product are generally the sounds that are smoother, warmer, and less strident.

Audio Examples 4-6 to 4-8 demonstrate totally different distortion sounds. In each case, the guitar is plugged into the distortion unit, then the distortion unit is plugged directly into the mixer.

The box in Audio Example 2-16 has a strident, buzzy distortion and isn't really usable.

Audio Example 2-16
Buzzy Distortion

The distortion box in Audio Example 2-17 is one manufacturer's attempt at simulating a tube amplifier distorting. This can be a very usable sound on a lot of commercial songs.

Audio Example 2-17
Simulated Tube Distortion

The distortion box in Audio Example 2-18 is another manufacturer's attempt at simulating the rock stack-type amp. This is a little more aggressive sound and can also work well in many settings.

Combining these sounds with the sound of a good amp can give them much more life and punch.

All-in-One Effects

These multi-effects processors are unbeatable for their convenience and power. Companies such as Line 6 and Roland have really led the way with great-sounding and powerful effects. Internal routing capabilities often let the user determine which order the signal path takes through the various effects. The ability to save a custom sound to memory for recall later is irresistible to most players.

As these devices have gotten more powerful and as the sounds have become more accurate, all-in-one effects pedals have become useful at any level. There is, however, an occasional trade-off, in which the simple convenience of the system tempts us to compromise the sound we really want for the music.

Whenever you're recording guitar through a multi-effects processor, try to save the application of reverberation and delay for mixdown. Effects are so easily applied and sounds are so quickly built, and they can sound so good with the track, that you might want to just print the sound with delay and reverb. Once you print the sound, there's no way to minimize the effects during mixdown. If you truly love the sound of the reverb and delay in your guitar rig, you can use it as an outboard effect during mixdown. Simply build an effect with reverberation and delay, feed it with an aux bus, then return the device outputs to the mixer channels.

Almost all of these effects pedals provide stereo outputs. On certain effects these outputs act as one big mono output; on others there is a distinct stereo image. Sounds that include chorus, phase shifting, and flanging effects are almost always stereo. In addition, most reverbera-tion effects are stereo. Many amp simulation algorithms offer multiple speaker outputs. If you're using basic compression and overdrive sounds, there is little benefit to recording the stereo outputs—mono will work well.

If you have the tracks available, go ahead and record the stereo outputs. It won't hurt anything, and you might create a nice psycho acoustic effect created by panning the channels during mixdown.

Stomp Boxes

There has been a movement toward the all-in-one guitar effects boxes and pedals because of their ease of use and powerful sound-shaping tools. However, the all-in-one devices don't always sound the best for certain applications. Hence, the single guitar effects pedal—the stomp box—still lives.

These small and inexpensive effects pedals let the musician shape a more characteristic and unique sound. Getting out the most popular multi-effects pedal is often inspiring for the player. Many of the small stomp boxes have become classic in their sound. The MXR Dyna-Comp still has a sound that I can't find on other devices. The Ibanez Tube Screamer is the same way. Even in a world-class studio, where the room is full of ultimate gear, engineers and producers are turning to some of these inexpensive vintage tools in the quest for a unique sound.

Digital Modeling

One of the exciting developments of the digital era is digital modeling. When I plug my Les Paul into my old Fender Deluxe amp, it produces a very characteristic and recognizable sound. That combination not only makes a characteristic sound that I could recognize a mile away, it also creates a unique and recognizable waveform that can be duplicated and repeated. It's a simple matter of mathematics to calculate the difference between the waveforms of the sound coming directly from the instrument and the sound after it has gone through the amplifier and out the speakers. Once we calculate the difference between the direct and amplified signal, that formula can be applied and added to any direct instrument sound. In this way, sonic character of nearly any amplification system can be cloned with incredible precision and accuracy.

The folks at Line 6 created an amplification system that uses this modeling principle in a very effective way. They have modeled the sounds of many different guitar amplifiers—the original Fenders, Marshalls, Rolands, Hi Watts, and so on. They've also modeled the classic guitar effects, including specific types of compression pedals, delays, choruses, and reverbs. They've even modeled the sound difference between various speaker cabinet configurations, from a single 10" speaker to a cabinet with four 12" speakers. I've played through most guitar amplification setups and I'm amazed at how accurate these models are. Most guitar effects manufacturers currently offer their own rendition of the modeling system.

Listen to the guitar sounds in Audio Example 2-19. I have a Gibson Les Paul plugged straight into the Line 6 amp, then running directly into the console. Those who have played guitar through these amps should recognize the sounds as very accurate and authentic. Because the modeling is so accurate, the amplification systems on these units must be clean and sonically transparent enough to faithfully reproduce the modeled sounds.

Audio Example 2-19

The Fender, Marshall, Roland JC-120, and Vox Sounds

This innovative company also offers The Pod, which has several different amps and effects available, along with a software interface for storing effects and creating patches.

As a purist, one might or might not appreciate the accuracy of these models. There is something special about the sound of the real thing that's difficult to quantify mathematically. However, there's no denying that these modeling systems provide vast flexibility to the home recordist who probably doesn't have all the classic amps and instruments readily available.

Equalizing the Guitar

The recording purist's approach to equalization has always been to record the signal without EQ. It's true that recording with a very extreme EQ can cause problems, but with many guitar sounds, you're endeavoring to create unique sounds. The tone is a key ingredient in these sounds so it's usually best to go ahead and print the equalized guitar signal.

There are certain EQ ranges that add specific qualities to guitar sounds. Depending on the type of guitar and style of music, EQ changes can have varying results. Here are some good starting points for equalizing a guitar.

Boosting 100 Hz can add a good, solid low end to most guitar sounds. Boost this frequency sparingly. It can be appropriate to turn this frequency up, but most of the time a boost here will conflict with the bass guitar. I end up cutting this frequency quite often on guitar. Listen as I turn 100 Hz up and down on the guitar sound in Audio Example 2-20.

Audio Example 2-20

Boost and Cut 100 Hz

200 Hz tends to be the muddy zone on many guitar sounds. A boost here can make the overall sound of the guitar dull. A cut at 200 Hz can expose the lows and the highs so that the entire sound

has more clarity and low-end punch. Cutting this frequency can help a double-coil pickup sound like a single-coil pickup. Audio Example 2-21 shows the effect of cutting and boosting 200 Hz.

Audio Example 2-21

Boost and Cut 200 Hz

The frequency range from 250 Hz to 350 Hz can add punch and help the blend of a distorted rock sound. Notice the change in texture of Audio Example 2-22 as I boost and cut 300 Hz.

Audio Example 2-22

Boost and Cut 300 Hz

The frequency range from 500 to 600 Hz often contains most of the body and punchy character. Try to hear the body of the sound change as I cut and boost 550 Hz on the guitar in Audio Example 2-23.

Audio Example 2-23

Boost and Cut 550 Hz

The frequency range from 2.5 kHz to about 5 kHz adds edge and definition to most guitar sounds. I'll boost and cut 4 kHz on the guitar sound in Audio Example 2-24.

Audio Example 2-24

Boost and Cut 4 kHz

Boosting 8 kHz to around 12 kHz makes many guitar sounds shimmer or sparkle. These frequencies can also contain much of the noise from the signal processors, so cutting these frequencies slightly can minimize many noise problems from the guitarist's equipment. Listen as I boost and cut 10 kHz on the guitar sound in Audio Example 2-25.

Audio Example 2-25
Boost and Cut 10 kHz

Video Example 2-2
Equalizing the Guitar Sound

The recording purist's approach to equalization has always been to print the signal to tape without EQ. It's true that recording with a very extreme EQ can cause problems, but with many guitar sounds, you're endeavoring to create different and unique sounds. The tone is almost always a key ingredient in these sounds, so it's usually best to go ahead and print the equalized guitar signal.

A word of caution: If the sound is heavy in bass frequency content, it's generally better to print with less lows than you think you'll need in mixdown. These frequencies are easy to turn up in the mix, and you won't lose anything by saving the addition of lows for mixdown. Low frequencies contain the most energy of all the frequencies and virtually control the VU readings. A sound with too many lows will read unnaturally hot on your meters. If you end up needing more high frequencies in the mix, they can be buried in the mass of lows. When this happens, your tracks become very noisy. As you try to recover the clarity by boosting the highs, you end up boosting processor noise and tape noise.

Delay

The use of delay on a guitar sound has the effect of placing the sound in a simple acoustical space. Delays of between 250 and 350 ms can give a full sound for vocal and instrumental solos (especially on ballads). This is a very popular sound. It's usually most desirable if the delay is in time with the music in some way. Audio Example 2-26 was recorded at a tempo of 120 bpm. I've added a 250-ms delay, which is in time with the eighth note at this tempo.

Audio Example 2-26

The 250-ms Delay

A slapback delay of 62.5 ms is in time with the thirty-second note, at 120 bpm, and gives an entirely different feel to Audio Example 2-27.

Audio Example 2-27

The 62.5-ms Delay

Regenerating a longer delay of about 200 to 350 ms can really smooth out a part. All of these effects usually make the guitarist sound like a better player than he or she really is. Guitarists love that! This enhancement can be advantageous to all concerned, but don't overdo the effects, or the part will get lost in the mix. It might lose definition and sound like it's far away.

Should I Print Reverb or Delay to Tape?

There are many different effects that a guitarist can show up with, and most of them sound pretty good. It's tempting to go with whatever sound the guitarist has up at the time and record it to tape. This approach can work well and might be preferred if you don't have much processing gear.

Ideally, have the guitarist get a good sound using whatever compression and distortion is needed for the part, but save the addition of all reverbs, delays, and choruses for mixdown. Record the raw sound and finish shaping it in the mix. This approach lets you get just the right delay length, delay amount, reverb sound, and chorus after you can hear the part in the context of the rest of the arrangement.

Be flexible. If a guitarist has come up with a great sound that might take you a while to duplicate, and if he or she wants to print the sound to tape, give it a try. Be conservative in the amount of reverb and delay that is included.

There are no hard and fast rules when it comes to creating innovative and exciting new sounds, so be open to trying new tricks.

Electronic Doubling

Doubling a guitar part is a very common technique. Doubling can smooth out some of the glitches in the performance and can give the guitar a very wide, bigger-than-life sound. Pan the double apart from the original instrument, and you'll usually get a multidimensional wall of guitar that can sonically carry much of the arrangement. Doubling works well in rock tunes in which the guitar must sound huge and impressive.

This doubling effect can be achieved in a couple of ways. Electronic doubling involves patching the instrument through a short delay, then combining that delay with the original instrument. A live double simply involves playing the part twice onto different tracks or recording two players (playing the identical part) onto one or two tracks. Both techniques sound great. Experiment! Let the music help you decide.

To set up an electronic double, use a delay time between 0 ms and about 35 ms. Short doubles, below about 7 ms, don't give a very broad-sounding double, but they can produce interesting and full sounds and are definitely worth trying. Pan the original guitar to one side and the delay to the other.

Audio Example 2-28 demonstrates a guitar part doubled electronically using a 23-ms delay and no regeneration.

Audio Example 2-28

The 23-ms Double

The Panned Electronic Double

1. *Plug aux out of the mixer into the digital delay line input.*
2. *Turn up the original guitar alone in the aux bus and raise the aux master level.*
3. *Plug the line output of the digital delay into the line input of an available mixer channel or effects return.*
4. *Set the delay time on the digital delay between 0 ms and 35 ms.*
5. *Pan the original guitar track to one side and the delayed signal to the other. Adjust the balance between original and delayed signals on the mixer's input faders.*

Aux Out

Input
Digital Delay
Output

Guitar

Delay

Audio Example 2-29 uses the same musical part as Audio Example 4-11, this time with a live double.

Audio Example 2-29

The Live Double

Always check a double in mono to make sure the part sounds good in both stereo and mono. Slight changes in delay time can make the part disappear or cut through strong in mono. Find the delay time that works well in stereo and mono. If you've panned the original full left and the delay full right, the sounds are very impressive in a stereo mix, but these hard-panned tracks often disappear when the mix is played in mono. Try repositioning the pan adjustments so they are only partially left and partially right.

Multi-Effects

The current arsenal of guitar effects includes several units that contain many different, high-quality digital effects. These multi-effects units are relatively inexpensive and can produce excellent premium-quality sounds. Take advantage of these effects and the guitarist's diligence in finding great sounds, but be conservative in printing reverb and delay to tape.

Chorus/Flanger/Phase Shifter

Chorus, flanger, and phase-shifting effects are very common and important to most styles of electric guitar. A smooth chorus or flange can give a clean guitar sound a ringing tone. It can add richness that's as inspiring to the rest of the musicians as it is to the guitarist. Listen to the chorus on the clean guitar part in Audio Example 2-30.

Audio Example 2-30

Chorus

A smooth phase shifter can add color to a ballad or interest to a funky rhythm guitar comp. Notice the interest that's added to Audio Example 2-31 by the phase shifter.

Audio Example 2-31

Phase Shifter

The chorus effects are often part of a solo guitar sound used together with distortion, compression, and delay. The guitar in Audio Example 2-32 is plugged into the compressor first, then the distortion, next the delay, and finally the chorus.

Audio Example 2-32

Multiple Effects

Reverberation

Reverb is a useful ingredient in the final mix and is used primarily to smooth out the guitar sound when it must blend into the mix. Too much reverb can spell disaster for the clarity and definition of a good guitar part. On the other hand, reverb can hide many flaws in a marginal guitar part. Adapt to your situation.

Most electric parts sound good with a bright hall reverb sound, a decay time of about 1.5 seconds, a predelay of about 80 ms, high diffusion, and high density. This kind of setting offers a good place to start shaping most guitar reverbs. Audio Example 2-33 demonstrates a guitar with this set of effects.

Audio Example 2-33

Hall Reverb

There are several other types of reverb that can sound great on many different musical parts. Experiment. Often, the sound of the guitar is so interesting with the delay, distortion, and chorus that there's really no need for much (if any) reverb. Clean guitar sounds typically benefit the most from interesting and more complex reverberation. For instance, slow, open ballads and arena rock projects sound good with hall and chamber reverb using decay times in the range of 1.5 to 3 seconds. Faster, punchy productions usually work well with plate, inverse, and gated reverbs that have a decay time between .5 and 1.5 seconds.

Try adjusting the predelay to add a different feel to the reverb sound. Longer predelays that match the tempo of the eighth note or quarter note can make the part sound closer to the listener and as if it was played in a large room. Listen as I adjust the predelay during Audio Example 2-34.

Audio Example 2-34

Adjusting Predelay

Panning

There might be two or more separate guitar parts with totally different sounds in the same song. Though this is common, it can cause a bit of a problem during mixdown, in which each part should be audible and understandable. Panning can play a key role in helping you separate these different-sounding parts for the listener's sake. When used along with different EQ settings for each guitar part, panning the instruments to very specific locations can produce excellent results.

When positioning guitars in the left to right spectrum, be sure you maintain an even balance for the overall mix. It's common for the guitar to be playing the primary harmonic rhythm part. If that part is panned even slightly to one side, the entire mix can sound one-sided.

Sometimes the main guitar part gets in the way of the lead vocal or some other instrument that's panned to center. Rather than panning the two parts apart from each other, try leaving the lead vocal in the center, then running the guitar through an electronic double. Pan the original guitar and the double apart from each other. This keeps the presence and aggressive sound of the guitar but lets the vocal be heard and understood better with less interference from the guitar.

Most modern guitar effects are stereo. They accept the single input from the guitar and have stereo outputs. These stereo outputs usually come from a stereo delay, chorus, flanger, or phase shifter that is built into the guitar effects processor. If I have enough available tracks I'll usually print both of those outputs to tape. When there aren't many tracks left, you generally can't print both outputs from the effect to tape. This is not really a problem. If we need to, we can run the guitar through a stereo chorus, flanger, or phase shifter during mixdown.

A major problem with multiple guitar parts arises when the mix is played in mono. All those tricky panning positions are laid on top of each other as everything goes to the center. It's crucial that each instrument has unique and different EQ characteristics to maintain some identity in a mono mix. The song in Audio Example 2-35 has three guitar parts. Listen to each part separately and notice that the sound on each is similar. Equalizing like this might sound okay in stereo, but when switched to mono, these parts don't retain much of their identity.

Audio Example 2-35
Conflicting Guitars

In Audio Example 2-36, first you hear each guitar part separately. Notice that each has very different-sounding EQ. I'll pan them to acceptable positions in the mix. Finally, see if you can still hear all the parts when I switch to mono at the end of the example.

Audio Example 2-36
Equalized for Mono

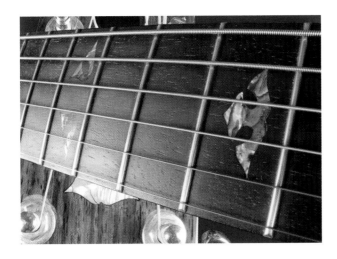

Recording Great Acoustic Guitar Tracks

Sound Characteristics

The sound of an acoustic guitar is amazingly pure and sonically rich. Like most of the symphonic instruments, year after year, generation after generation, the acoustic guitar sound remains fine just the way it is in its natural environment. Capturing the natural sound of an instrument that is so universally accepted and recognized is an important and fundamental skill in the recording world.

Experimentation with this acoustic instrument is not unheard of, but it's most common that the acoustic guitar is used for the natural depth it offers. A good acoustic guitar sound includes the natural transient of the string attack along with the fullness and body of the instrument.

At least 50% of the recorded sound—maybe it's 100%—is because of the musician. A bad player can't make the best guitar sound good; however, a great player can make music on almost any guitar. In your quest to find the ultimate sound, don't forget to give yourself a break if the player isn't cutting it musically.

Preparing the Instrument

Strings

If the strings are dead and lifeless on any acoustic guitar, the recorded sound will be dead and lifeless. No amount of equalization of effects will restore the rich tone that a good set of new strings provides.

Keep in mind that heavier-gauge strings provide more low frequency content. Most acoustic players use a medium-gauge set of strings because of the excellent balance of high and low frequencies they produce, along with reasonable playability. A lot of electric guitarists use light-gauge acoustic strings simply because their fingers are accustomed to playing on guitars with low action and thin strings.

Light-gauge acoustic strings produce adequate highs but weak lows. For the player, it's important to weigh the options. If you need a full strum sound from the acoustic guitar, you might have better luck using medium-gauge strings. However, the guitarist might perform a much more musical and technically acceptable part on lighter-gauge strings simply because he or she doesn't need to struggle to provide adequate finger pressure.

When recording acoustic guitar as part of a complex arrangement, it is sometimes preferable to use lighter strings because low-frequency information is typically removed to decrease cluttering in the mix.

There's one problem with new strings. They squeak more when the guitarist moves around on the neck. This can be a problem when recording. The best players usually have enough technique and finesse to play on brand new strings without much of a problem. For the rest of us, there can be other solutions. The quickest way to get the strings to squeak less is to put something slippery on them. Unfortunately, slippery products usually contain some sort of oil. Your local music store has access to commercially manufactured products designed to make guitar strings more slippery. These products can work very well. I even know people who put the thinnest possible coat of vegetable oil on their strings. Use any of these products sparingly. Oil on strings causes them to lose brilliance and clarity. You might end up with no squeaks at the expense of all that great acoustic guitar sound.

Picks

Another very important factor in the sound of an acoustic guitar is the pick. Playing with a thin pick gives a sound that has clearer high frequencies. The thin pick slapping as it plucks the strings becomes part of the sound. Playing with a thick pick produces a full sound with more bass and fewer highs, plus you don't get as much of the pick sound.

Audio Examples 3-1 and 3-2 use the same guitar and mic setup. The only change is the guitar pick. Audio Example 3-1 was performed with a very thin pick.

Audio Example 3-1

Thin Pick

Audio Example 3-2 was performed with a very thick pick.

Audio Example 3-2

Thick Pick

Alternate Tunings

Acoustic guitar has embraced the concept of alternate tunings for a long time. Whereas electric guitarists often do everything they can to avoid open strings, acoustic players rely on the open strings to provide the basis of richness and depth.

There are many alternate tunings that are regularly implemented in acoustic music. Some have become more common than others, but often tunings are selected in the heat of a session, with a player adjusting to the requirements of a specific piece of music.

Some of the most common alternate tunings are:

+ Dropped D tuning – DADGBE
+ Dropped G tuning – DGDGBE
+ Open G tuning – DGDGBD
+ Major D thord – DADF#AD
+ High-strung guitar – EADGBE Bottom four strings tuned up one octave. This tuning requires a change of string gauge on the lower strings. Try, from bottom to top, .034, .024, .013, .010, 016, .013.

Audio Example 3-3

Alternate Tunings

The Impact of Different Wood Configurations on Tone

Spruce Top

Spruce is the most common wood used for the acoustic guitar top. It provides a bright and full tone.

Rosewood Sides and Back

Rosewood is commonly used for the sides and back of the acoustic guitar. It provides a clean and bright tone, with tonal stability and transparency.

Mahogany Sides and Back

Guitars with mahogany sides and backs typically produce a warmer tone with a smoother midrange than guitars with rosewood. Whether mahogany or rosewood produces a better sound is not the question. They both provide a different musical feel and both are very applicable to any number of musical applications.

Electric Acoustic Guitars

Acoustic guitars with pickups can work well in a live performance situation—simply plug directly into the mixer, amplifier, or through a DI into the snake box on stage. You can get a passable sound and eliminate one microphone in the setup. However, though the sound can be okay for live performances, it's hardly ever a great sound for recording. The sound from an electric acoustic pickup typically sounds sterile and small, and it doesn't have the broad, full, interesting sound of the acoustic instrument. To run an electric acoustic guitar directly into a mixer, follow the same procedure as with any electric guitar.

The frequencies that tend to be over-accentuated by most acoustic guitar picks are typically between 1 and 2 kHz. Try using a parametric equalizer; set up a narrow-bandwidth cut and sweep the frequencies between 500 Hz and 3 kHz. You'll probably find one specific point that eliminates much of the brittle, edgy sound. Once you seek and destroy this problem frequency, the electric sound is passable. Most of the time, I find the problem frequency ends up between 1.2 and 1.5 kHz, but it really depends on the guitar, the room, and the sound system.

When the mid-range problem is solved, try adding a little clarity in the highs between 5 and 10 kHz—whatever sounds best in your application. In a recording situation, you might want to warm up the low end by boosting around 100 Hz; however, in a live setting this is a recipe for a very boomy feedback.

Recording Electric Acoustic

Recording acoustic guitar from its pickup rather than a microphone should be reserved for live recordings, special effects, artistically experimental recordings, or when there is no other option. At best the sound is usually thin, lacking the warmth of a recording made using a high-quality condenser microphone. Pickup configurations have gotten much better in recent years; however, in a recording application, miking the acoustic is still the preferred technique.

Connecting the electric acoustic is the same as connecting the regular electric guitar. You can either connect the guitar output directly into the mixer line input or through a DI to the mic input.

There is an amazing difference in the sound quality between direct boxes. Use a high-quality DI and be sure to test several on your guitar. I have found the Radial JDI, Countryman, and Demeter DIs provide excellent sound quality in this application.

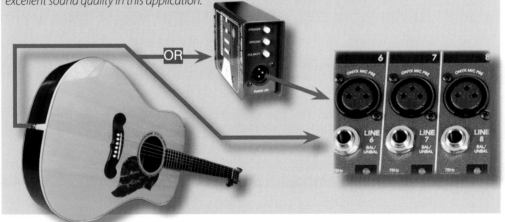

Audio Examples 3-4 and 3-5 use the same acoustic steel string guitar. Audio Example 3-4 demonstrates the acoustic guitar run directly into the board from the instrument pickup.

Audio Example 3-4

Acoustic Guitar Direct In

Audio Example 3-5 is the same guitar as Audio Example 3-4, using a microphone to capture its sound to tape.

Audio Example 3-5

Miking the Acoustic Guitar

The miked guitar has more tone and character; it sounds better. If you don't want the true sound of the instrument, running direct can produce some unique and usable sounds. There are all sorts of variables that can cause us to record in atypical ways. We need to be open to almost any approach in the interest of finding a new and exciting sound.

Video Example 3-1

Equalizing the Electric Acoustic Guitar

Recording Acoustic, Acoustically

Finding the Right Environment

It's very important to record any acoustic instrument in a space that sounds good, or at least makes the instrument sound good. If the recording space affects the guitar sound in a negative way, you'll have a very tough time getting the sound just right, even with the best and most expensive microphones, preamps, and recording systems.

Audio Example 3-6

Acoustic Guitar Recorded in Different Spaces

Mic Techniques

Mic Type

Typically, the best kind of mic to use on any acoustic guitar is a condenser mic. Condensers capture more of the subtlety of the attack, the sound of the pick on the strings, and the nuance of artistic expression. Also, condenser microphones produce a full sound when miking from a distance. Moving-coil mics and ribbon mics can produce passable acoustic guitar sounds, especially if that's all you have, but the accepted mic of choice for acoustic guitars is a condenser.

The steel string acoustic is the most common acoustic guitar. These guitars come in many different shapes, sizes, and brands. Each variation has a characteristic sound, but the primary trait of the acoustic guitar is a very clear and full sound. The second most common type of acoustic guitar is the nylon string classical guitar. Classical guitars have a warm, full, and mellow sound.

Audio Example 3-7 demonstrates the sound of a steel string acoustic guitar.

Audio Example 3-7

The Steel String Acoustic Guitar

Audio Example 3-8 demonstrates the sound of a nylon string classical guitar.

Audio Example 3-8

The Nylon String Classical Guitar

Mono Mic Techniques

In most cases it's best to keep it simple when miking an acoustic guitar. Selecting one great mic (typically a small-diaphragm condenser mic) and moving it to the one place that provides the sound you're looking for is a highly successful approach. The advantage of a single-mic technique is the assurance of mono compatibility and simplicity.

There are distinct regions on the acoustic guitar that provide pre-dictable tonal character. Aiming the mic at the sound hole provides a boomy, bass-heavy sound.

Video Example 3-2

Changing the Single Mic Position

In Audio Examples 3-7 and 3-8, I used a condenser mic about eight inches away from the guitar. With a condenser mic six to eight inches from the guitar, we can potentially get a sound that has too much bass, especially as we move over the sound hole. We can control the frequency content of the acoustic guitar sound dramatically by changing mic placement. If there are too many lows in your acoustic guitar sound, try moving the mic up the neck and away from the sound hole, moving the mic back away from the guitar to a distance of one or two feet or turning the low frequencies down.

One way to turn the low frequencies down is by using the bass roll-off switch. Most condenser microphones have a switch to turn the bass frequencies down. These switches may have a number by them to indicate the frequency at which the roll-off starts. The number is typically between 60 and 150. If there's no number, there might be a single line that slopes down to the left. When you use a condenser mic for close-miking, you'll usually need to use the bass roll-off switch to keep a good balance between lows and highs.

If we point a mic at different parts of the acoustic guitar while it's being played, we find that each zone has a different sound. There are all sorts of tricky ways to combine these different sounds from different places on the guitar, but it's usually best to keep it simple. More mics mean more chances of problematic phase interaction and more chance that your great stereo sound will turn to mush when your mix is heard in mono.

I've tried many techniques for miking acoustic guitars, using up to four or five mics. The method that consistently works the best for me uses one good condenser mic placed in the position that gets the sound I need for the track.

There are three common positions to mike the guitar: in front of the sound hole, behind the bridge, and over the neck. Though each instrument has its own characteristic sound, each of these possible mic positions holds a consistent type of sound from one guitar to the next: Over the neck contains the highs, over the sound hole contains the lows, and over the body behind the bridge contains the mids.

We'll use a steel string acoustic for the next set of Audio Examples, but all the techniques are worth trying on any acoustic steel string, nylon string or 12-string guitar.

Acoustic Guitar Mic Positions

Select the microphone position that provides the sound that best suits the music. Each mic position offers a different tonal balance. When you're setting the mic, try wearing headphones while you move the mic to different locations around the instrument. It's likely that you'll find the perfect sound, and you might be surprised at the mic position when you find it.

I typically prefer the sound I get when I place the mic six to eight inches away from the point where the neck joins the body, in front of the guitar—but each song, player, and guitar is different.

Mids — Lows — Highs

If you position the mic directly over the sound hole, the sound you'll capture will be bass-heavy and boomy, like the sound in Audio Example 3-9.

Audio Example 3-9

Microphone over the Sound Hole

If you position the mic over the top and behind the bridge, the sound will be strongest in mids, like the sound in Audio Example 3-10.

Audio Example 3-10

Microphone behind the Bridge

Point the mic at the front of the neck to hear more highs from the guitar, like the sound in Audio Example 3-11. This mic position can produce a good usable sound, but you might have a problem with string and finger noise.

Audio Example 3-11

Microphone over the Neck

The sound I get from one condenser mic pointed at the front of the neck, between the sound hole and where the neck joins the body of the guitar, is very often the most usable. That doesn't mean that I don't use other techniques, nor does it mean I'm not always trying new approaches on these instruments. In reality, we can do almost anything in almost any way and still get away with it if the sound supports the musical impact. Take these standard techniques and build on them. Push the limits.

When we miked the electric guitar amp, the room began to play an important part in the sound of the instrument. The same is true for miking the acoustic. As we move the mic away from the instrument, the character of the sound changes dramatically. The music you're recording determines the usefulness of room sound.

The acoustic guitar in Audio Example 3-12 was recorded with the mic six inches in front of the instrument, pointed between the sound hole and where the neck joins the body.

Audio Example 3-12
Over the Neck, Near the Sound Hole

Audio Example 3-13 demonstrates the guitar from Audio Example 3-12 with the mic three feet away from the instrument and pointed at the sound hole.

Audio Example 3-13
Three Feet Away

Video Example 3-3
Moving the Mic from behind the Bridge to above the Twelfth Fret

Audio Example 3-14 uses the same acoustic guitar as the previous two examples. The mic is still three feet from the guitar, but the guitar is in a smaller room than in Audio Example 3-13.

Audio Example 3-14
Smaller Room

Audio Example 3-15 keeps the same guitar and player as Audio Examples 3-12 to 3-14. This time the guitar is recorded in a bathroom.

Audio Example 3-15
The Bathroom

The acoustic guitar sounds in Audio Examples 3-12 to 3-15 are all different, though theoretically usable in a musical context. Sometimes we get so caught up in wanting more and more reverb and effects units that we forget what great sounds are right in front of us, in our own living or working space. They're always at hand at no additional cost. What a deal! In addition, if you add effects to some of these interesting acoustic sounds, you might end up with some unique textures that add individuality to your sound.

Individual acoustic guitars often produce different tonal balance when miked at different spots. In other words, there isn't one microphone placement that works best for every guitar. Experiment with each instrument to find the sounds you like.

Stereo Mic Techniques

Many engineers prefer to record acoustic guitar using stereo mic technique. Overall, it's usually best, especially in your formative years, to record acoustic using a single microphone. However, there are many musical situations in which a unique stereo image provided by two well-placed microphones is very desirable. Try these techniques and decide for yourself which approach fits the way you do music. There is no right or wrong approach. Simply choose the technique that provides the emotionally and musically appropriate sound.

Any time you implement a stereo mic technique, adhere to the 3:1 rule to minimize negative phase interactions.

The 3:1 Rule

The 3:1 rule provides a guideline for multiple mic placement that will typically produce an acceptable amount of separation—with minimal phase degradation—between the recorded and live tracks. It simply states that, considering any two microphones in the same acoustic space, the distance between the two microphones should be at least three times the distance from either mic to the intended source.

Coincident miking techniques, such as the XY, offer the exception to this rule, since their purpose is to capture a phase-coherent stereo image of one source, rather than separation between sources in the same acoustic space.

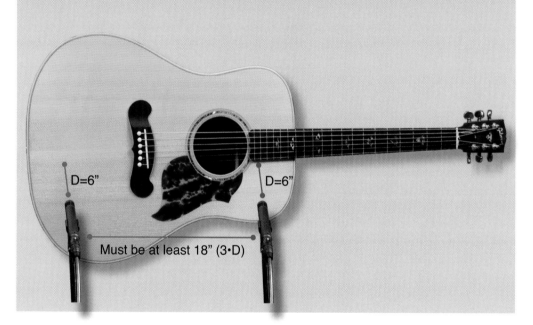

Spaced Pair

+ One mic over the twelfth fret
+ One mic over the bridge

XY at the Twelfth Fret

+ Position a traditional XY configuration, aimed at the twelfth fret, from a distance of 6 to 10 inches.

XY Distant Technique, Moving the Mic to Find the Sweet Spot

+ Create an XY configuration and from a distance of 1 to 4 feet, move the mics to locate the sweet spot.

Spaced Pair

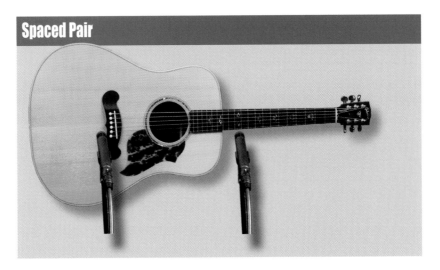

If you have the pleasure of including an assistant in your setup, have the assistant move the mics to the position of your choice. Be sure the assistant is wearing headphones so you have easy communications. Another good technique is to actually move your head around the guitar to find the spot that sounds the best to you. The right position for any distant mic placement is always dependent on the sound source, the placement in the room, and the inherent room acoustics.

XY at the Twelfth Fret

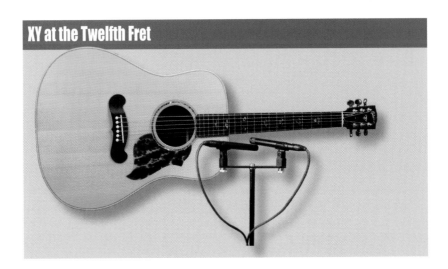

Player's Perspective Spaced Pair

- One mic over the twelfth fret
- One mic at the player's right ear, pointing down at the guitar

This one is touchy in terms of phase interaction. Slight movement of the mics results in substantial changes in mono.

One Mic in Front and One Mic in Back

Because this technique involves microphones pointing at each other through the guitar, it's typically necessary to invert the phase of the back mic.

Video Example 3-4

Spaced Pair, Player's Perspective Spaced Pair,
XY at the Twelfth Fret, and XY Distant Technique

Recording Acoustic Guitar and Voice Together

There will be times when the singer needs to play the acoustic guitar and sing at the same time. This is absolutely not ideal from a technical perspective; however, it is sometimes the only way to capture a truly musical performance. A struggle to record better music always wins over a struggle to record more technically precise bits and bites.

All you can do in this situation is optimize the details over which you have control. Initially, close-mike the guitar and voice separately. Use what you already know about microphones. Microphones with a hypercardioid polar characteristic exhibit the narrowest pickup pattern, so using this kind of mic will minimize leakage.

The biggest drawback in this scenario is that it's nearly impossible to overdub the guitar or the voice. It's also very difficult to apply effects separately to the voice and the guitar because the leakage from one feeds the effect being applied to the other.

Using a computer-based digital system provides editing flexibilty to combine multiple takes into one solid performance. Record both mics to individual tracks, repeating the process for as many takes as are required to cover all the parts well, then comp them together after the fact. You might need to record several complete takes, then fix it later—if the player can't separate playing from singing, there's a good chance he or she won't be comfortable with starting and stopping to duplicate a phrase with a little different interpretation.

Given plenty of patience and a good singer/player, you can make this technique work well. It is well worth the hassle as long as the music benefits.

Tuning/Instrument Selection

The age of the strings plays a very important role in the sound of any guitar. It's especially important on acoustic guitars. New strings add clarity and high frequency. Old strings produce a sound that's dull and muffled.

Guitar strings come in different gauges, or sizes. Light-gauge strings are thinner than heavy-gauge strings. Light-gauge strings produce a sound that has less bass and more highs—the sound is thinner. Lighter strings also give less volume than heavy strings and don't project as well in a group. These strings might not work well in a live acoustic performance situation, but in the studio they can give you a very clean, transparent, and usable sound. This kind of sound works very well for single-note-picking parts and arpeggiated chords.

Medium- and heavy-gauge strings produce more volume and bass frequencies than light-gauge strings; they give the guitar a full sound.

The sound of heavier strings is typically even in level, from lows to highs. This kind of sound works very well for rhythm-strumming parts.

Dynamic Processing and the Acoustic Guitar

Acoustic guitars have a wide dynamic range. A compressor can help even out the volume level of the different pitch ranges and strings. Some instruments even have individual notes that are much louder than others. Low notes (on the larger strings) will often produce a lot more energy and volume than higher notes on the smaller strings—it all depends on the instrument.

Try this approach to compressing the acoustic guitar:

+ Set the ratio control between 3:1 and 5:1.
+ Adjust the attack time. Slower attack times accentuate the sound of the pick. The fastest attack times will de-emphasize the sound of the pick.
+ Adjust the release time. Setting this control between one and two seconds usually results in the smoothest sound.
+ Adjust the threshold for a gain reduction of 3 to 7 dB on the loudest part of the track.

Audio Example 3-16 demonstrates the acoustic guitar without compression.

Audio Example 3-16
No Compression

Audio Example 14 uses the same acoustic guitar as Audio Example 3-17. This time the signal is compressed with a gain reduction of up to 7 dB.

Audio Example 3-17
Compressed

Acoustic Guitar Note before Compression

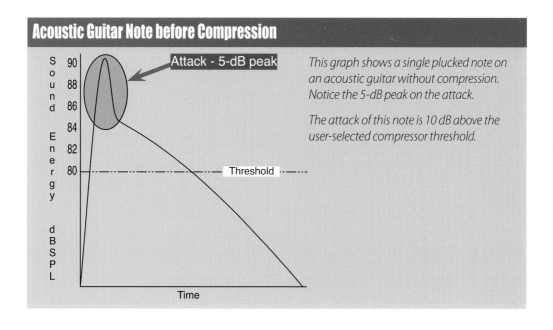

This graph shows a single plucked note on an acoustic guitar without compression. Notice the 5-dB peak on the attack.

The attack of this note is 10 dB above the user-selected compressor threshold.

Compressed Guitar Note with a Fast Attack

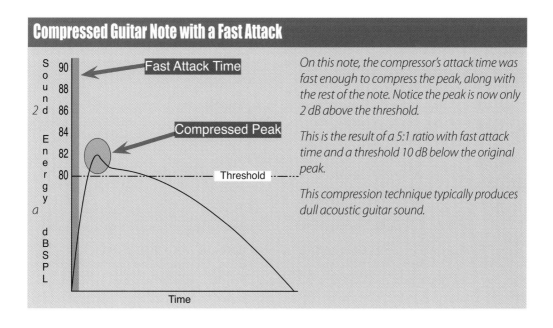

On this note, the compressor's attack time was fast enough to compress the peak, along with the rest of the note. Notice the peak is now only 2 dB above the threshold.

This is the result of a 5:1 ratio with fast attack time and a threshold 10 dB below the original peak.

This compression technique typically produces dull acoustic guitar sound.

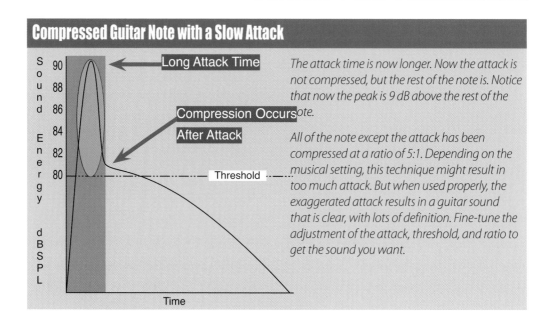

Compressed Guitar Note with a Slow Attack

Long Attack Time

Compression Occurs After Attack

Threshold

Sound Energy dB SPL

Time

The attack time is now longer. Now the attack is not compressed, but the rest of the note is. Notice that now the peak is 9 dB above the rest of the note.

All of the note except the attack has been compressed at a ratio of 5:1. Depending on the musical setting, this technique might result in too much attack. But when used properly, the exaggerated attack results in a guitar sound that is clear, with lots of definition. Fine-tune the adjustment of the attack, threshold, and ratio to get the sound you want.

Double-Tracking the Acoustic Guitar

One way to get a really full sound from the acoustic is to do a live double track. If you play the original track in the headphones, a good guitarist should be able to duplicate the part with a fair degree of accuracy. Pan these two tracks apart during playback. This creates a chorus-delay-flange-phase shifting effect that happens naturally as the two parts work together.

Audio Examples 3-18 and 3-19 demonstrate this double-tracking technique. Listen to Audio Example 3-18 for the original track.

Audio Example 3-18

Acoustic Guitar

Audio Example 3-19 shows how adding the double-tracked acoustic adds fullness and depth, especially when the two parts are panned away from each other in the stereo spectrum.

Audio Example 3-19

Adding the Double Track

Constructing Acoustic Guitar Parts

It helps in the recording process if the engineer has an idea of how acoustic guitar parts are constructed. A few basic concepts are used over and over. They work well in a song, and they can work well when combined during the same song.

Arpeggios

In an arpeggio the guitarist holds a chord and plays the individual notes, typically letting each ring while the chord is held. The notes are played in whatever order is most musical for the song. Arpeggios provide a very solid and interesting foundation for a song; however, avoid including multiple instruments arpeggiating together. Too many musicians playing random chord tones ends up sounding muddy very quickly.

Strum Patterns

It's most common for the acoustic guitarist to develop a rhythmic strum pattern that repeats throughout the tune. Sometimes the verse is a strum pattern and the chorus is arpeggiated, or vice versa. Strum patterns are typically based on the rhythmic background unit. If the player has a great sense of timing and beat placement, all is well. If the player is rhythmically handicapped, the song could be in jeopardy.

Digital editing allows you to move beats in time to create the proper musical feel. This is where you need to be an excellent musician, too. There are countless musical decisions we make from the technical side, and the more you know about good music, the greater your value will be in the recording community.

Sometimes it's necessary to create an acceptable verse or chorus and then copy it to the other verses and choruses. It might seem at first like you're putting a lot of time into a small ingredient—welcome to the wonderful world of recording. You must do what it takes to provide the foundation for an excellent musical work. Anything short of that lofty goal is a waste.

Single Lines

Single lines (streams of single notes) on the acoustic guitar can add great emotional depth and tension, especially when combined with a strum pattern or arpeggio. Whether or not single-line parts have great musical power is typically dependent on the performance.

Single lines, in the form of acoustic guitar solos, are common in some styles.

Whenever you're recording single-note parts or solos, compression helps smooth out the volume differences between the notes. It's best to save more severe compression for the mixdown process so you can fine-tune the positioning and intensity of the musical part.

Mixing Acoustic Guitar

Equalizing the Acoustic Guitar

We use equalization on acoustic guitar to shape the sound for the space in the mix that we want the guitar to fill. From our audio examples, you can tell that much of the sound can be shaped through mic placement, string selection, and pick selection. If we have a well-maintained guitar with the correct mic placed precisely where it should be and a great player playing the appropriate strings with the perfect pick, using impeccable technique to play wonderful parts that have phenomenal artistic expression, we might not need to use much EQ, if any.

Let's look at some common solutions to equalization problems you might encounter when recording acoustic guitars. The most common equalization of the acoustic guitar involves cutting the low frequencies, below 150 Hz. Lows can be predominant and boomy on an acoustic guitar. These low frequencies can clash with the bass guitar, bass drum, piano, or any full-range instrument. In Audio Example 3-20, I'll turn the frequencies below 150 Hz down. This can make the guitar sound a little thin when it is by itself, but this sound generally works best in the mix.

Audio Example 3-20

Cut 150 Hz

Another common EQ for acoustic guitar involves adding a high-frequency shimmer at about 10 to 12 kHz. On the guitar in Audio Example 3-21, I'll boost 12 kHz.

Audio Example 3-21

Boost 12 kHz

If the guitar is sounding muddy, we can usually clean the sound up by turning the lower mids down (between 200 and 500 Hz). Listen to the change in the guitar sound in Audio Example 3-22 as I turn down the curve centered on 300 Hz.

Audio Example 3-22

Cut 300 Hz

When you need more edge or definition from the sound, boost a frequency between 3 and 5 kHz. Audio Example 3-23 demonstrates the sound of boosting the acoustic guitar at 4 kHz.

Audio Example 3-23

Boost 4 kHz

Adjust a frequency between 1.5 and 2.5 kHz to emphasize or de-emphasize the sound of the pick hitting the strings. The actual frequency you select depends on the type of strings, the gauge of the strings, the physical makeup of the guitar, and the pick. In Audio Example 3-24, I boost and then cut 2 kHz.

Audio Example 3-24

Boost and Cut 2 kHz

Video Example 3-5

Adjusting EQ on the Acoustic Guitar

Reverberation

The choice of reverberation when recording acoustic guitar is dependent on the musical style and arrangement of the song. In folk, country, or blues, the acoustic guitar might use little or no reverb. Any reverberation used in these styles is typically very natural-sounding. Hall and chamber settings on digital reverbs can smooth out the sound without being intrusive or obvious. Decay times of one to two seconds work very well. These reverberation settings can help the part blend into the mix without dominating the sound of a song.

On the folk-style part in Audio Example 3-25, I start with no reverberation, then I add a small amount of chamber reverb with a 1.5-second decay time.

Audio Example 3-25

Chamber Reverb

Pop and commercial rock musical styles are more likely to use chorus-type effects and unnatural sounding reverb. Even in these styles, the acoustic guitar is often treated as a natural instrument. If chorus effects or delays are used, they're typically intended to simulate the effect of double tracking.

Ballads are more likely to use more effect on the acoustic guitar. The rich texture of the reverberated guitar can be heard and appreciated in the open texture of a pop ballad.

In the proper context, any of the chorus, flanger, or phase shifter effects can sound great on acoustic guitar. The guitar in Audio Example 40 has a stereo flanger and slapback delay set to the same speed as the eighth note. This is a very usable sound, although it doesn't reflect the purist's approach to the acoustic guitar.

Classical Guitar (Nylon String Guitar)

When we use the term *acoustic guitar*, we typically refer to the steel-string guitar, although technically the acoustic family includes all guitars producing a viable and recordable acoustic sound (steel string, classical, 12-string, etc.).

Classical guitar is sometimes used as the foundation for a song, but often the mellow tone it produces gets buried in a group context. Therefore, it is commonly recorded as a single instrument backup to a vocal track or as a solo instrument with a band track. When used for a solo, the classical guitar provides a warm and very intimate tone that draws the listener into the music.

There is abundant classical literature written specifically for this instrument. Some of the most emotionally wrenching pieces for classical guitar come from this well-respected library.

Use the same mic techniques for classical guitar that you use for the steel string guitar. Adjust positioning and proximity to fine-tune the guitar tone. The orchestration and the musical texture should guide your decisions.

Recording Great Drum and Percussion Tracks

The Percussion Family

You must listen to excellent examples of the genre that you're recording. Specifically, drum and percussion sounds define the character and impact of any musical style. Most people haven't listened enough with analytical ears to decide what they like and dislike about certain drum sounds. They have nothing on which to base their opinions.

When considering drum sounds, some common characteristics exist in drum sounds that most of us would call good. The term good is obviously subject to individual opinion. A good drum sound must also be appropriate for the musical style of the song that it's in.

Good drum sounds will almost always have:

- Clean highs that blend with the mix
- Solid lows that blend with the mix
- Enough mids to feel punch
- Not so many mids that the sound is muddy
- Natural sound that possesses a warm tone
- Dimension, often sounding larger than life
- Believably appropriate reverberation
- Balance and blend in the mix

The most important thing you can do at this point is listen to many different styles of music that have been recorded in a lot of different studios by many different top-notch professionals. Subject yourself to a large quantity of music. Try to be very analytical about the sounds you're hearing. It's one thing to let the music passively cross your ears; it's another to actually hear what's going on texturally, musically, and sonically.

Drum Conditioning

To get good drum sounds, it's necessary to be familiar with drum tuning and dampening techniques. A bad-sounding drum is nearly impossible to get a good recorded sound from. A good-sounding drum can make your recording experience much more enjoyable.

If the drum heads are dented and stretched out, cancel the rest of your appointments for the day. You'll be spending a substantial amount of time getting an acceptable drum sound.

If the drums aren't high-quality instruments, there's a good chance that the shells aren't smooth and level, and there's a possibility that the drums aren't even perfectly round. If this is the case, the heads won't seat evenly on the drum shell and there'll be a loss of tone, detracting from the drum sound.

Tuning

Often, the difference between a good-sounding drum and a bad-sounding drum lies simply in tuning. The standard approach to tuning involves

- Tuning the top head to the tone you want
- Making sure the pitch is the same all the way around the head by tapping at each lug and adjusting the lugs until they all match
- Duplicating the sound of the top head with the bottom head

If the head isn't tuned evenly all the way around, the head won't resonate well. You'll probably hear more extraneous overtones than smooth tones.

Audio Example 4-1

A Poorly Tuned Tom

Drumsticks

The drummer's choice of sticks and their condition can make a big difference in the sound of the drums. Nylon-tipped sticks have a brighter-sounding attack than wood-tipped sticks, especially on cymbals. Hickory sticks have a different sound than oak sticks, and they both sound different than graphite or metal sticks. Heavy sticks have a completely different sound than light sticks.

Most experienced studio drummers carry several different types of drumsticks with them, even though they each probably have an overall favorite.

If you want to be prepared when recording drums, it's worth the investment to have some extra sticks available that vary in size and physical composition.

Muffling Drums

There are several techniques for muffling and dampening drum tone. Trends shift with time and genre. Whereas drums of one era and style are highly controlled and dampened, drums of the next are open and free. It's your job to stay in touch with current trends, adjusting your techniques accordingly.

Don't use muffling as a substitute for a well-tuned drum. It's hard to beat the sound of a great drum with great natural tone. I try to use a dampening technique to lightly control unwanted overtones that I know will be difficult to deal with during mixdown.

Try each of the illustrated dampening techniques to hear the difference in the sound of each approach. I've gotten great sounds by using self-adhering weather stripping and a product called Moon Gel, applying the amount of material in the positions that create the sound I want. Moon Gel is a jello-like solid rectangle, approximately 1 x 1.5 x .125 inches. This is a very flexible approach. Both Moon Gel and the foam weather stripping are easy to move around for the desired sound and they provide an even, natural sound and appealing dampening. Moon Gel sticks to the head much like weather stripping, without the sticky residue.

Hardware

Hardware matters. It provides a stable and solid foundation for drum tone. The drum hardware is a good indicator of overall product quality and attention to detail. Drums with excellent hardware will almost always sound better than drums with substandard hardware.

Shells that are true and hoops that are meticulously crafted make your job a lot easier. If the head does not make even contact around the shell it's very difficult to get good tone from the drum.

Mounting hardware is also crucial, especially tom mounts. Any mount system that lets the drum float with no screwed-in hardware provides the drum the opportunity to sing. Imagine screwing a large bracket to the face of an acoustic guitar—it's easy to imagine there might be a change in the sound. The same is true for drums. A company called RIMS makes a great mount system that holds the drum by a set of lugs, and the difference in sound is notable. Most major drum manufacturers currently have free-floating tom mount systems.

I've never had good luck miking floor toms with legs. The tone seems to transfer through the legs to the floor. Whenever possible mount floor

Free-Hanging Tom Mount Systems

Toms are typically the most difficult of the drums to find the perfect sound for. The tone is often full of dominant overtones, or even just a lack of tone. This is especially true of drum sets that use a mounting bracket that attaches to the tom shell and is held in position by a tube that penetrates the bracket and clamps into place. Attaching any solid bracket to any drum (kick drums or toms) chokes the sound and provides an unimpressive tone.

Mounts like the one pictured, which let the drum hang freely, allow the drum to vibrate naturally, providing an excellent tone with much less tinkering by the drummer and engineer.

toms on a stand and suspend them from a free-floating mount such as the RIMS system.

Avoid mounting anything on the kick drum. Toms and cymbals should be mounted on separate stands, not on brackets screwed into the kick drum. The more freedom any drum has from contact with any other solid object, the better it will sound.

Room Acoustics

This size and shape of the acoustical environment is very influential on the sound of the drums. If the drums don't sound good in the room, they probably won't sound good recorded. A drum set requires a certain amount of space for the sound of the kit to fully develop. In addition, the overall sound of the kit becomes trapped in a small room. Leakage and immediate reflections off the surrounding surfaces combine in damaging phase relationships at each of the microphones—especially the overheads and room mics.

Larger studios tend to provide adequate space for the drum sounds to develop their full potential. Not only does the size of the room affect the sound of the drums, but where you place the drums in the room affects the sound. To determine the best position of the drums in room, first carry the floor tom around the room, striking it at each location to determine where it sounds good. Because the floor tom is often the most difficult to get to sound good, once you find the position where this drums works well, most of the rest of the kit will also sound good.

Even once you find a good location for the drumset, listen to the entire kit at that location, then determine whether you like the sound. During planning, allow plenty of time to get a good drum sound. Spending the time necessary to find the best location, the best microphones, and the best drum kit is a very worthwhile investment in the sound of the recording project.

The density and absorption characteristics of the acoustical environment are as important to achieving a great drum sound as the size of the environment. If a room is too dead, the sound loses life and character. If the room is too live, it's difficult to achieve an intimate sound. Because each song and each style of music is unique, experiment with microphone techniques and acoustical spaces. Find the sound for the drums that best supports the musical vision.

Theories of Drum Miking

Most of the drum sounds you hear on albums are achieved through the use of several microphones recorded separately to several tracks that are blended and balanced during the mixdown. This is ideal. Practically speaking, most people don't have a pile of microphones to use at home, let alone eight to 12 available tracks on the multitrack for drums. Most people have one or two microphones, and these microphones weren't purchased with drums or percussion in mind, but as your setup and skills build, you'll want to build your arsenal of task-specific microphones.

Essential Microphones

You should have a good condenser mic for over the drum set and for cymbals. Condensers are the mic of choice for percussion, and they do the best job of capturing the true sound of each instrument. The fact that condenser microphones respond to transients more accurately than the other types of microphones makes them an obvious choice for percussion instruments, such as tambourine, shaker, cymbals, triangle, claves, or guiro.

Mic Choices

The mic of choice for close-miking toms, snare, and kick is a moving-coil mic, such as a Shure SM57, Sennheiser 421 or Electro-Voice RE20. Though they don't have the transient response of condenser microphones, moving-coil microphones work great for close-miking drums because they can withstand intense amounts of volume before distorting. Also, most moving-coil microphones have a built-in sensitivity in the upper frequency range, which provides an EQ that accentuates the attack of the drum.

Most reasonably priced condenser and moving-coil microphones provide good results. Don't overlook the obscure. As trends come and go we all start hunting for unique and interesting sounds that imprint a sonic personality. Keep all the mics you can get your hands on. Even a cheap lo-fi mic might be the perfect tool to create an interesting and musical sound.

Positioning the Microphones

Keep the mic out of the drummer's way because a stick hitting the mic can ruin a take or even a microphone. Most mic manufacturers make microphones that are designed for getting into tight spots like drum sets. If the mic has to be pointing straight across the drum due to space restriction, there will be more leakage between drums. It's best to point the mics at the drums, 1 to 2 inches away, and at an angle of 30 to 45 degrees.

It's best to use a mic stand for each drum mic, rather than using stands that mount on the drum rims. The less that touches the drum, the better the tone.

Phase Interaction between Mics

Whenever you're close miking the kit, be particularly aware of phase interactions between microphones. With up to 10 microphones placed in a small acoustical environment, the leakage between microphones can enhance or rule that sound of the drum set.

Keep in mind the 3:1 rule. When placing microphones, the distance from one microphone to its intended source should be no more than one-third the distance between it and another microphone. Adhering to this suggested ratio between microphones at least provides some assurance that native phase influences will be minimal.

When placing microphones, movements of an inch or two by one microphone make an amazing difference in the overall sound of the drum kit. Experiment with placement and position to get the perfect

The 3:1 Rule

The distance between microphones in any multi-mic setup should be at least three times the distance from either mic to its intended source. This is especially true in drum mic setups. The fact that there are often several mics used to record the kit provides ample opportunity for destructive phase interactions. Always maximize your efforts to find the perfect mic positions. Small changes can produce huge changes in the overall drum sound.

Distance between mics must be at least 3 times D

Distance = D

Distance = D

sound. If you settle for the wrong sound, everything else will be difficult. Phase interactions and leakage increase the likelihood that small changes in mic position produce large changes in overall sound quality.

Recording Level

Digital

If you're using a digital recorder, don't push the drum levels above the meter's peak. The digital recording process has a pretty hard ceiling. There is no benefit to exceeding the preset maximum digital recording level. A couple of the mastering engineers I work with push digital levels beyond their intended maximum in an effort to create compact discs that are the loudest on the block. Their equipment is meticulously maintained and they have plenty of headroom in their systems, which are designed to push the limits. They win most of the awards for doing it the best, but when engineering a digital recording, we don't need to exceed maximum digital recording levels.

Analog

Sometimes it's very desirable to record drums tracks (except the overheads and hi-hat) at analog levels exceeding 0 VU. A drum that's been recorded hot (in the range of +2 to +5 VU) won't usually give a buzzing kind of distortion; as the analog tape reaches the point where it can't handle more magnetism, it will usually produce compressed rather than distorted sound. This point is called the *point of oversaturation*. The sound of analog tape approaching the point of oversaturation has become an effect in its own right for recording drums. It's common for kick and toms to be recorded very hot to analog tape specifically for the sound this technique produces. It's also common for kick, snare, and toms to be recorded at 0 VU (or colder) to ensure that the transient will be accurately recorded. These are musically based decisions that you can make if you're stylistically aware or creatively attuned.

Acoustic Considerations

Music is about creativity and passion. It is as valid to capture drums with one mic as with 20. The pertinence is determined by musical and artistic evaluation, not the track count.

Mic placement is the main concern when using one mic to record the drums. Where you place the mic in relation to the drums is the primary determining factor of balance between the drums and intimacy of the drum sounds.

Including the acoustic sound of the room that the drums are in makes a big difference in the sound of the track. The amount of room sound that you include in the drum track can totally change the effect of the drum part. The sound of the room that the drum set is in plays

Portable System

Technology is changing the way we do business. A small system like this is easy to take to the location of your choice. Try recording your drum track in a theater, concert hall, or gymnasium.

This system includes a Macintosh PowerBook, software, some microphones, and a Mackie Onyx mixer. This mixer includes the FireWire card option. All I had to do was plug the FireWire into my PowerBook and my recording software instantly recognized the mixer and functioned flawlessly with it as a digital interface and mixer.

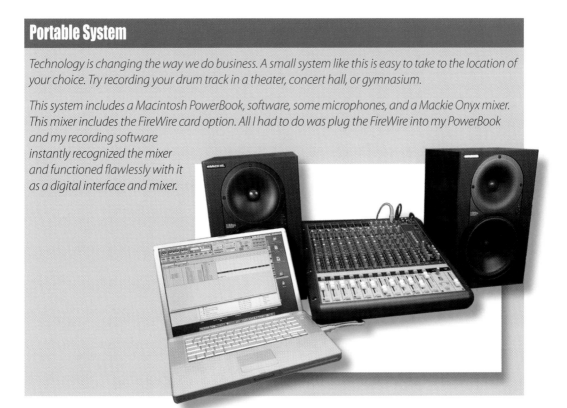

a very important role in the sound of the drum track, especially if you use a distant miking technique.

With the advent of high-quality portable recording systems based on a laptop computer and a small audio interface, you're no longer limited to recording the drums in one substandard acoustical space. Try moving the recorder and the drums into a warehouse, concert hall, or gymnasium. Recording in these larger spaces can give your drum sounds punch, life, and character that simply can't be electronically duplicated.

Recording a Drum Set with One Microphone

Listen to the examples of a complete drum set recorded with one microphone. Audio Examples 2 to 5 all use the same drum set in the same studio.

One Mic in Front

This setup uses a condenser microphone with a cardioid pickup pattern positioned in front of the set, pointed at the set, approximately 6' above the floor.

One Mic over the Drummer's Head

This setup uses a condenser microphone with a cardioid pickup pattern behind the kit, directly over the drummer's head, pointed at the set, about 6' above the floor.

In Audio Example 4-2 the drum set was recorded with one mic directly in front of the kit, pointed at the set, and about six feet from the floor.

Audio Example 4-2

Mic in Front

One Mic Overhead

This setup uses one cardioid condenser microphone pointed down at the drums from a distance of about 4'.

In Audio Example 4-3 the mic is behind the kit, just above the drummer's head, and pointed at the kit.

Audio Example 4-3
Mic over the Drummer's Head

In Audio Example 4-4 the mic is about four feet above the set and is pointed down at the drums. When a mic is placed over the drums and points down at the set, it's called an *overhead*.

Audio Example 4-4
Overhead

Finally, in Audio Example 4-5 we hear the drum set from one mic, positioned about eight feet away and pointed toward the kit.

Audio Example 4-5
Eight Feet Away

One Mic Eight Feet Away

This setup uses a condenser mic with a cardioid or omni pickup pattern 8' from the kit, pointed toward the drums.

Recording a Kit with Two Mics

With two microphones on the set there are two primary options: You can use both mics together in a stereo configuration or you can use one mic for overall pickup while using the other for a specific instrument.

In Audio Example 4-6, I've set one mic directly over the kit with the second mic in the kick drum. When you use one of the microphones for the overall kit sound you can place the second mic on the kick drum (or possibly the snare) to get individual control, punch, and definition in the mix. Choosing to close-mike the kick or the snare is purely a musical decision that's dependent on the drum part and the desired effect in the arrangement. This mic setup is more flexible than the single mic technique, but we're still limited to a monaural sound because the kick or snare would almost always be positioned in the center of the mix with the rest of the set.

One Mic Overhead, One in the Kick

1. *One cardioid condenser micro-phone is pointing down at the kit.*
2. *One cardioid moving-coil micro-phone is inside the kick drum, aimed at the head, about halfway between the center of the head and the shell.*

One Mic over the Kit, One in the Kick

Audio Example 4-7 uses the two condenser microphones with cardioid polar patterns as a stereo pair. The two mics are placed in a traditional X-Y configuration, directly above the drum set, at a distance of approximately three feet above the cymbals, pointing down at the drums. With this configuration, we can get a sound that has a stereo spread. As we get into the mixing process, we'll see that positioning supportive instruments away from the center of the mix helps us hear the solo parts that are typically positioned in the center of the mix.

Stereo X-Y

Stereo X-Y Overhead

Two condenser microphones are 3' above the cymbals. The mics are at a 90° angle to each other, pointing down at the drums. With this X-Y configuration, the mic capsules should be positioned on the same horizontal and vertical plane. They should be close enough to each other so that they're nearly touching.

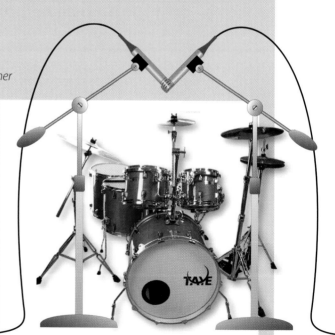

Try the X-Y configuration from different distances and in different rooms. Stereo mic technique is often the best choice for a very natural drum sound, but for contemporary commercial drum sounds, it lacks flexibility.

Another good two-mic technique involves placing one mic on each side of the drummer's head, level with his or her ears, pointing forward toward the drums. Position the microphones with their capsules three to six inches from the drummer's ears to achieve a good stereo image. The drummer's skull will act as a baffle between the two microphones. Audio Example 4-8 demonstrates this technique.

Audio Example 4-8

Head Baffle

Recording a Kit with Three Mics

If you use one mic on the kick, one mic on the snare, and one overhead mic, separate control of the kick and snare is possible. With three

X-Y Mic Technique

The traditional X-Y technique uses two cardioid condenser microphones positioned together to form a 90° angle. The mics should be overlapping and nearly touching.

This is called a coincident mic technique because the capsules are very close to each other and they share the same horizontal and vertical planes.

Coincident stereo mic techniques such as the X-Y configuration exhibit the least amount of adverse phase interaction when combined in a mono mix. Because the mic capsules are as close together as they can possibly be without touching, they hear the sound source nearly simultaneously; they receive the sound waves in the same phase.

Head Baffle

Two cardioid condenser microphones are positioned level with the drummer's ears, pointing toward the front of the kit. The mics are 4 to 8" from the drummer's head. This technique provides a very natural and balanced rendition of the kit.

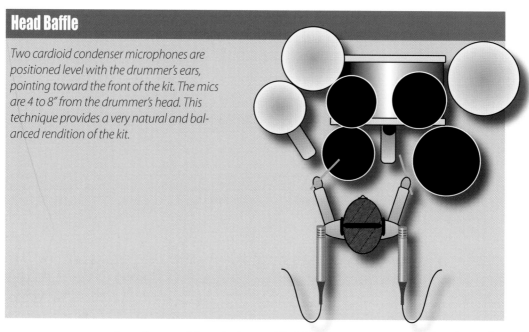

microphones, this technique will yield the most commercial and punchy sound. The kick and snare are the two main contributors to the definition of style. Being able to fine-tune their levels, EQ, and effects is an advantage. The drum set in Audio Example 4-9 was miked with one mic inside the kick, one mic two inches above the snare, and one mic about two feet above the cymbals. This configuration produces the most commercially viable results so far, but it doesn't provide a stereo image of the set. The kick, snare, and overhead are almost always positioned together in the center.

Audio Example 4-9

Three Microphones

If we use a kick and two overheads, we can get a stereo image of the kit, but we lose individual control of the snare. Another option is to put the single mic on the snare instead of the kick, combining that mic with the two overheads. This can be a usable option, but we sacrifice control of the kick. Audio Example 4-10 demonstrates the sound of a drum set with two microphones overhead, in an X-Y configuration, combined with one mic inside the kick.

Audio Example 4-10

X-Y Overhead, One in the Kick

Recording a Kit with Four Mics

With four microphones on the set, you begin to have good control over the kick and snare sounds, plus you can get a stereo image. Some very acceptable drum sounds can be achieved using a setup with one kick mic, one snare mic, and two overheads. You'll need to experiment with placement of the microphones (especially the overheads), but solid

Recording the Kit with Three Microphones

1. One cardioid condenser mic placed 2' above the cymbals, pointing down at the set.
2. One cardioid moving-coil mic pointing at the snare, from a distance of approximately 2".
3. One cardioid moving-coil mic inside the kick, positioned for the best sound.

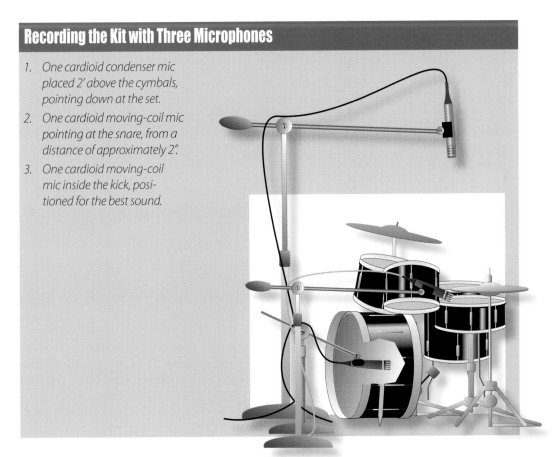

and unique kick and snare drum sounds are possible with this mic technique. The individual microphones plus the overheads used in a stereo configuration can provide an excellent stereo image. The set in Audio Example 4-11 was miked with one kick mic, one snare mic and two overheads in an X-Y configuration.

Audio Example 4-11

Snare, Kick, and X-Y

Kick, Snare, and X-Y

1. Two cardioid condenser microphones in a traditional X-Y configuration above the kit. Experiment with placement and distance above the kit to find the appropriate musical sound.

2. One cardioid moving-coil mic inside the kick.

3. One cardioid moving-coil mic pointed at the top of the snare drum, from a distance of about 2" above the top head.

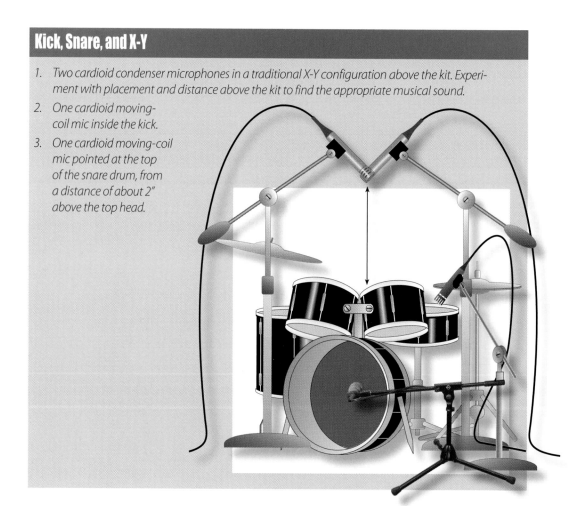

Close-Mike Technique

The most common approach to getting good, punchy drum sounds that have unique character is to use the close-mike technique. Each drum will typically have its own mic. Each of these microphones plus two overheads will be printed to separate tracks of the multitrack. These tracks will either stay separate until the mixdown, or they might be combined with the assignment buses and bounced to stereo tracks, making room for more instruments or voices.

The drum set in Audio Example 4-12 is set up with one kick mic, one snare mic, one mic on each tom, two microphones overhead in an X-Y pattern, and one hi-hat mic.

Kick, Snare, Toms, and X-Y

1. *Two cardioid condenser microphones in a traditional X-Y configuration above the kit. Experiment with placement and distance above the kit to find the appropriate musical sound.*

2. *One cardioid moving-coil mic inside the kick.*

3. *One cardioid moving-coil mic pointed at the top of the snare drum from a distance of about 2" above the top head.*

4. *One cardioid moving-coil mic pointed at the floor tom.*

5. *One cardioid moving-coil mic aimed between the upper two toms and positioned so that the two drums are balanced and blended.*

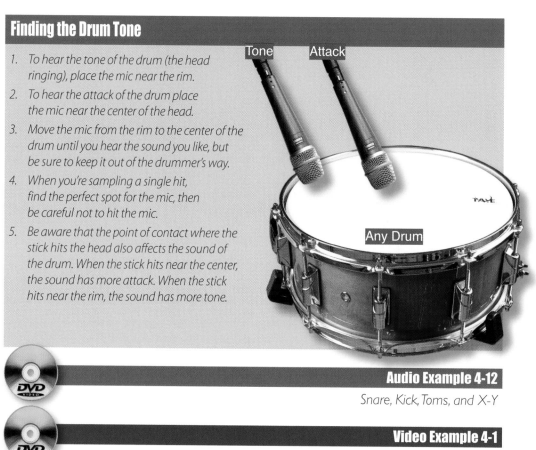

Finding the Drum Tone

1. To hear the tone of the drum (the head ringing), place the mic near the rim.

2. To hear the attack of the drum place the mic near the center of the head.

3. Move the mic from the rim to the center of the drum until you hear the sound you like, but be sure to keep it out of the drummer's way.

4. When you're sampling a single hit, find the perfect spot for the mic, then be careful not to hit the mic.

5. Be aware that the point of contact where the stick hits the head also affects the sound of the drum. When the stick hits near the center, the sound has more attack. When the stick hits near the rim, the sound has more tone.

Audio Example 4-12
Snare, Kick, Toms, and X-Y

Video Example 4-1
Recording the Drum Set with Various Microphone Configurations

Equalizing Drums

These equalization guidelines apply to the recording of basic tracks as well as mixdown. It's best to be conservative in the application of EQ on the actual recorded track. Save the extremes and "fancy" stuff for mixdown. Radical EQ and sound shaping are difficult to undo after the fact. However, a good solid tone can be molded and formed into whatever is musically appropriate during mixdown.

Always find the microphone, mic placement, and tuning that sound the best on any drum before beginning the equalization process.

Dampening the Kick Drum

1. *Set a pillow or blanket inside the kick with the front head off the drum. A duck-down pillow is most adjustable and results in a full, punchy sound with good tone.*

2. *Use something like a brick or mic stand base to keep the pillow or blanket in place.*

3. *The pillow or blanket should touch the head. The more it touches, the greater the dampening.*

4. *There are some excellent commercially produced kick drum muffling systems that incorporate these techniques in a very visually appealing package.*

Weight on Pliiow

The nature of close-miking a kick drum typically produces a raw sound that's overly abundant in lower midrange frequencies between 200 and 600 Hz, and the sound usually needs EQ to be usable.

When I listen to a raw close-miked drum sound before it's been equalized, I first listen for the frequencies that are clouding the sound of the kick. That frequency range is almost always somewhere between 200 and 600 Hz. Listen to the kick in Audio Example 4-13 as I turn down a one-octave wide bandwidth centered at 300 Hz.

Audio Example 4-13

Cut 300 Hz

Once the lower mid frequencies are turned down, I'll usually address the low frequencies between 75 and 150 Hz. On the kick drum and maybe the low toms I might boost a frequency bandwidth in this range. On toms, snare, hi-hat, and overheads I'll typically cut the frequencies below 100 to 200 Hz. This opens up the sound of the set and lets you isolate the sound of these higher drums.

Next, I'll typically locate an upper frequency to boost that will emphasize the attack of the beater or stick hitting the instrument. Boosting a frequency between 3 and 5 kHz will usually emphasize this attack. Listen to the kick in Audio Example 4-14. A moving-coil mic is pointed halfway between the center of the drum and the shell, from a distance of six inches. At first, this drum has no EQ. First I'll cut at 300 Hz, next I'll boost the low end at about 80 Hz, then I'll boost the attack at about 4 kHz.

Audio Example 4-14

Cut 300 Hz, Boost 80 Hz and 4 kHz

Choose your equalization changes with the big picture in mind. If your drum tracks have a lot of isolated tom fills that need to sound full and powerful, leave some low-frequency power in the track. It might be necessary to change EQ throughout the course of the track. Don't boost the same high frequencies on each track. The overheads might respond well to a boost of all frequencies above 7 to 10 kHz. Conversely, a tom track might sound best with a narrow bandwidth boosted at 4 kHz or so.

Kick Drum

The kick drum (bass drum) is very important to the impact of the drum sound. Different styles demand different kick sounds. Some sounds, such as jazz and heavy rock kicks, have less dampening and ring longer.

Often in the jazz idiom and some hard rock settings, the kick is not dampened, but the most common kick sound is lightly muffled,

Typical Kick Drum EQ

The actual amount of cut or boost you use is solely dependent on what it takes to get the sound you want out of the instrument you're miking. First use mic choice and placement to get the best and most musical sound, then use the amount of EQ necessary to create the appropriate sound.

1. *A low-frequency boost between 75 and 150 Hz adds a low, powerful thump to the kick drum sound.*
2. *A mid-frequency cut between 250 and 600 Hz helps clean up the thick, cloudy sound of a close-miked kick.*
3. *A high-frequency boost between 3 and 5 kHz adds defini-tion, attack and impact to the kick drum sound.*

Adjust the bandwidth on each of these bands to fine-tune the overall tone.

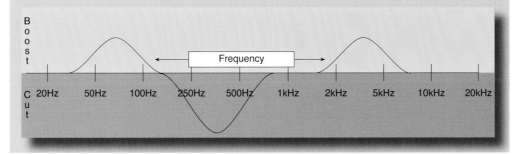

with good low-end thump and a clean attack. To achieve this sound, remove the front head and place a blanket or a pillow in the bottom of the drum. The blanket or pillow should be positioned for the desired amount of dampening—the more contact with the head, the more muffling. The weight of the pillow or blanket affects the sound. I've found that a down pillow works great; I'll usually place a brick or a mic stand base on the pillow to hold it in place.

For a little more tone, leave the front head on the drum, still dampening inside using a pillow or blanket. It has become popular to cut a six- to eight-inch hole in the front head, typically slightly off center. Use this hole to position the mic inside or slightly outside the drum. Move the mic in or out to achieve the balance of tone and attack that best supports your music.

A moving-coil mic, positioned inside the kick about six inches from the drummer's head and about halfway between the center of the head and the shell, will usually produce a good sound.

Experiment with mic placement to get the best sound you can before you equalize the sound. On any drum, the attack is strongest at the center of the drum, and the tone is strongest toward the shell. Move the mic to the center of the head if you want more attack. If you need more tone, move the mic toward the shell.

Audio Example 4-15 demonstrates the sound of a kick drum with the mic inside the drum pointing directly at the center of the head, where the beater hits, from a distance of six inches. Notice the attack.

Audio Example 4-15

Kick Attack

Audio Example 4-16 demonstrates the same kick as Audio Example 4-15 with the same mic aimed at the head about two inches in from the shell and about six inches from the head. Notice the tone.

Audio Example 4-16

Kick Tone

Another factor in the sound of the kick is the distance of the mic from the drum head. Audio Example 4-17 demonstrates the kick with the mic three inches from the head and about halfway between the center of the head and the drum shell.

Audio Example 4-17

Kick Three Inches Away

The mic in Audio Example 4-18 is about one foot outside of the drum, still pointed about halfway between the center and the shell.

Audio Example 4-18

Kick 12 Inches Outside

Video Example 4-2

Adjusting the Kick Drum Equalization

As you can tell by these different examples, positioning is critical to the sound of the drum. Not only is the placement of the mic critical, but the tuning of the drum can make all the difference. The tension should be even around the head, and there should be appropriate dampening for the sound you need. It's common to hear a very deep-sounding kick that has a solid thump in the low end and a good attack. In search of this kind of sound, most drummers tend to loosen the head to get a low sound. This can be a mistake. If the head is tuned too low, the pitch of the drum can be unusable and might not even be audible. To get a warm, punchy thump out of a kick, try tightening the head.

Another very important consideration in the kick sound is the drummer's technique. Drummers that stab at the kick with the beater can choke an otherwise great sound into an unappealing stutter-slap.

Snare Drum

Snare drums usually fall into one of two categories: very easy to get a good sound out of or almost impossible to get good sounds out of. Fortunately, there are some tricks we can pull out of the hat to help the more difficult drums sound good. It's important for you to know some quick and easy techniques for getting the snare to work. It's amazing how many decent drummers are lost when it comes to drum sounds.

First, make sure the heads are in good shape. A lot of times the top snare head has been stretched and dented so much that the center of the head is actually loose and sagging, even though the rest of the head

The Snares

If the snares are in bad shape or unevenly tensioned, you will have difficulty achieving a full-bodied and smooth sound. Pay attention to these details and you'll have an easier time recording this important instrument. Keep in mind that often the snare drum sound is fundamental to the stylistic impact of your recording.

Snares

1. *Be sure the snare strands are even in tension.*
2. *If the snares are loose or broken, cut them off.*
3. *If the snares can't be adjusted for constant tension or if there are too many strands missing, replace the entire set of snares.*
4. *Applying tape to loose snares can minimize extraneous buzzes, but the tape chokes the sound of the drum.*

is tight. This isn't good. Replacing the head will make a huge difference in the sound.

A good snare sound is dependent on a lot of factors working perfectly together. If you can handle drum-tuning basics, it'll make a big difference in the sound of your live drum recordings, plus you'll have an insight and perspective on drums that will prove to be a valuable asset.

Two Mics on the Snare

Often, it's a good idea to place a microphone on the top of the snare drum and another microphone underneath the drum. This sound from the top of the head is usually full, with plenty of tone. The sound from the bottom of the drum provides the edgy high frequencies from the rattling snares. It is, however, very important to understand that the microphone on the top is pointing down and the microphone on the bottom is pointing up. Any time two microphones point at each other, they are 180 degrees out of phase. When these two microphones

Two Mics on the Snare Drum

Depending on the snare drum you're recording, the mic on the top head might not produce a sufficient amount of buzz from the snares rattling on the bottom head. When this is the case, simply position a mic aiming up from the bottom at the snares; blend these mics to produce a sound with just the right amount snare sound.

Invert the phase of the bottom mic

Anytime two mics point at each other, like the mics described herein, they are 180 degrees out of phase. Notice that when these mics are combined to one track, or both panned to the center position, the resulting sound is thin and unappealing. Simply invert the phase of the bottom microphone, and the combined sound becomes smooth and very usable.

combine to one track several frequencies cancel, causing a very thin and weak sound. This solution to this is to reverse the phase of the bottom microphone, therefore forcing the two microphones to work together to create one good sound instead of working against each other to create one bad sound. Audio Example 4-19 demonstrates this concept as two microphones work together to capture the complete sound of the snare drum.

Audio Example 4-19

Two Mics on the Snare Drum

There are times when the snare sound has an unappealing and dominant tone. The right solution to this problem is to retune the drum so the obtrusive tone is gone. We can, though, use this opportunity to

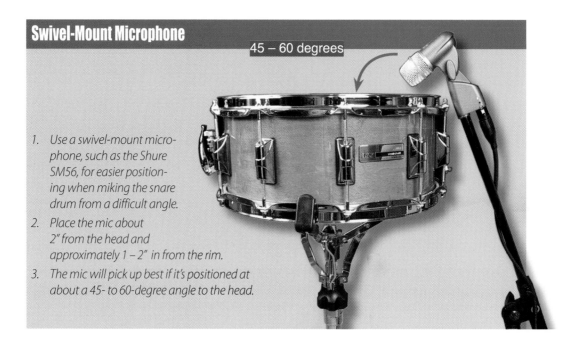

Swivel-Mount Microphone

45 – 60 degrees

1. Use a swivel-mount microphone, such as the Shure SM56, for easier positioning when miking the snare drum from a difficult angle.
2. Place the mic about 2" from the head and approximately 1 – 2" in from the rim.
3. The mic will pick up best if it's positioned at about a 45- to 60-degree angle to the head.

learn something about equalization. If this happens to you, and for one reason or another you can't get rid of the obnoxious ring, try this technique—it actually applies to shaping many different types of sounds.

On a parametric equalizer, set up a very narrow bandwidth and an extreme boost. Next, sweep the boost until the unwanted tone is obviously as loud as it gets—this procedure is simply locating the problem frequency by sweeping until it reaches the maximum level. After you've located the problem frequency, all you need to do is change the boost to a cut, eliminating the problem ring to whatever degree you desire.

Video Example 4-3

Eliminating an Unwanted Ring in the Snare Tone

Toms

Recording toms is similar in many ways to recording the kick drum and snare drum. It's important that the heads are in good shape, that they're tuned properly, and that the dampening gets the appropriate sound for the track. Tune the top and bottom heads to the same tone and be sure the tension is even around each head.

If you want more attack in the sound, move the mic toward the center of the drum, but keep it out of the drummer's way. A miked drum sound has more attack when the microphone is positioned near the center of the drum and more tone when the microphone is positioned near the rim.

Choose reverb for the toms that blends with the snare sound. It's normal to use the same reverb on the toms that you use on the snare. If you use another reverb sound, be sure it complements the overall sound of the snare drum. Avoid selecting sounds that indicate completely different acoustical environments unless you're intentionally conforming to a musical judgment.

Listen to the different tom sounds in Audio Example 4-20. Note what you like and dislike about each sound. Is the sound boomy? How do the lows sound? Can you hear the attack? Does the drum sound full? Is the drum thin-sounding? Do you hear much tone?

Audio Example 4-20

Lots of Toms

Video Example 4-4

Equalizing the Toms

Overhead Microphones

Once you've positioned the close microphones for the snare, kick, and toms, use mics over the drums to capture the cymbals and fill in the overall sound of the drums. It's amazing how much separation we can achieve close-miking the kit. One or two mics over the drums are essential to a blended, natural sound.

Position condenser microphones in a stereo pattern (like the examples of a two-mic setup). A good pattern to use is the standard X-Y configuration, with the microphones pointing down at the set at a 90 degree angle to each other. This will provide the excellent stereo image necessary for a big drum sound and will work well in mono.

If the drummer's kit is large and covers a wide area, try spreading the X-Y out. Move the microphones away from each other, but be sure they're still pointing away from each other. Also, keep the microphones on the same horizontal plane to minimize adverse phase interactions when listening to the mix in mono.

Overheads on a close-miked kit give definition and position to the cymbals and fill in the overall sound. There isn't much need for the low frequencies because the close microphones give each drum a full, punchy sound. I'll usually roll the lows off below about 150 Hz, and I'll often boost a high frequency between 10 and 15 kHz to give extra shimmer to the cymbals.

We want the overheads to accurately capture the transient information. Because the transient level exceeds the average level by as much as 9 dB, recording levels on the overheads should read between -7 and -9 VU at the peaks to ensure accurately recorded transients. Digital meters should not reach overload (OL).

Pan the overheads hard right and hard left for the most natural sound. The X-Y technique will provide a sound that is evenly spread across the stereo spectrum. The overheads in Audio Example 4-21 are about three feet above the cymbals in an X-Y configuration and are panned hard right and hard left. The lows below 150 Hz are rolled off, and the highs are boosted at 12 kHz.

Wide Stereo Overhead Microphones

- *For a wide stereo image, use two cardioid condenser microphones over the drum set spaced 1 – 3' apart.*
- *The mics should be at 90° angles to each other and pointing away from each other.*
- *If you point the mics toward each other, you'll encounter problems, especially when summing the stereo mix to mono—essentially they become one big mono microphone with phase problems.*

Audio Example 4-21

X-Y Panned Hard

We can add different character to the sound of the drums by moving the overheads closer to or farther from the kit. Positioning the mic farther away from the set includes more room sound on the track. This can be good or bad depending on the acoustics of the recording environment.

It isn't typically necessary to add reverb to the overheads in a close-miked configuration. The reverb on the snare and toms is usually sufficient to get a smooth, blended sound.

The Hi-Hat Mic

Sometimes it's desirable to put a separate mic on the hi-hat. The choice for or against a hi-hat mic should be based on the style of music and

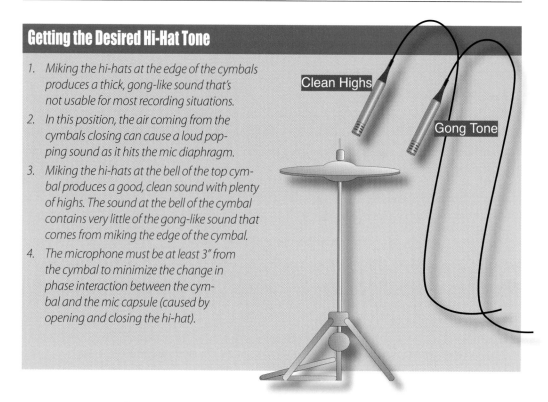

Getting the Desired Hi-Hat Tone

1. Miking the hi-hats at the edge of the cymbals produces a thick, gong-like sound that's not usable for most recording situations.

2. In this position, the air coming from the cymbals closing can cause a loud popping sound as it hits the mic diaphragm.

3. Miking the hi-hats at the bell of the top cymbal produces a good, clean sound with plenty of highs. The sound at the bell of the cymbal contains very little of the gong-like sound that comes from miking the edge of the cymbal.

4. The microphone must be at least 3" from the cymbal to minimize the change in phase interaction between the cymbal and the mic capsule (caused by opening and closing the hi-hat).

Clean Highs

Gong Tone

the importance of the hi-hat in the drum part. Most of the time the microphones on the kick, snare, toms, and overheads pick up plenty of hi-hat, but a separate track for the hat adds definition to the hi-hat attack and provides pan control in the mix.

Audio Example 4-22

Panning the Hi-Hat

Audio Example 4-23 demonstrates the sound of a hi-hat miked at the outer edge.

Audio Example 4-23

Hi-Hat Miked at the Outer Edge

Audio Example 4-24 demonstrates the sound of the hi-hat with the mic pointing down at the bell of the top cymbal.

Audio Example 4-24

Hi-Hat Miked at the Bell

The Mono Room Mic on the Floor

Whenever extra tracks and mics are available, it's a good idea to record a mono room microphone to a separate track. Use a large-diaphragm condenser microphone close to the floor and about 10 to 20 feet from the kit to capture a mono sound that is full of low and mid frequencies. Sometimes this track ads dimension and realism to the overall sound of the kit. As a mixdown resource, the sound from this microphone provides a track that can be soloed and processed for an interesting breakdown sound. I always record this track when I can, and often I don't use it. However, sometimes it provides the sonic diversity—at just the right time—to help create an interesting textural change.

Gating the Drum Tracks

Sometimes we need to isolate the drum tracks to equalize them separately, to pan them, or to add effects to an individual instrument or group of instruments.

Patch the drum track through a gate. Adjust the attack time to its fastest setting and the release time to about half a second. Adjust the range control so that everything below the threshold will be turned off. Finally, adjust the threshold so that the gate only opens when the drum is hit. This will isolate the drum. After the drum is isolated, you can process it alone with minimal effect on the rest of the kit. For example, you can add as much reverberation as you want without leakage adding reverb to the rest of the drums. Listen to the kit in Audio Example 4-25. I'll solo the snare track, then adjust the gate to get rid of the leakage between the snare hits.

Audio Example 4-25

Adjusting the Gate

After the gate is adjusted properly, you can put drastic amounts of reverb on the snare by itself. Listen to Audio Example 4-26 as I put a lot of reverb on this gated snare track.

Audio Example 4-26

Reverb on the Gated Snare

In Audio Example 4-27, listen to the complete kit with a lot of reverb on the gated snare track. After a few seconds, I'll bypass the gate on the snare. Notice the change in the reverb.

Audio Example 4-27

Bypassing the Gate

Application of Techniques

Aiming the Mics

It's important to get into the habit of aiming microphones away from sounds you want to exclude from a track. Use the cardioid pickup patterns to your advantage. For example, if you're miking a hi-hat and the mic is pointed at the bell of the top cymbal, that's good. Not only should you point the mic at the bell of the hi-hat, but you should point the back of the mic at a cymbal that's close by. Pointing the back of the hi-hat mic at the crash cymbal helps minimize the amount of crash that is recorded by the hi-hat mic. Use the cardioid pickup pattern to reject the unwanted sound while it captures the intended sound.

Phones

It's necessary for the drummer to have a good, well-balanced headphone mix. Headphones are the best way for the drummer to monitor the rest of the musicians or tracks. A good drummer is always trying to lock

Minimizing Leakage

1. *Aim the cardioid mic at the bell of the hi-hat to pick up a good, clean hi-hat sound.*

2. *Position the microphone so that it aims directly away from the instrument you want to minimize—in this case it's the crash cymbal. This technique won't eliminate an unwanted instrument, but it will decrease leakage and increase separation.*

into a strong rhythmic feel with the rest of the group. The drummer and bass player, especially, need to hear each other well. Be sure both the bass player and the drummer can hear the attack of the kick, snare, and hi-hat. Don't make them guess where the beat is. Adjusting the headphone mix can be your most important contribution to the feel of a song. Listen to the headphone mix yourself through headphones, so that you can tell exactly what the players are hearing. Respond to their requests for changes in level. Spending the time to make the phones an asset rather than a detriment is time well spent.

Baffles, Gobos, and Screens

Ideally, the drums will be the only sound in the room at the time they're being recorded. This provides ultimate flexibility during mixdown. However, there are times when guitar, bass, and drums must be recorded in the same room, usually due to a lack of space or time. When this happens, isolate the instruments as much as you can. Use baffles around the drums to shield the drum microphones from other sounds. *Baffles* are small, freestanding partitions with either two soft, absorptive sides or one soft side and one hard, reflective side. They typically measure about four feet square and are four to eight inches thick. They're also called *gobos* or *screens*.

Gobos, Baffles, and Screens

Place baffles around the drums to isolate the mics from other live instruments in the studio. A baffle will only effectively isolate frequencies smaller than it is. The overheads in this illustration are obviously not baffled; additionally, neither are the low frequencies longer than four feet.

There is still value in using this baffle setup. The baffles do more than just minimize leakage into the drum mics; they also decrease the drumset volume in the room, therefore minimizing leakage of the drums into other instrument or vocal mics.

Some baffles are six to eight feet tall, utilizing glass or plexiglass in the upper portion so that musicians can still get visual cues from one another while at the same time being acoustically isolated.

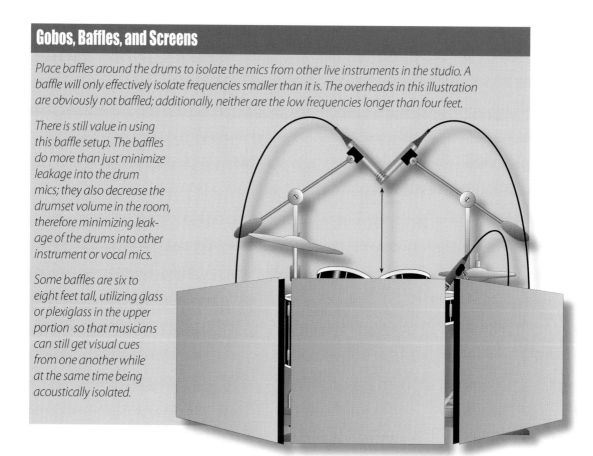

When baffling drums, be aware of the surfaces behind the drum set. Hard, reflective surfaces behind the kit send strong reflections all around any room. Baffles are often as effective behind the drums as they are in front.

Baffles can also be placed around the guitar amp, or blankets can be placed over the amp and the mic. The blanket will shield the guitar mic from unwanted sounds, plus it will muffle the guitar to help keep it from the drum mics or other microphones in the room.

Though we strive for ultimate separation between tracks and complete control over the sound of each instrument, some great recordings have been achieved with the entire band in one room playing the tracks live. Blues, jazz, some country and some rock styles can benefit from the natural, open sound that a live one-room recording offers.

Click Track

One feature of a professional-sounding recording is a solid rhythmic feel that maintains an even and constant tempo. A sure sign of an amateur band and an amateur recording is a loose rhythmic feel that radically speeds up and slows down.

Most drummers need some assistance to maintain a constant tempo. We call this assistance the *click track*. A click track can simply be a steady metronome pulse, like that from a drum machine or an electronic metronome. It gives the drummer a rhythmic reference to keep the tempo steady.

A drum machine is a good source for the click because it offers the ability to change the sound. Click sounds with good transients work the best because the transient attack unquestionably defines the placement of the beat.

It's very important that the drummer hears the click well, but the biggest problem with a click track is leakage of the sound of the click from the headphones into the drum microphones. It's difficult to deal with click leakage into the overheads on a quiet or texturally open part of a song. The click has to be at a certain level for the drummer to hear it, but if it's too loud and it's audible on the drum microphones, the drum track might not be usable. The solution lies in finding headphones that enclose the drummer's ears well enough to conceal the click from the microphones. There are many phones available that will perform well. They usually have solid housings and fluid- or air-filled soft plastic pads that completely surround the ears.

Effects on Drums

Whenever possible, wait until mixdown to add reverb to the drums. If you have enough tracks, print each drum to its own track, then during mixdown, assess the need for effects. You won't really know the musical impact of the effects on the entire mix until the mix is up and running.

If you're combining the drums to one or two tracks at the time of the initial recording but you have a separate mic for each drum, you might need to print the reverb to the multitrack. This process can work well, but it takes practice and experience to second-guess what the track will really sound like in the final mix.

The amount of reverb and ambience that you incorporate in your drum sounds depends on stylistic and musical factors. We seem to see-saw from very wet sounds to very dry sounds in all pop genres. It's up to you to stay in tune with the trends in your musical arena. Be informed to create a competitive and commercial sound, or at least know what you're doing when you break all the rules in pop-dom.

Remember, the more reverb you apply to any sound, the farther away and less intimate it feels.

Compressing Drums

Compression is a common drum recording and mixing technique. Compression has two primary effects on drum tracks. First, because the compressor is an automatic level control, it evens out the volume of each hit. This can be a very good thing on a commercial rock tune. The compressor keeps the level even so that a weak hit doesn't detract from the groove.

The second benefit of compression is its ability, with proper use, to accentuate the attack of the drum. If the compressor controls are adjusted correctly, we can exaggerate the attack of the drum, giving it a very aggressive and penetrating edge. This technique involves setting the attack time of the compressor slow enough that the attack isn't compressed but the remaining portion of the sound is.

The following steps detail how to set the compressor to exaggerate the attack of any drum:

1. Set the ratio between 3:1 and 10:1.

2. Set the release time at about .5 seconds. This will need to be adjusted according to the length of the snare sound. Just be sure the LEDs showing gain reduction have all gone off before the next major hit of the drum. This doesn't apply to fills, but if the snare is hitting on 2 and 4, the LEDs should be out before each hit.

3. At this point, set the attack time to its fastest setting.

4. Adjust the threshold for 3 to 9 dB of gain reduction.

5. Finally, readjust the attack time. As you slow the attack time of the compressor, it doesn't react in time to compress the transient, but it can react in time to compress the rest of the drum sound.

Panning the Drums

Panning the drum requires a decision about the concept of the final mix. If you're trying to create a final product that sounds like a live band with a live drummer, you'll need to pan accordingly. Imagine the drummer's position on stage, and place all of the drums within that space. Because the drums are usually center stage, the toms are usually panned very close around the center when using this approach.

Panning from high to low between about 10:00 and 2:00 can still give the impression of the drums being center stage while clearing out the middle of the stereo image for lead instruments.

Kick and snare drums are almost always panned center because they provide the foundation of the mix. The low-frequency content of the kick needs to be dispersed evenly between the left-right spectrum, and the constant repetition of the snare dictates its center position. A snare panned to one side or the other continually pulls the listener to that side and distracts from the balanced feel of a mix.

Overheads are often panned hard left and right. The acoustic mix of the drums in the room keeps them grouped together in most settings.

Toms panned hard left to hard right can interrupt the natural feel of a mix.

Listen to the drum balance through a good set of headphones. Some pan settings sound good on monitor speakers but are very distracting in headphones. If you ignore these guidelines, do it intentionally with great artistic and musical resolve.

Compare Your Work

I've never known anyone who didn't want his or her work to sound competitive next to other commercially released music. Check your work against your favorite album in your genre. Set up the mixer so the reference CD is playing at the same time as your mix. Select back and forth between the two, evaluating how they compare sonically. This is very instructional. Listen specifically to the high-, mid-, and low-frequency content.

The most difficult frequencies to dial in are the lows. It's important to be very selective and intentional when boosting and cutting low frequencies. When the same low frequency is boosted on several instruments (kick, bass, guitar, keys, and so on), energy accumulates and the mix level becomes artificially hot—the meters register hot but the mix sounds cold.

To create a mix that's powerful and punchy, start with the drum and bass mix. Where you boost low frequencies on one instrument, cut low frequencies on another. Fit the mix together like a jigsaw puzzle throughout the frequency spectrum.

It's more important to establish a clean attack on each drum track than it is to establish powerful lows. When you turn down the midrange, you'll find that both the lows and highs can be heard better.

Continue to craft your mix until it matches the reference CD in every way.

+ At the same meter reading does it sound as loud? If not, try fitting your equalizations together tighter.

+   On a track that doesn't need lows, roll them off to the point at which you can just start to hear a difference. (High-pass filters work best for this.)

+   On a track that doesn't need highs, roll them off to the point at which you can just start to hear a difference. (Low-pass filters work best for this.)

+   Try eliminating some ingredients from the mix. Simpler is louder.

+   Locate ingredients that might be momentarily causing deceptively high levels. Toms are often the guilty party where this is concerned. If the low frequencies are turned up too far on a floor tom, your mix might go crazy every time the drum is hit. Typically, the mixing engineer can't even hear the frequencies that are causing the buildup. Turning the low frequencies down on the floor tom often provides the perfect cure—the drum still sounds just as good and the mix level is controlled.

Does Your Mix Sound as Clean in the High Frequencies as the Reference?

It's amazing how bright many commercial pop mixes are. This is true because experienced mix engineers have discovered that a bright mix cuts through on the radio. They've also discovered that if a mix is a little devoid of low frequencies, the problem is easily repaired during mastering. In addition, they've gotten the maximum level on the master media, providing a cleaner, smoother, and punchier mix in both the analog and digital realms.

Evaluate the sound of each drum and each instrument for frequency content, comparative level and balance, and musical effect. After you've completed this process, you'll be amazed at how great your mix sounds.

It is very satisfying to listen to your work and be able to realistically proclaim its competitive integrity.

Triggering during Mixdown

It's common in certain genres to use the recorded drum tracks to trigger sampled drum sounds. I've used this technique and gotten some incredible results. Current digital workstation software packages facilitate automatic replacement with great ease. Your digitally recorded drum sounds can be replaced with those of your favorite drummers. The libraries of samples are readily available—and they sound really good.

However, this technique can create a sterile and nonmusical mix. It is very difficult to recreate the expression of a real performance on a great kit. Don't let triggered sounds become a cop-out—a substitution for spending the time to record innovative, fresh, and musical drum sounds. If you use triggered sounds, use them for musical augmentation or if there's just no other way to get decent-sounding drum tracks.

There are numerous ways to replace recorded sounds with pre-sampled sounds. Verify the approach by consulting the documentation for your software or DAW.

Automation

Take advantage of the automation features available on many of the current mixers, digital software packages, and digital audio workstations. Listen through your song and turn the tom tracks on only when the toms are hit. This will tighten the entire drum sound. Use automated mutes to add precision to releases and punches. Listen carefully to the entire drum part and meticulously craft the drum levels, pans, and EQ.

Then combine the drums and bass. Be sure they're blended and tight. Ride their levels throughout the mix to maintain punch, power, and transparency. I like to add the lead vocal next and automate its levels throughout. After this is accomplished, the rest of the ingredients have a place to go; you know where they're needed and where they're not needed.

Conclusion

All of the techniques and principles contained in this book work during tracking and in final mixdown. Build the drums from the kick drum to the overheads. Strive to maintain intimacy while at the same time providing the illusion of controlled size and depth. Have fun developing your drum sound.

Recording Great Bass Guitar Tracks

B ass is an interesting instrument. Its function, in most musical settings, is to give a solid rhythmic and harmonic foundation for the rest of the arrangement. As the engineer, it's your job to get a great bass sound that blends with the rest of the song. It's the bass player's job to play a solid rhythmic part with the correct musical touch. Without both player and engineer working together in any recording situation, things can become difficult.

Electric Bass

A bass player who's unfamiliar with the recording process can cause some problems. Live players usually develop a brutal performance approach to bass. They get used to playing as hard as they can to help themselves feel the beat and to just get into the music. This heavy touch results in a lot of string buzzes and rattles that are usually covered up or forgiven in a live performance. But in recording, the same noises can be both distracting and destructive to an otherwise good song.

Bass Guitar Parts

Throughout this section I'll refer to certain parts of the electric bass. Recording each instrument requires knowledge, not only of the physical design of the instrument, but of the tonal characteristics. Become familiar with the physical and tonal characteristics of every instrument you record.

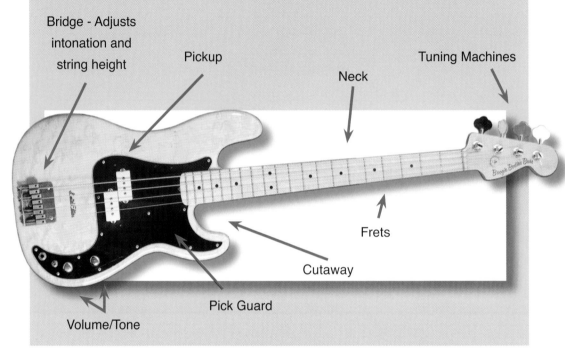

Bridge - Adjusts intonation and string height

Pickup

Neck

Tuning Machines

Frets

Cutaway

Pick Guard

Volume/Tone

A player with a solid but controlled touch can get a great rhythmic feel and a clean sound. Listen to Audio Example 5-1. The bassist is playing very hard and causing buzzes and clacks that will distract from the song.

Audio Example 5-1

Buzzes and Clacks

Audio Example 5-2 demonstrates the same bass part performed with a controlled touch.

Audio Example 5-2

The Controlled Performance

As engineers, we don't usually get to pick the bassist for the session, so we need to be capable of getting the best from each situation within the given time restraints.

Offering a couple of politically delicate and emotionally sensitive suggestions can help an inexperienced bassist through a tough situation. If I've learned anything in my years of recording it's that a musician's ego, though often sizable, is usually fragile. It's the "bigger they are, the harder they fall" theory. Be diplomatic and constructive in your suggestions.

I've found that the best way to suggest a change in a musician's approach is to simply play back a take. If you turn the bass track up and the bassist hears a lot of fret buzz and rattle, that says it all. Most of the time, a conscientious player will hear and adjust his or her playing technique accordingly. If a suggestion is necessary, having the tape as your reference helps the player instantly understand what you're talking about. As a rule, musicians want to do whatever they can to get a good recording, and they'll almost always do anything within their abilities to accomplish that.

A good player, playing with a solid touch that's completely controlled, makes your job easy. A player who consistently overplays and is out of control makes your job difficult.

Condition of the Bass

If you have any control over the condition of the bass, be sure the strings are in good condition and that the intonation, string height, and pickups are adjusted for the desired sound.

Old, dull-sounding strings are rarely good for recording. Some players like old strings for certain styles, such as traditional rock, country, or jazz, because they feel that older strings have a smoother sound with less string squeak and rattle. This is true in certain settings, but most great players that use bass strings for a long time keep the strings very clean and in good condition.

There is a point in the life of any string when it starts to vibrate unevenly throughout its length, causing dead spots, dull-sounding notes, and unpredictable intonation at different positions on the neck.

Many players frequently boil their bass strings to clean out the built-up oils and dirt that detract from the clarity of the sound. This can greatly increase the life and clarity of the strings. Audio Example 5-3 demonstrates a bass that I've had in the closet for a while. It's a good bass with custom pickups and a custom neck and body, but the strings were old. Listen to the bass guitar before I boiled the strings.

Audio Example 5-3

Dull Bass Strings

Listen to Audio Example 5-4 to hear the bass after the strings were removed, boiled, and reinstalled. Notice the difference in clarity.

Audio Example 5-4

Boiled Strings

Poor string height adjustment can cause fret and string buzz, uneven volume from string to string, or (if the strings are too high) intonation problems, especially in the higher frets.

Intonation is set by the string length adjustment at the bridge. This is the adjustment that determines the accuracy of the notes at each fret. It is best done by an experienced guitar technician. Inaccurate adjustment of the guitar intonation results in an instrument that can be in tune in the open position but out of tune everywhere else on the neck.

If the pickups aren't adjusted properly, the strings might not have even volumes, and the sound of the instrument can change drastically. Pickups that are too close to the strings can produce a sound that's muddy or distorted. Pickups that are too far from the strings can produce a signal that's weak or thin-sounding. There's usually a position that gets the right combination of clarity and raw punch for the music.

As the recordist, it's not typically your position to start readjusting these settings on the instrument, but be aware that these are some of the most important factors in finding a great bass sound.

Direct Box/Direct In (DI)

Bass guitar typically sounds best when run directly into the mixer, either through a direct box or by plugging directly into line in.

If you're using a direct box, plug into the direct box, then plug the XLR out of the direct box into the mic input of the mixer. This approach usually produces the best sound and offers the advantage of long cable runs from the direct box to the mixer.

A passive direct box simply transforms the high-impedance output into a low-impedance signal suitable for the mic input of the mixer. The bass in Audio Example 5-5 is running through a passive direct box directly into the mic input with no EQ or dynamic processing.

Audio Example 5-5

Bass through the Passive DI

An active direct box contains circuitry that, besides matching impedance, enhances the signal. Active direct boxes usually have more

Bass Guitar through the Direct Box

1. Plug the bass guitar into the direct box input.
2. Plug the XLR output of the direct box into the mic input of the mixer.
3. Send the bass guitar signal to the recorder using the bus assignments.
4. Set the levels and record.

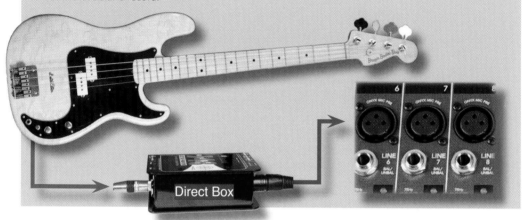

Direct Box

high-frequency clarity and more low-end punch. Audio Example 5-6 demonstrates the same bass as the previous example run through an active direct box.

Audio Example 5-6

Bass through the Active DI

Pickup Output Level

It's almost always best to set the instrument's volume control at maximum. This sends the hottest signal to the board, resulting in a better signal-to-noise ratio.

Many of the newer pickups, especially pickups using active electronics, have very strong output levels. These strong levels can overdrive the circuits of some direct boxes and mixers. If the active bass electronics are overdriving the direct box or mixer inputs, try turning the volume down at the bass until the sound is clean and distortion-free.

I've had excellent results plugging basses with active electronics directly into the line input of the mixer, bypassing the direct box. This way, you've eliminated a circuit. Always try to include the least number of circuits in the signal path while still achieving the appropriate musical sound. Fewer circuits in the signal path usually means less noise and less distortion. Many stock instrument pickups produce a weak signal. If your bass produces a low-level signal, you might have an insufficient level when plugging into the line input of a mixer that operates at +4 dBm. On the other hand, the same bass might work very well when plugged into the line input of a mixer that operates at -10 dBV. Each situation is a little different, so you must rely on your ears and make an informed decision. Know your options and try each of them until you find the sound you're looking for. Start with the method that you expect will work best. As your experience level increases, you'll probably be able to accurately predict the results of several different types of setups. Here are a few rules of thumb I use:

1. If the bass is an early model Fender, Gibson, Ibanez, etc. with stock pickups, use a passive or active direct box and set the instrument volume at maximum.

2. If the bass is a Fender, Gibson, Ibanez, etc. with active electronics, use a direct box and, if necessary, turn the instrument volume down from maximum to keep from overdriving the direct box or the mixer input. Also, try plugging directly from the instrument into the mixer's line input.

3. If the bass has active EMG pickups, plug into line input of the mixer. Also, try plugging the bass into a direct box—but you'll probably need to turn the output of the instrument down.

Instrument Differences

Aside from instrument adjustment, the player's touch, and the choice of direct box, choice of instrument is very important, When you consider that many different manufacturers make many different models, it makes sense that the sound difference from one instrument to the next can be so dramatic that even two identical basses made by the same manufacturer can sound different.

Listen to the basses in Audio Examples 2-7 through 2-10 and note the differences in sound quality. Use the chart in the following illustration to evaluate each instrument's sound. Each bass was plugged into the same mixer input, without EQ, using the same direct box.

Audio Example 5-7 demonstrates a Fender Precision Bass. The *Precision Bass*, sometimes referred to as the *P-Bass*, is the all-time most popular bass guitar. It has a good, solid low end that provides an excellent foundation for most musical styles. This has become the standard bass sound, and we can use it as a reference for the other sounds.

Audio Example 5-7
Bass 1: P-Bass

Audio Example 5-8 demonstrates a very inexpensive bass.

Audio Example 5-8
Bass 2: Inexpensive Bass

In Audio Example 5-9 you hear a custom-built version of a Precision Bass that uses DiMarrzio pickups.

Audio Example 5-9
Bass 3: Custom P-Bass

The bass in Audio Example 5-10 uses active electronics within the bass itself. Active electronics add punch in the lows and clarity in the highs.

Audio Example 5-10

Bass 4: Active Electronics

As we study some of these fundamental differences between basses, it's apparent that many of the initial variables can make or break the sound. Recording the bass sound that's right for the song can be tricky. The techniques that we cover will help you out of some tight spots, but your recording life will be much easier if the source is good. Work from the instrument to the tape recorder. Give each point along the signal path detailed attention.

Bass Guitar Parts

This is a subjective survey for your own benefit. Rate each instrument from 1 to 10 in each category. 10 is the best or most pleasing. 1 is the worst (annoying, least pleasing, or awful). These are the key sound characteristics in most sounds, so practice evaluating other instruments with these same qualities in mind. Once you've rated these bass guitars, you should have a better idea of what you think a good bass sound is.

	Lows	Mids	Highs	Clarity	Punch	Sustain
Bass 1 Precision Bass Audio Example 5-7						
Bass 2 Inexpensive Bass Audio Example 5-8						
Bass 3 Custom P-Bass with DiMarzio pickups Audio Example 5-9						
Bass 4 Active Electronics Audio Example 5-10						

Musical Style

Each style of music has its own appropriate bass sound and playing style. When referring to a player's touch, we're basically indicating the intensity of the right-hand attack. Some players lightly touch the strings, while others pluck with great aggression and fire. Style, in contrast to touch, includes everything about how the notes are plucked or struck, along with how the rhythmic feel is interpreted, as well as the passivity or aggression of the musical performance.

Bass is an instrument that contains many different sounds depending on the style preference of the player. Musicians who play jazz make music that sounds like jazz. Musicians who play rock all the time seem to fit well stylistically into almost any rock song. Country players sound good playing country music, R&B players sound good playing R&B music, and on and on. We encounter a problem when a player who only knows the idiosyncrasies of one style tries to play another style. It often just doesn't feel right. A player who understands the nuances and correct interpretations of several styles greatly increases his or her value in any musical setting, especially recording. If you analytically listen to many different types of music, you'll be able to discern many of the characteristics that make a particular style correct.

The type of attack used to pluck the bass string plays a very important part in stylist interpretation. Audio Examples 5-11 through 5-15 will help you recognize some of the different ways a bass can be played.

Most parts are played with the first two fingers of the player's right hand. This technique produces a solid low end with good definition in the attack of each note.

Audio Example 5-11

Finger Plucking

Some players pluck the bass with their thumb only. This usually gives a sound that is fuller in the lows.

Audio Example 5-12

Thumb Plucking

Some parts are played with a pick. Using a felt pick produces a sound that's similar to the sound produced by using the fingers, but without quite as much low end.

Audio Example 5-13

The Felt Pick

Using a regular plastic pick produces a sound that has a lot of attack and a clear sound.

Audio Example 5-14

The Plastic Pick

When playing with a pick, the player might mute the strings slightly with the heel of the right hand, producing a good attack with a tight, solid low note. This is a common sound in country music.

Audio Example 5-15

The Plastic Pick, Muted

Sometimes when you're recording bass, you'll simply need a sound that's warmer and fuller; other times you might need a sound that's thin, with more definition. It's not always possible to bring in different instruments. If you ask the bassist to pluck the strings closer to the bridge, the sound will have less low end and the notes will penetrate through the mix. If the bassist plucks the strings closer to the point where the neck joins the body, the sound will be smooth and warm in the low end, but the definition of each note might decrease.

Asking the bassist to adjust his or her right hand position is a great way to get the raw sound that you need for a song. If you need a smooth, sustained, low-end bass sound, you could EQ all day and never get the effect of simply asking the bassist to pick the strings a little closer to the neck. Or, if you need the bass to cut through the mix a little better, the best solution could be to simply ask the bassist to pluck a little closer to the bridge.

Audio Example 5-16 demonstrates the sound of a bassist plucking back by the bridge. This sound generally works best for punchy rock, fast country, or some R&B songs.

Audio Example 5-16

Plucking by the Bridge

Audio Example 5-17 demonstrates the sound of a bassist plucking up by the neck. This sound is generally best for slow ballads that need a full, sustained bass sound to support the rest of the arrangement.

Audio Example 5-17

Plucking by the Neck

Most bass parts sound best if plucked somewhere between the two extremes demonstrated in Audio Examples 5-16 and 5-17. Being aware of this sound-shaping technique can save you a lot of time and energy. Audio Example 5-18 demonstrates the sound of the same bass as the previous two examples, plucked about halfway between the point where the neck joins the body and the bridge.

Audio Example 5-18

Plucking between the Neck and the Bridge

Recording Levels for Bass

Record the bass with the hottest part of the track peaking at about 0 VU. If the sound is strong in the low end, it's usually OK to push the bass level to +1 or +2 VU. If the bass sound is particularly thin with lots of snaps and pops, record at -1 to -3 VU to compensate for the transient attacks.

Mic Techniques

Most of the time the direct sound is best because of its definition and clarity. During mixdown, a direct bass sound is usually hard to beat for defining the low end in a controlled way. Sometimes, especially on harder rock songs, it sounds good to mike the bass cabinet. If a player has a characteristic sound that comes from a unique amplifier setup, miking that setup might be the best way to get the appropriate musical sound to tape.

When miking a bass cabinet, keep the mic close to the speaker cabinet to get a good, tight sound. When the mic is close to the cabinet, you might need to be conservative in adjusting the amp volume. If the amp is too loud, the sound from the amp could overdrive the mic. Moving coil mics, such as the Shure SM57, Sennheiser 421, Electro-Voice RE20, or the AKG D-12E, are good for close-miking the bass cabinet and will also handle a lot of volume before they overdrive.

The electric and acoustic guitar sound benefits from adding natural room ambience to the sound on tape. That's not usually true on the bass. If the bass sound contains too much ambience, the low end of the mix tends to become muddy and unclear. Room ambience isn't usually equal in all frequencies, and your bass sound can take on a boomy character that's not good for the sound of your mix.

Try to keep the mic within one to three feet of the cabinet. If the cabinet contains multiple speakers that each cover a different frequency

Miking the Bass Speaker

1. *Pointing the mic at the center of the speaker produces a sound with more high-frequency edge.*
2. *Pointing the mic at the outer edge of the speaker cone, away from the center, produces a warm, smooth sound with less edge.*
3. *When miking the bass cabinet you'll almost always get a tighter, more controlled sound if you get the cabinet up off the floor. Try placing the cabinet on a chair or other type of stand. This approach will help control the low frequencies.*

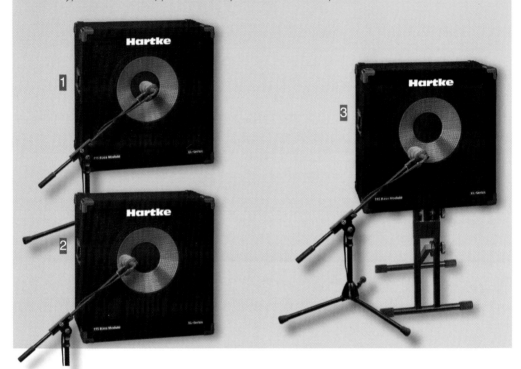

range, move the mic back two or three feet from the cabinet to get the full range of the sound.

If the cabinet contains just one speaker or multiple identical speakers, move the mic close to one speaker. Usually one of the speakers sounds better than the others. If so, mike the best-sounding speaker. Keep in mind, the center of the speaker has more edge and highs, and the outer edge of the speaker produces more warm, smooth lows.

Audio Example 5-19 demonstrates the sound of a bass cabinet with the mic aimed at the center of the speaker, from a distance of about one foot. Notice the clarity in the upper midrange.

Audio Example 5-19

Bass Cabinet Miked at the Center

Audio Example 5-20 uses the same speaker as Audio Example 5-19, miked with the same mic pointed at the outer edge of the speaker. Notice the full sound that comes from miking this part of the speaker.

Audio Example 5-20

Bass Cabinet Miked at the Outer Edge

When miking a bass cabinet, you'll almost always get a tighter, more controlled sound if you get the cabinet up off the floor. Setting the cabinet on a chair or other type of stand can help control the low end of a miked bass cabinet.

As with the guitar, we can combine the direct sound and the miked sound to get the best of both worlds. If we combine the tight, clean sound of the direct signal with the character of the miked signal, we can get a unique sound that adds to the musical feel of the song. It's some-times possible to pan the direct and miked sounds apart in the mix, but be careful with this technique. Always check your mix in mono before you commit to panning the two bass tracks apart, and be sure the bass volume sounds balanced between the left and right channels.

Listen to the direct bass sound in Audio Example 5-21.

Audio Example 5-21

The Direct Bass Sound

Audio Example 5-22 demonstrates the sound of the miked bass speaker.

The Miked Bass Speaker

Most of the time you'll keep both the miked and the direct sound panned to center, blending for the sound you want. Listen as I blend the

Bass into Direct Box and Amplifier

- *Plug the bass into the direct box input.*
- *Patch the THRU (out to amp) jack into the amplifier input jack.*
- *Patch the low-impedance XLR output of the direct box into the mic input of the mixer.*
- *Place a mic in front of the speaker and connect the mic cable to a separate mic input on the mixer.*

This setup lets you use the mixer to blend the direct and miked sounds. Record both of these sounds onto one tape track in the desired proportions or record each signal to a separate tape track. It's best to record the miked and direct signals to separate tracks if you can spare them. That way, you give yourself freedom in the mixdown to blend the sounds in the way that supports the music best.

Direct Box

two sounds. You'll hear the direct sound first, then the miked sound. Then I'll pan the two tracks apart for a stereo sound.

Audio Example 5-23

Blending the Direct and Miked Sounds

Compressing the Electric Bass

Bass is usually compressed. There's a big difference in level between notes on many basses. Some notes read very hot on the VU meter and some read very cold. Because the compressor automatically turns down the signal above the user-set threshold, it helps keep the stronger notes under control.

If the bass notes are evened out in volume by the compressor, the bass track stays more constant in the mix and supplies a solid foundation for the song. If the bass is left uncompressed, the bass part can tend to sound especially loud and boomy on certain notes and disappear altogether on others. More consistent levels from note to note typically provide the best foundation for most recordings.

A compressor becomes especially useful if a player snaps a high note or thumps a low note because the level changes can be extreme. Not only does the compressor help control the louder bass sounds, but it also helps the subtleties come through more clearly. If the loud sounds are turned down, the entire track can be boosted to achieve a proper VU reading. As the track is turned up, the softer sounds are turned up, which makes them more audible in the mix.

The bass part in Audio Example 5-24 is not compressed. Notice the difference between the loudest and softest sounds.

Audio Example 5-24

Non-Compressed Bass

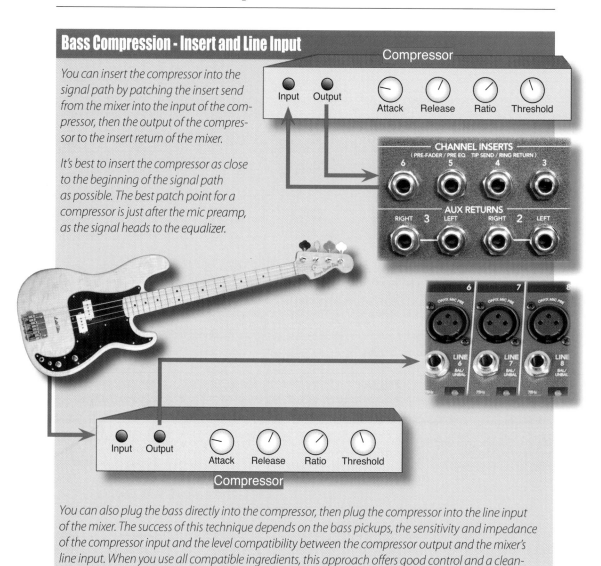

Bass Compression - Insert and Line Input

You can insert the compressor into the signal path by patching the insert send from the mixer into the input of the compressor, then the output of the compressor to the insert return of the mixer.

It's best to insert the compressor as close to the beginning of the signal path as possible. The best patch point for a compressor is just after the mic preamp, as the signal heads to the equalizer.

Compressor

Input Output Attack Release Ratio Threshold

CHANNEL INSERTS
(PRE-FADER / PRE EQ   TIP SEND / RING RETURN)
6   5   4   3

AUX RETURNS
RIGHT 3 LEFT   RIGHT 2 LEFT

Input Output Attack Release Ratio Threshold
Compressor

You can also plug the bass directly into the compressor, then plug the compressor into the line input of the mixer. The success of this technique depends on the bass pickups, the sensitivity and impedance of the compressor input and the level compatibility between the compressor output and the mixer's line input. When you use all compatible ingredients, this approach offers good control and a clean-sounding bass track. Be sure you've matched operating levels (+4, -10) and impedances.

Audio Example 5-25 uses the same bass used in Audio Example 5-24. This time the bass is compressed with a ratio of 4:1 and gain reduction of up to 6 dB. This example peaks at the same level as the previous example, but notice how much more even the notes sound.

Compressed Bass through the DI

- *Plug the bass into the compressor.*
- *Patch the output of the compressor into the input of the direct box.*
- *Patch the XLR output of the direct box into your mixer's mic input.*

Direct Box

Input   Output   Attack   Release   Ratio   Threshold

Compressor

Audio Example 5-25

Compressed Bass

If the bass part is very consistent in level and the player has a good, solid, predictable touch, you might not even need compression. I've been able to get some great bass sounds without compression. This only happens when you have a great player with predictable and disciplined technique, a great instrument, and the appropriate bass part. Aside from these factors, most bass parts need compression.

If the bass part includes snaps and thumps, consider limiting. With a limiter, most of the notes are left unaffected, but the snaps and thumps are limited. Limiting is the same as compression, but with a ratio above 10:1.

If the limiter is set correctly, the bass part can be totally unprocessed on everything but a strong thump. The thump might exceed the threshold by 10 dB, but if the ratio is 10:1 or higher, the output of the compressor won't show more than a 1-dB increase.

Follow this procedure to correctly adjust the limiter:

1. Set the ratio control to about 10:1.
2. Set the attack time to fast.
3. Adjust the threshold so that gain reduction only registers on the snaps and thumps.

The bass part in Audio Example 5-26 isn't limited. Notice how much louder the snaps are than the rest of the notes. Also, note that the normal level is low to keep the snaps from oversaturating the tape.

Procedure for Compressing Bass Guitar

1. Set the ratio (typically between 3:1 and 7:1).
2. Set the attack time. The attack time needs to be fast enough to compress the note but not so fast that the attack of the bass note is removed. If the attack time is too fast, the bass will sound dull and lifeless.
3. Set the release time. Start at about 0.5 seconds. If the release time is too slow, the VCA will never have time to turn the signal back up after compressing. If the release time is too fast, compression might be too obvious, because the VCA reacts to each short sound by turning down, and then back up.
4. Adjust the threshold control for the desired amount of gain reduction (typically about 6 dB at the strongest part of the track).

Audio Example 5-26

Snaps Not Limited

The bass part in Audio Example 5-27 is limited. Notice that now the snaps aren't much louder than the rest of the notes, and the entire part sounds louder because the limiter has squashed the peaks.

Audio Example 5-27

Limited Snap

Equalization of the Bass Guitar

Of all the parts of a mix, the low frequencies are the most difficult to deal with, especially at first. If you're listening on large far-field monitors powered by many watts of clean power, it's fun to boost the bass and sub-bass frequencies between 30 and 70 Hz. It sounds good and you can physically feel the bass. But this approach presents two primary problems:

1. Most home and car stereos can't reproduce these low frequencies. Your music might sound weak in the low end if it's played on an average system, even though it sounded warm and smooth in the studio.

2. The bass and sub-bass frequencies contain a lot of energy. The low-frequency level can dominate and control the overall mix level. If you've boosted sub-bass frequencies, the VU level of the mix will rise (pretty much in direct proportion to the boost). If your mix is played back on a regular home stereo, these lows will be inaudible. Also, in order to achieve an acceptable listening level, you'll need to turn up the volume. When the volume is turned up, the noise is turned up, so your mix ends up sounding noisy and thin in the low end.

Audio Examples 5-28 through 5-30 are all mixes of the identical rhythm track. In Audio Example 5-28, I've boosted 50 Hz on the bass guitar by about 6 dB.

Audio Example 5-28

Mix with 50 Hz Boosted on the Bass Track

Audio Example 5-29 demonstrates the same mix as Audio Example 5-28 without the boost at 50 Hz on the bass track. Both of these mixes peak at the same level on the VU meter, but notice that Audio Example 5-29 seems louder.

Audio Example 5-29

Mix without 50 Hz Boosted on the Bass Track

Now listen to the two mixes together in Audio Example 5-30. The first eight bars have 50 Hz boosted on the bass. The second eight bars have no boost.

Audio Example 5-30

Alternating between 5-28 and 5-29

The same results occur if you're just recording the bass track. If you have a question about how much bass frequency to print to the multitrack, print slightly less than you think you might need in the mix. You can always turn the lows up in the mix. But if you've recorded to the multitrack with too much sub-bass or bass, the track might be unnaturally noisy because of the artificial levels from the overabundance of inaudible lows.

It's often appropriate to roll off the frequencies below about 40 Hz. This can get rid of frequencies that might never be heard but are adding to the overall level of the mix. To add a good low-end foundation to a bass sound, try boosting between 80 and 150 Hz. This frequency range will produce a very solid feel, and these frequencies can be heard on almost all systems. On the bass in Audio Example 5-31, I boost at 80 Hz then sweep the boost from 80 Hz up to 150 Hz.

Audio Example 5-31

Sweeping from 80 Hz to 150 Hz

If the bass sounds muddy and thick in the lower mids or upper bass, try cutting at a frequency between 250 and 500 Hz. Cutting these frequencies can help a stock P-Bass sound like a bass with active electronics. This is one of the most common requests from bassists. Cutting in this range and running the bass through an active direct box can usually produce the desired effect. In Audio Example 5-32, I'll cut at 250 Hz, then sweep the cut from 250 to 500 Hz.

Audio Example 5-32

Sweeping the Cut between 250 Hz and 500 Hz

In Audio Example 5-33, I'll boost at 250 Hz, then sweep the boost from 250 to 500 Hz.

Audio Example 5-33

Sweeping the Boost between 250 Hz and 500 Hz

The frequencies between about 700 and 1200 Hz contain the sound of the bass string being plucked, plus the harmonics that can help the listener recognize the pitch of the bass notes. Listen to Audio Example 5-34 as I boost, then cut at 1000 Hz.

Audio Example 5-34

Boost Then Cut at 1000 Hz

The upper clarity and string noise on a bass usually resides in the frequencies between 2 and 3 kHz. Listen to Audio Example 5-35 as I boost at 2 kHz, then sweep from 2 kHz to 3 kHz.

Audio Example 5-35

Sweeping the Boost between 2 kHz and 3 kHz

Video Example 5-1

Equalizing the Bass Guitar

On most bass sounds, the frequencies above 3 or 4 kHz don't add much that's usable. Even though the upper frequencies contain important harmonics, they aren't usually boosted because they also contain most of the string and fret noises. The key to getting a great sound is in determining what sound best complements the mix. Always compare the bass sound to the kick drum sound and shape the bass to work with, not against, the kick. If the kick is heavy in one particular low frequency, avoid that frequency on the bass.

Panning the Bass

Bass is almost always panned straight down the center of the mix. Bass frequencies are omnidirectional, so panning isn't usually very effective from a listening perspective. The upper frequencies of the bass are directional and can indicate placement, but panning the bass track is not good for the stereo level of the mix. If the bass is panned to one side, the mix will read much hotter on that side because of the low-frequency energy in the bass. The bass needs to be centered to distribute the low-frequency energy equally to the left and right sides of the mix and to provide a solid foundation for the rest of the arrangement.

In Audio Example 5-36, I'll pan the bass from left to right, then to 12:00. (When we speak of pan positions, we often indicate pan placements in relation to clock times.) Notice the difference in the sound of the mix. If you're listening on a system that has meters on the playback of this CD, watch the meter change as I pan the bass track.

Audio Example 5-36

Panning the Bass

Reverberation and Bass Guitar

It's usually best to keep the bass clean and dry. You can set up a bass sound that's incredible by itself with delays, reverb, chorus, and even distortion, but as soon as the bass is combined with the drums, guitars, and keys, the interest of the bass effects is buried and the bass loses definition and punch. The best approach when recording bass is to keep it simple. I'll give you a couple of tricks that I use to make the bass sound bigger without losing clarity in the mix, but even these should be used sparingly and with caution. If you put effects on the bass, you might end up with a mix that's thin or unpredictable. If you use a clean, simple, dry bass track, you'll have a good foundation for the rest of the arrangement.

Reverb is usually inappropriate for bass. In the context of a rhythm section, there's generally too much going on with the other instruments to be able to appreciate or hear the sound of the reverberation on the bass. Adding reverb to the bass can cause your mix to sound distant or muddy. In the mix in Audio Example 5-37, I'll add reverb to the bass track. Notice the difference in the clarity of the overall sound.

Audio Example 5-37

Adding Reverb to the Bass

As with other solo instruments, if you're recording a solo bass track, reverb can add rich, full sound. A smooth, rich-sounding hall reverb can add interest to most solo bass sounds. Listen to Audio Example 5-38 as I add hall reverb to the solo bass part.

Solo Bass with Reverb

Even though it's best to keep the bass sound simple and clean, here's one technique that works very well, especially on stereo mixes. Use a digital delay to create a stereo bass sound. First, set up a short delay time, between about 5 and 23 ms. Be sure that there's no regeneration. This effect involves panning the original bass to one side, then panning a short delay of the bass to the other side. This creates enough difference in the sound of the left and right channels to make the bass seem to come separately from the left and the right instead of from the center. It sounds like stereo! Adjust the levels so that left and right read the same on the VU meter when the bass plays alone.

Listen to the solo bass track in Audio Example 5-39. It starts with the original bass panned to the center position. Next, the original track pans to the left, then the delay is turned up and panned right.

The Stereo Bass Sound

This technique opens up the center of the mix to make room for lead vocals, solos, and other instruments that need to occupy that space. The exact delay time is dependent on the sound of the bass track, but it should generally be below about 23 ms. If you try this technique, always check the sound in mono and stereo. This technique can sound very good in stereo, but when the same part is played back in mono it can sound very bad. The delay of the bass combined with the original bass in mono can result in the canceling and summing of certain frequencies. The delay time determines which frequencies will cancel and sum.

The best way to set this sound up is to listen in mono while you adjust the delay time. Changing the time as little as a fraction of a millisecond can drastically change the sound of the bass in mono, even though the bass still sounds the same in stereo.

Once you have the sound that you need in mono, you can feel confident that this stereo bass technique will work well for your song. The bass in Audio Example 5-40 starts out stereo. Listen as I combine left and right to mono and then adjust the delay time in one-millisecond increments. You can hear how extreme the change can be. Once I've found a sound that's full in mono, I switch back to stereo.

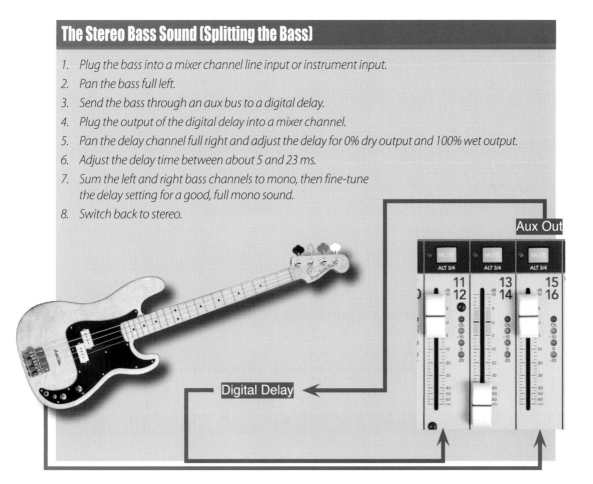

The Stereo Bass Sound (Splitting the Bass)

1. Plug the bass into a mixer channel line input or instrument input.
2. Pan the bass full left.
3. Send the bass through an aux bus to a digital delay.
4. Plug the output of the digital delay into a mixer channel.
5. Pan the delay channel full right and adjust the delay for 0% dry output and 100% wet output.
6. Adjust the delay time between about 5 and 23 ms.
7. Sum the left and right bass channels to mono, then fine-tune the delay setting for a good, full mono sound.
8. Switch back to stereo.

Adjusting Bass Delay for Mono Compatibility

This technique can also work well using a chorus, flanger, or phase shifter. Pan the original dry bass to one side and the 100% wet-effected bass to the other side. These effects are even more important to monitor in mono than the simple delay because the oscillator that varies the delay time can cause the bass to constantly change from very thin to very boomy in mono, even though the sound might be great in stereo. Listen to Audio Example 5-41. The dry bass is panned left and the chorus is panned right. Notice the difference in sound as I switch between stereo and mono.

The Bass with Chorus

These bass effects are best left until mixdown. If you don't check the sound in mono, printing a double, chorus, flanger, phase shifter or reverb to the multitrack could result in a great bass part that's not usable in the mix. If at all possible, record a clean and simple bass track to the multitrack.

Recording Synth Bass

When recording a synthesized bass, there's a good chance that the sound is pretty good coming directly out of the keyboard or sound module. If the keyboard has a stereo output, use both left and right if you have enough tracks. The stereo bass sounds on keyboards are usually created in the same way we made the electric bass stereo. A short delay or chorus-type effect is used to widen the stereo image. Using the stereo outputs lets you pan the bass away from the center position while maintaining a full and balanced sound. Audio Example 5-42 demonstrates a stereo bass sound from a sound module. It starts in stereo then switches to mono, then switches back. Even though the levels stay the same on the left and right meters, there's a big difference in the sound.

Audio Example 5-42

Stereo Synth Bass

Using the stereo outs from a keyboard presents the same dangers we had when we delayed or chorused the electric bass guitar. The bass might sound great in stereo but thin and wimpy in mono. If you really want the stereo bass sound, listen to the bass in mono and adjust the delay settings until the bass sounds good. If you don't have access to the delay settings on your sampled sound and if the bass sound is unacceptable in mono, use one side of the bass sample for a mono sound. You can always create your own stereo bass sound that is mono-compatible using an outboard delay, phase shifter, or chorus.

Plugging In the Synth Bass

Most of the time the keyboard outputs work best running directly into the line inputs of the mixer. If you're plugging into the line input of a mixer that operates at -10 dBV, you'll almost always have plenty of gain from the keyboard to get sufficient recording levels with the mixer settings at their normal levels.

If you're plugging into the line input of a mixer that operates at +4 dBm, your keyboard or sound module will seem to have a weaker signal. Sometimes you'll barely have enough signal to get sufficient level to tape—even when the input fader, output fader, and keyboard volume are at maximum. This will result in more noise being included with your signal. If you're plugging into the line input of a +4-dBm mixer and the level from your keyboard is too low, plug the keyboard into a direct box, then plug the XLR output of the direct box into a mic input of the mixer. This will give you plenty of gain, and you'll be able to use the mic preamp to optimize the levels at each point of the signal path.

The simplest approach to recording keyboard is simply plugging into the line inputs. If the levels are sufficient, this is usually the purest approach because it includes the least amount of circuitry. Also, it's less expensive because you don't need a direct box for every keyboard or sound module output. Home recording equipment often operates at -10 dBV. Professional recording equipment operates at +4 dBm. A lot of the newer keyboards have higher output levels, which increases their compatibility with mixers operating at +4 dBm. I use a few keyboards regularly that have plenty of output to run into any mixer.

To maintain a better signal-to-noise ratio, always turn the keyboard volume control up as far as possible without overdriving the mixer input. Most of the time you'll be able to set the keyboard at maximum gain.

If you need to use a DI, there will be times when the keyboard output will be too hot for the direct box input. There might be a pad on the direct box to help optimize this initial gain setting. It's important that the pad be adjusted properly to maintain a good signal-to-noise ratio without distortion. There might be a one- or two-position pad that will attenuate the input by 10 to 40 dB.

Listen to the keyboard sound without attenuation. If there's distortion, pad the signal with the attenuator on the direct box. If there's still distortion, use more pad. (10 to 20 dB of attenuation is usually enough to clean up the sound at this initial gain point.)

Miking the Synth Bass

The normal procedure for recording synth bass is plugging directly into the recording console. There's usually enough control over the sound within the keyboard to get the sound you need going directly into the mixer. That's not to say you shouldn't try miking the bass speaker cabinet if you're in search of a different sound. Some very high-quality recordings are made with a synth run into an amplifier, then miked. This approach has the potential of adding acoustic interest to your sounds that differentiates them from the stock sounds coming straight out of the synth. Listen to the differences between Audio Examples 5-43 through 5-45.

Audio Example 5-43 demonstrates a good, solid sampled bass sound recorded directly into the line input of the mixer.

Audio Example 5-43

Synth Bass Direct In

Audio Example 5-44 demonstrates the same part played into a bass amp and miked with a moving-coil mic from a distance of about two feet.

Audio Example 5-44

Synth Bass Miked

Notice in Audio Example 5-45 the blending of the direct synth bass sound and the miked synth bass sound.

Audio Example 5-45

Blending Direct and Miked Synth Bass

Synth Bass Range and EQ

Using keyboard bass has become such a common technique that the range of acceptable bass sounds has increased greatly. The usable range of the instrument has even been affected. Most musicians in the earlier days of synthesized bass sounds tried to stay within the natural range of a four-string bass. It was thought that using any notes below low

E on the bass guitar would result in a part that wasn't believable or natural-sounding.

It didn't take too long to break that barrier because the full, rich sound of the low-pitched, synthesized bass notes sounded and felt good. Now it's not uncommon to hear a bass part that goes as low as the C or even the B below low E on a four-string bass guitar. In fact, five-string and six-string bass guitars have become commonplace as real bass players try to match the full sound of the synthesized bass.

When recording these low bass notes, always listen to the bass parts on small speakers before you commit to any EQ settings. On large, far-field monitors, the low bass notes can sound great. They might be warm and full on the big speakers if you boost the bass or sub-bass, but when the mix is played back on a boom box the bass part could be inaudible. A small stereo might not even reproduce frequencies below 100 Hz or so. If you've recorded a part with lots of low notes and boosted the very low frequencies, you'll be dissatisfied with the sound you hear from a small set of speakers.

Consider that low E, the lowest note on a four-string bass guitar, has a frequency of 41.20 Hz. If you're using bass notes lower than low E, it becomes increasingly important to EQ for smaller speakers. The fundamental frequencies of the common notes below E are 36.71 Hz for low D and 32.7 Hz for low C. The only way to make these notes discernible on small systems is to boost the harmonics rather than the fundamental frequencies. The way to get a fuller sound from that note and be assured that the note will be heard on any setup is to boost a harmonic of that note. If you boost 30 to 40 Hz, you'll be raising the overall level of the mix with a frequency that won't be heard on most systems, but if you boost a harmonic the note will sound stronger on more systems. The first harmonic above 40 Hz (low E) is 80 Hz, so boosting between 60 and 80 Hz is a good choice for a song that contains a lot of lower bass notes.

The notes in the bass part in Audio Example 5-46 go down to low C. I've boosted a one-octave-wide band centered at 40 Hz, essentially boosting fundamental frequencies between about 30 and 60 Hz. This sounds very warm and powerful on the far-field monitors in my studio, but it is less than impressive on most systems.

Audio Example 5-46

Bass Boosted at 40 Hz

In Audio Example 5-47, I've equalized the bass to sound good on smaller speakers by boosting at 80 Hz rather than 40 Hz. The bass still sounds good on larger monitors and also sounds good on smaller near-field monitors.

Audio Example 5-47

Bass Boosted at 80 Hz

In Audio Example 5-48, I've boosted at 160 Hz. This helps the part come alive more on small speakers, but we're losing a little punch on the large far-field monitors.

Audio Example 5-48

Bass Boosted at 160 Hz

Now listen to the previous three examples in a row. You'll hear eight bars with 40 Hz boosted, eight bars with 80 Hz boosted, then eight bars with 160 Hz boosted. Play these examples on a few different systems to hear the real difference.

Audio Example 5-49

The Previous Three Audio Examples

Compressing the Synth Bass

Low notes from a keyboard are almost always pretty even in output, so compressing the synth bass part isn't common. Using the compressor to accentuate the attack of a note might be a good plan if it weren't for the fact that the envelope of the sound is usually controllable within the keyboard. If you need more attack from a note, the place to get it is from the keyboard. Even sampled bass sounds are typically pretty even in volume, and compressing isn't needed.

Recording Level for the Synth Bass

Recording level for the synth bass depends on the tonal character of the sound. For most full but not boomy bass sounds, the VU meter can read up to +1 or +2 VU at the hottest part of the track. If the sound is thin in the low end with lots of attack, recording levels should be more conservative, around -3 VU.

Audio Example 5-50 demonstrates a bass sound that can be recorded at 0 VU.

Audio Example 5-50
Bass Sound Recorded at 0 VU

Audio Example 5-51 demonstrates a bass sound that should be recorded at about -3 VU.

Audio Example 5-51
Bass Sound Recorded at -3 VU

Panning Synth Bass

Keyboard bass, such as the electric bass, should be panned to the center in order to distribute the low-frequency information evenly between the left and right channels. If the keyboard has stereo outputs, it's usually okay to pan the bass hard right and hard left, but always be sure to check the bass sound in mono. Most stock stereo synth bass sounds work pretty well in stereo and mono, but never assume—always check.

When tracks are panned hard left and right, they'll often be easy to hear in a stereo mix but will get buried in a mono mix. This is especially true if there aren't other instruments hard-panned. As we get more into mixing, we'll see that giving an instrument its own space in a stereo mix will isolate that instrument and help it to be easily heard.

If your bass track is very audible in stereo but buried in mono, try soft-panning the stereo bass. Listen to the stereo key bass sound in Audio Example 5-52. First it's hard-panned apart, then you'll hear it summed to mono. Notice how the level of the bass seems to change when I switch to mono.

Audio Example 5-52
Switching between Stereo and Mono

Audio Example 5-53 demonstrates the same bass sound used in Audio Example 5-52, this time panned to about 9:00 and 3:00. Notice that the bass still sounds stereo, but when I switch to mono the apparent volume of the bass stays more constant than in the previous example.

Audio Example 5-53
Bass Panned to 9:00 and 3:00

Effects and the Synth Bass

Approach reverberation on key bass the same way you approach electric bass. Reverb isn't usually appropriate except on flowing ballads, in which you need the bass to blend into a smooth pad.

The same delay and chorus techniques that work well on the electric bass sound good on key bass. In fact, most of the stock stereo key bass sounds from the manufacturer use these techniques. Again, check the sounds in mono before you commit them to tape.

Acoustic Bass

The *acoustic bass*, also called the *stand-up bass*, *string bass* or (more traditionally) the *double bass*, is an instrument that's uncommon in most commercial, pop, country, and rock recording situations. Unless you're regularly recording symphony orchestras or full-blown film scores, you don't encounter acoustic bass very often.

In addition to symphonic settings, string bass will sometimes show up in a jazz group, whether small ensemble or big band. Occasionally the bassist in a '50s rock-and-roll band will use stand-up to give the band a different edge and drive, but it's generally a novelty in commercial rock.

There are two approaches to recording this instrument—symphonic and pop, including rock, jazz, country, blues, and so on.

When recording string bass for a traditional symphonic setting, the key considerations are

1. Room ambience
2. Blending between basses if there are more than one
3. Blending with the rest of the string section
4. Blending with the rest of the orchestra
5. Separation

Essentially, we're looking for a bass sound that's smooth, blended, and supportive of the rest of the orchestra. If the strings are plucked (pizzicato), we're looking for a smooth, blending sound. If the bass is being played with a bow (arco), we're trying to capture the smooth, supportive sound of the bass, not the scraping sound of the bow pulling across the strings.

First of all, find a good-sounding hall or room. If you're recording a symphony, you're probably already in a pretty sizable studio or concert hall, but if you have an option, find the best-sounding room to record in. Orchestras have been know to go to great extremes to record in just the right concert hall for a particular piece of music.

In any recording situation where the goal is to capture the instrument and the room sound, mic placement is a critical factor. Use a condenser mic with flat frequency response and place it at the spot that gives you the balance you need between the instrument and the ambience. The distance from the sound source will usually be between about three feet and 15 feet.

The determining factor in mic placement is the room. Sound will react differently in different sized rooms, different shaped rooms, and rooms constructed with hard or soft materials. Trust your ears to help

Distant Miking Upright Bass

To get a smooth, blended sound, set the mic between three and 15 feet from the bass or basses. Adjust the mic distance to include the desired amount of room ambience. This technique is good for an orchestral sound but isn't typical for a jazz or pop rhythm section sound.

To capture a section sound with equal level between the basses the mic must be equidistant from each instrument.

you find the sound you need. If the mic is too close to the bass, the sound won't blend with an orchestral texture. Pizzicato will feel too close and arco will have too much of a grind.

If you're not able to record in a room that sounds good naturally, try adding hall reverb to the bass sound. This reverberation should blend the sound with the rest of the mix and give the bass a warm, smooth sound.

When you're recording string bass for a commercial rock, pop, or jazz song, the key considerations are

1. Capturing a close, tight sound
2. Capturing good punch from each note
3. Capturing good attack to each plucked note
4. Capturing a sound that fits with and complements the rest of the rhythm section

Miking the string bass with these goals in mind demands an entirely different approach than miking the string bass for an orchestral setting.

Close-Miking the String Bass

It's best to use a condenser mic with a good, full range. Mike the bass from a distance of one to three feet, depending on just how close you want the sound to be. If you place the mic so it's pointing at the area where the strings are plucked, the sound will be tighter and each note will have more attack.

If you place the mic so it's pointing at the F hole, the sound will be fuller in the lows and low mids, but the attack might not be as clear.

Close-Miking the String Bass

For clear attack and punch on each plucked note, point the mic at the spot being plucked. Mic distance is typically one to three feet from the instrument. This technique works well for jazz or pop rhythm section sounds, but isn't typical for an orchestral sound.

For more lows and low mids, point the mic at the F hole from a distance of between one and three feet. This technique works well for a jazz or pop rhythm section sound, but isn't typical for an orchestral sound. However, if you have a bad-sounding room and a good-sounding reverb, you can usually simulate an orchestral sound by adding a little hall or chamber reverb to the sound you get when miking the F hole.

For a natural orchestral sound, it's best to avoid compression on string bass. Typically on pop styles, if the bassist is inconsistent in his or her playing attack, it's necessary to compress the upright bass in the same way you do the electric bass. This helps keep the part even in level and supportive, both harmonically and rhythmically.

Equalization of acoustic bass should be applied to compensate for any booming frequencies that might be present as a result of the instrument's individual character.

Conclusion

We've covered a lot of very useful points that will help you get more out of your bass parts. Each instrument and player is unique, so the variables are always a factor. In recording, all we can do is build a bag of tricks to draw from. The more you learn, the more accurately you'll be able to guess the outcome of each different recording situation.

Recording Great Vocal Tracks

This chapter demonstrates some proven techniques for recording vocals, providing pointers on getting good, commercially competitive lead and backing vocal sounds.

The art of vocal recording is very involved. It's amazing how sensitive, both mentally and physically, the vocal instrument is. Singing is an interesting blend of technical ability, physical talent, and emotional interpretation. There must be a good balance between these factors. The same singer with the same ability can perform in totally different ways depending on the recording environment, the mood we create during the session, the singer's physical and emotional well being, the mix we set up in the headphones, and the kind of vocal sound he or she hears while recording. Awareness and understanding of these factors will help you bring out the best in the singers you record.

Vocals are the focal point of almost all commercial songs. If the vocals sound good, the song will probably sound good. If they sound bad, the song will probably sound bad. The vocal tracks typically contain the most apparent emotional content and impact of the song. Most listeners focus on the vocals first (consciously, at least).

The vocal tracks must capture the appropriate emotional and musical feel for the song. For most styles, it's important that they're understandable, in tune, and that the lyrics are sung in a way that gives the song meaning. Conveying the meaning of the lyrics usually takes precedence over other factors. Small flaws in technical presentation can be justified by an authentic, emotional, heartfelt performance.

Vocal recording techniques are very subjective. Approach the audio examples in this chapter with that fact in mind. Some of these techniques will jump out at you, and you'll easily hear a difference between the before and after. Other examples will be more subtle, and you'll need to replay the CD and really focus on the sounds. If you can't hear the difference on a technique that I've presented, try harder. Make a list of everything you hear in each sound, then compare lists. Include the subjective feeling each example evokes. Note the high-, mid-, and low-frequency content. Describe the sounds with words such as thick, thin, meaty, or chunky. Try to hear everything you can about these sounds. Listen on different systems, at different listening levels, and on a good set of headphones.

Some of the scenarios I've set up, such as the wind screen comparisons, are very subtle. Whether you use a foam wind screen or panty hose on an embroidery ring isn't going to make or break your recording, but attending to this kind of subtle detail throughout the recording process will make a very big difference in the sound of your recordings. I repeat: Listen closely!

Let's start by looking at some techniques that'll help you record a good sound. Commit this information to memory and practice the techniques until they're practically instinctive. Concentrate on recording an excellent vocal take rather than simply an excellent vocal sound. An excellent take includes style, emotion, inspiration, and a good sound. A good sound by itself doesn't do much to make a song appeal to anyone.

Vocal Phrasing

The more you understand about vocal phrasing and interpretation, the better you'll be at recording—period. When I was putting this chapter together, this section was way down in the outline, but it just hit me that the first sentence out of my head was the most profound of the chapter. We can spend a fortune on gear to get a great vocal sound and we can figure out what to tweak and where, to capture the finest resolution digital or analog signal, but if we record bad musical phrasing and interpretation, we're left with nothing but—should I say it—CRAP!

Breathing

Work the phrases out with the singer. Use your judgement. Some very natural and raw singers will freak out if you start putting them in a box. Once they think about where they need to breath, they might forget to breathe altogether. How can that be good? Most singers, however, are fine with just a couple suggestions on phrasing and where to breathe— and it really doesn't usually take much to make things better.

There are a couple of advantages to stabilizing phrasing.

+ You'll magnify the musical flow and impact.
+ As you combine takes to find the magical take, everything will fit together much better if the phrasing is consistent from take to take.
+ If the phrasing is musical and well thought out, the singer should feel more comfortable—virtually empowered by the musical momentum.

Every great singer I've ever worked with has been completely in control of many aspects of the song, including the rhythm of their breaths. Many singers—in fact, most singers—do this subconsciously. They breathe in time with the groove somehow. If you are recording a singer who has problems with rhythmic feel, he or she is probably starting the phrases on time but somewhere in the middle it gets off. Almost always, you can listen closely and hear that the singer is breathing in some random rhythm between phrases. This is a tough one to just get people to do properly because, if they were really feeling the groove, everything about them would be in time, including their breaths.

If you're aware of this, you might be able to help get more out a singer than he or she came to the session with. Something as simple as suggesting that he or she takes their breathe on the snare beat (usually count 4) just before the phrase starts can set the singer right in the pocket from the first note.

Choosing Breathe Points and Phrases

Phrasing should not be random. It should be manipulated to draw the listener through the song. Many phrases break in a natural rhythm—every two or four measures. However, there are many occasions when long phrases or phrases that carry over the normal phrase pattern are powerful and necessary to strong music.

Breaking lyrical flow provides the listener with rest. Music must provide the proper stylistic balance of tension and release, activity and rest, or aggression and passivity. As the musician, you are in control of how the listener feels at the end of the piece of music. Much of that feeling depends on your interpretation of phrasing.

If you really want to move from one musical section to another, continue the phrase at the end of one section and continue it into the next. At the end of a chorus, for example, sing over the natural break that occurs between the sections and continue the phrase into the bridge. Controlling the musical flow in this way holds the potential for undeniably exciting transitions.

Releases

Most decent singers can successfully and powerfully start a phrase. But the best singers really know how to end one. As you produce and develop all the vocal tracks, hold a high standard in every possible way, but if you truly want to end up with professional-sounding vocals, convince the singer to end each phrase with confidence and intentional power. Amateurish vocals typically diminish and even fade off at the end of the phrase. Phrasing like this diminishes musical flow and momentum. Every time the vocalist throws away the end of the phrase, he or she loses a listener.

Listen to some truly great singers and pay attention to how they end each musical phrase. I think you'll be surprised at how intentional and musical the releases are, and at the powerful momentum they create. I often ask singers to think past the end of the phrase. This approach almost always gets them to finish the phrase without killing the musical flow. Most of the problems I see with a young artist's phrasing result from an excitement to start the phrase and an unintentional finish.

Pronunciation

Pronunciation is very important! It must be stylistically correct and repeatable. In some genres, everything is about the message and the understandability of the lyrics. Other styles are about the groove and the vibe. It's not as important that each word is understandable as it is that the words sound good together and that they support the groove. As the producer/engineer, you must be familiar with the style in order to make critical suggestions.

Often, proper focus on consistent and understandable pronunciation and diction leads to better and more musical phrasing as well as improved intonation and timbre. If you're building backing vocals, uniform and consistent pronunciation and phrasing are essential. If everyone is phrasing together and if they all interpret the lyric and musical flow together, the backing vocals will not only be understandable and rhythmically consistent, they'll probably be musically and emotionally powerful.

Enunciation

Enunciation and vocal technique are very important. We need to record the most emotion-filled music possible—that's a fact. And the style of music determines the type of emotion we must capture. There are techniques that will provide endurance and stamina. There are principles of enunciation and diction that, when followed, nearly force good intonation and excellent phrasing. Never underplay the value of quality instruction. Whether you play an instrument or sing, fundamental skills support and lead the way to virtuosity and excellent. Though there are stylists who prefer a raw, unrefined sound and emotion, I've never met any musicians who wanted mediocrity from themselves or their recordings. Traditional training can always support your individuality. Grasp of fundamentals always leads to greater longevity, more endurance, and better health.

Smile—Mouth Shape Matters

It's important that vocalists control their facial expressions while singing in order to deliver the necessary style and impact, especially when building a group sound. Facial expressions tend to control intonation and pronunciation. Often, when a singer is under the pitch, a simple suggestion to smile a little more during a particular word or phrase pulls the pitch nicely into place. This can also tighten the sound in a negative way.

There is always a balance between technique and immediate results. Sometimes, the factor a vocalist really needs in order to perform an excellent take is practice or simple technique. Typically, in the studio, we need to get the best results possible for the moment, and we need them quickly. This is where you need to develop a sizable bag of tricks.

Whenever you're guiding pronunciation and mouth shaping, you absolutely must be in touch with the stylistic idiosyncrasies of the music you're recording. It's easy to produce a product that is "cheesy" if you're over-pronouncing and creating stiff and exaggerated phrases. In country music, much emphasis is placed on understandability of the lyrics. In alternative rock, it's all about the energy and feel. In pop rock, lyrics are important. In jazz it's about the vibe. Know your musical style!

When and How to Make Suggestions

It's a bad idea to start the session with your list of newly-found secrets to recording great vocal takes in hand, confidently walking the singer through the list of dos and don'ts. I always record a few takes of the track before I say anything other than really encouraging and uplifting stuff. In fact, if the singer has stamina, I record several takes all the way through, just making suggestions on a few things I hear.

Once you know you have a pretty good representation of everything in the song, then start going into detail. This is the particular area where digital hard-disk recording is wonderful because you can keep everything. In the analog domain, you must be more conscious of tape tracks and all those other limiting factors.

After I do a few complete run-throughs, I like to create separate tracks for each verse, chorus, and bridge. Then we focus on the first verse. I'll record a couple take of the verse straight through, make some suggestions, and really try to get a great full-sung verse. Once I think I have that, I'll really focus on each phrase so I know I have everything covered. Later, I go back and piece together all the best of the best takes. You must consider the music and the singer whenever you're going through this process. Some singers can only sing a song all the way through. Once you stop them, it's all over. They can't sing a separate phrase with any conviction or emotion to save their lives. Other singers thrive on going way into detail, and the finished combined track sounds musical and excellent in every way.

Anytime you piece phrases together, you run the risk that any natural musical flow might be completely lost. It might be stronger, musically, to take a less accurate full-sung take because it has a better emotional and musical flow. This is where you get to use everything you know about music, phrasing, and emotional power to determine what presents the strongest version of the song.

Always be as positive and constructive as you can possibly be with singers. You have the power to ruin the singer, the take, the recording, and the song! You will never get much out of a huddled mass of sobbing vocalist in a fetal position sucking his or her thumb under the grand piano! There is always a way to say what you need to say in a way that builds up and doesn't destroy. There is a point in a relationship at which bluntness is okay and appreciated because of its efficiency. However, people must know how much you care for them and how good you think they are before you can just stop the recorder and say, "Man, that take just sucked big time. How about we try it again with a little more punch?" Even if you get to that all-efficient point where you can say what you think, always attack an aspect of the take, not the singer in general.

Getting Vocals in Tune

Sometimes during a take it's obvious to everyone that the singer is consistently out of tune. This even happens with singers that always seem

Computer Assisted Automatic Tuning

A few years ago, Antares came out with a program called Auto-Tune. It's a software plug-in that works well with most digital audio recording software packages. It revolutionized intonation in vocals because it will automatically ride the pitch of any single-note audio track. It is an amazing tool.

This plug-in can be overused, but it can also be applied very taste-fully, naturally pulling vocal part into the correct pitch. I always try to use Auto-Tune in a way that sounds natural, leaving the amount of variance and toler-ance that provides the effect of live singers that have rock-solid intonation.

to have great intonation. So why do they, all of a sudden, start singing out of tune when it comes down to recording?

Many young singers simply haven't learned enough about their craft to endure the tedium and scrutiny of the recording world. Even though that fact is brutal, you as the engineer/producer are commissioned with the awesome duty of making the best of the situations you're given.

Often a singer is out of tune simply because the headphone mix is providing an inaccurate pitch reference or a pitch reference that's hard to pinpoint. Always listen to the headphone mix when you're getting the singer set up. It's even a good idea for you to plug headphones into the same mix they're getting so that you'll know instantly when something's not right.

Headphones

Often a singer is out of tune simply because the headphone mix is providing an inaccurate pitch reference or a pitch reference that's hard to pinpoint. Always listen to the headphone mix when you're getting the singer set up. It's even a good idea for you to plug headphones into the same mix the singer is getting so that you'll know instantly when something's not right.

Sometimes the mix isn't bad but the pitch reference is confusing. If the bass is the only pitched instrument in the mix and you're recording reference vocals, you can have a problem because it's often difficult to tell where the pitch center is on a bass guitar. Singing in tune to bass and drum accompaniment can be very difficult.

For pitch reference, the best instruments to include in the headphone mix are piano and clean guitar. Some of the big keyboard sounds include chorus, reverb, and other effects. These effects tend to obscure the pitch center, so they can transform the search for accurate intonation into the impossible quest. A clean, non-effected piano or guitar definitively identifies the tonal center, therefore showing the vocalist exactly where in tune is.

Singers demand different amounts of their own voice in the phones. Learn what helps them sing best, then strive to provide that at all times. The headphone mix is a key factor in the vocal recording process. Be aware of the headphone mix throughout all your vocal sessions.

Singers often sing with better intonation when they uncover one of their ears rather than letting the headphones cover both ears. Simply moving one side of the headphones behind the ear lets singers hear themselves more like they would in a live setting. This simple technique has the potential to fix intonation problems instantly!

Singers who prefer to listen through only one side of the headphones often like to cup a hand over the open ear with the open palm of the hand facing forward. The hand acts as a cup to capture the sound of the vocal as it reflects back to the ear. This is a very good way for singers to hear themselves. Singers who hear themselves accurately and have a supportive mix of the background accompaniment rarely sing out of tune. The best of singers struggle when they can't hear themselves well and are referencing to a confusing mix.

When the headphones are too loud or when they have fluid-filled earpieces (tightly enclosing the ear), most singers sing under the correct pitch. Open, foam headphones are good for intonation but bad for headphone leakage. The sound from the headphone that's picked up by the microphone is called *leakage*. Most major headphone manufacturers make headphones that offer an excellent compromise between completely open phones and completely sealed ears; these typically work best. Examples of excellent headphones for use in vocal recording are the AKG Model K240M and the Sony MDR-7506.

Singers usually like to hear a little reverb or echo in the phones while they're singing. This usually helps them get in the mood for the song. Like singing in the shower, singing with lots of reverb in the phones can be fun. But sometimes you sound too good in the headphones and the reverb might give the vocalist a false sense of security. Pitch and interpretation often sound fine when recording, but when it's time to mix the dry vocal might sound very marginal. A little reverb is usually okay when tracking, but less reverb in the headphones generally results in more accurate vocal tracks.

Mic Techniques

Placement

Placement of the microphone in relation to the singer is a key variable. Not only does it matter where the mic is, but the best placement changes depending on the type of mic you're using, vocal timbre, musical style, and personal taste.

Condenser microphones are usually the first choice for studio vocal applications. Commercial vocal sounds vary, but most professionally recorded hit vocals are recorded with a good condenser mic set on cardioid pickup pattern, from a distance of six to 12 inches. A vocal that's recorded at this distance sounds full and warm on most condenser mics. Recording at this proximity provides the recordist with the option of including the inherent

Vocal Acoustic Interaction

The singer's voice not only reaches the mic through a direct path, it also reflects off the surrounding surfaces. This illustration shows a few of the possible reflections of the walls at each end of the room, floor, and ceiling. Even though the sound waves lose energy with each reflection, it's amazing how much they influence vocal sound quality and timbre.

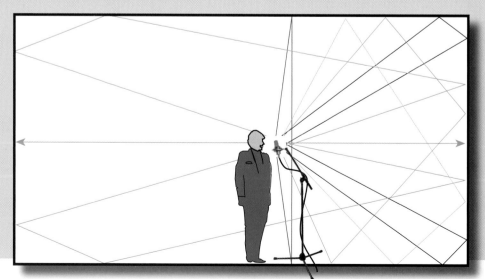

Side Wall Reflections

The vocal sound reflects off each surface in the room. The side walls often play an important role in the combination between direct and reflected sound. Not only does the sound combine at the mic in a varying phase relationship as it reflects off the walls, but reflections off any hard surface in the room influence the recorded vocal sound.

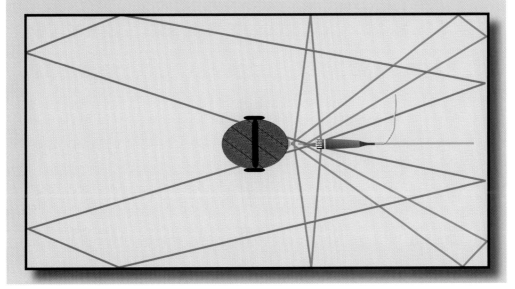

sound of the acoustical environment in varying degrees. Most lead vocals blend better in the mix when recorded with the microphone about a foot or so from the vocalist. Close-mike technique (from a distance of one to three inches) typically provides a sound that is a little too thick and cumbersome, especially when using a condenser mic.

If you're using a moving-coil mic, vocals sound thin and tinny from distances greater than six to eight inches. If you only have a moving-coil mic, you'll get the best results when close-miking solo vocals. When miking group vocals with a moving-coil mic, some fairly extreme addition of low-end EQ or subtraction of the appropriate high-frequency might be necessary to fill out the sound.

Distance

Let's look closer at what's happening with the vocal sound as we mike at one distance or another.

With any instrument, including vocals, the sound of the instrument or voice reflecting off the walls and other hard surfaces can be either very beneficial or very harmful to the recorded sound.

The vocalist's sound reaches the mic very quickly as it comes from the singer's mouth. When the sound travels from the mouth, reflects off a room surface, then comes back to the mic, the reflection arrives at the mic in phase or (in varying degrees) out of phase. We've already seen some of the results of undesirable phase interaction in previous chapters, and it's important to understand that any time you use a microphone to record a track, there is phase interaction between the

Combination of Reflections

Each reflection combines with the original sound wave, resulting in a completely new sound wave. The summing and canceling process that occurs when sound waves combine becomes very complex when all the possible reflections are considered.

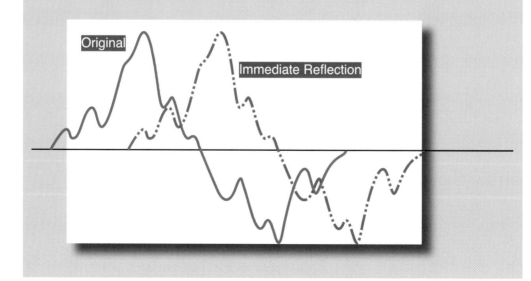

The Single Reflection

The sound of the direct voice and the single reflection combine to create a different vocal texture. Moving closer to or farther from a hard surface, such as a wall can affect the sound quality dramatically.

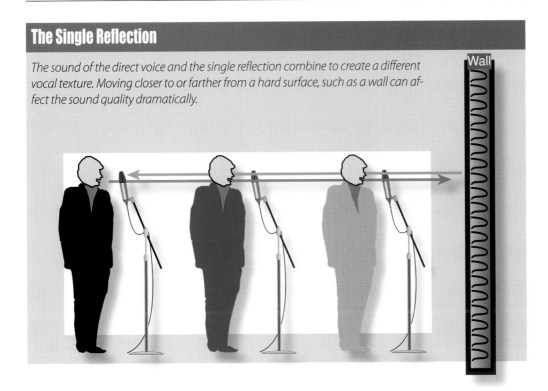

direct and reflected sounds. This phase interaction is the reason why a room adds its own signature to a sound.

Let's simplify in order to make it easier to understand. In Audio Example 6-1, I'll hand-hold a mic and walk slowly toward a hard surface.

Audio Example 6-1

Immediate Reflections

Imagine how complex this scenario becomes when the direct sound combines with every reflection in a room.

Small Room versus Large Room

If the reflections change the sound quality at the microphone, then we should also realize that, since the size and shape of the room determine the reflections, a singer can sound different when recorded in different rooms. Listen to Audio Examples 6-2 through 6-4. Each example demonstrates the effect of different rooms on my vocal sound. On each example, I'm holding the microphone about one foot from my mouth. Aside from the sound change, listen to the difference in natural room ambience. By room ambience I mean the sounds that just happen to be in the particular acoustical environment. Contributors to the ambient sound are things like furnaces, automobile sounds, office equipment, aircraft noise overhead, or electrical appliance noise.

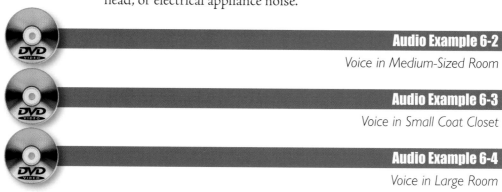

Audio Example 6-2
Voice in Medium-Sized Room

Audio Example 6-3
Voice in Small Coat Closet

Audio Example 6-4
Voice in Large Room

Based on the previous audio examples, it's clear that the room and mic distance play important parts in the sound of the vocal. We need a good set of rules about recording vocals to help provide a starting point for our choice of recording technique. Don't feel bound by these rules—many great vocal sounds have been recorded through techniques that break the rules—but use them as a foundation for your choices. Let's consider mics in two categories:

1. Moving-coil and ribbon
2. Condenser

Moving-Coil/Ribbon

Moving-coil and ribbon mics are almost always designed for close-miking applications and don't typically provide a full sound when the singer is more than six to eight inches from the mic. To get a full, natural sound from these mics, it's best to record the singer from a distance of two to six inches. Moving-coil mics and ribbon mics are the standard choice for live sound reinforcement applications because they work best at close range. In addition, moving-coil microphones are well-suited to live sound reinforcement use because they are the most durable of all the common mic types. Ribbon mics aren't very durable, but they provide a good sound when close-miking vocals.

The vocal in Audio Example 6-5 was recorded with a moving-coil mic about three inches from the singer.

Audio Example 6-5

Moving-Coil Mic from Three Inches

Audio Example 6-6 demonstrates the same set used in Audio Example 6-5 with the mic 12 inches from the singer. Notice the difference in fullness.

Audio Example 6-6

Moving-Coil Mic from 12 Inches

Audio Example 6-7 demonstrates the same vocal part, this time recorded through a ribbon microphone from a distance of about three inches.

Audio Example 6-7

Ribbon Mic from Three Inches

The ribbon mic in Audio Example 6-8 is 12 inches from the singer.

Ribbon Mic from 12 Inches

When recording vocals in a recording studio, condenser microphones are almost always the best choice. The condenser mic operating principle is best suited to accurately capture a singer's natural sound because it colors the sound less than other mic types. They also respond more accurately to transients, therefore producing a vocal sound that's very natural and understandable.

Unlike moving-coil and ribbon mics, condenser microphones sound full from a distance of one or two feet. The singer can stand back from the mic a bit, and you can still record a full, present sound while retaining the option to include more or less of the room's acoustical character. Miking vocals from one or two feet away often produces a unique and transparent sound. Sometimes when vocals are close-miked, especially with condenser microphones, they sound boomy and thick and don't blend well with the rest of the mix. The vocal line in Audio Example 6-9 was recorded with a condenser mic from about six inches.

Audio Example 6-9

Vocal Melody from Six Inches (Condenser)

Audio Example 6-10 demonstrates the same vocal line as Audio Example 6-9, this time recorded from a distance of about 12 inches. Notice that the line still sounds full.

Audio Example 6-10

Vocal Melody from 12 Inches (Condenser)

The condenser mic capsule doesn't respond well to moisture. If the singer is too close, the mic might suddenly quit working and remain inoperable until the capsule dries out. When the capsule dries off suf-

The Wind Screen

There are many different types and shapes of foam wind screens. They work very well when used in the proper context but can adversely affect sound quality. When a wind screen is placed over a mic capsule, the sound arriving at the capsule through the foam wind screen is affected mostly by the type of foam material rather than physical shape.

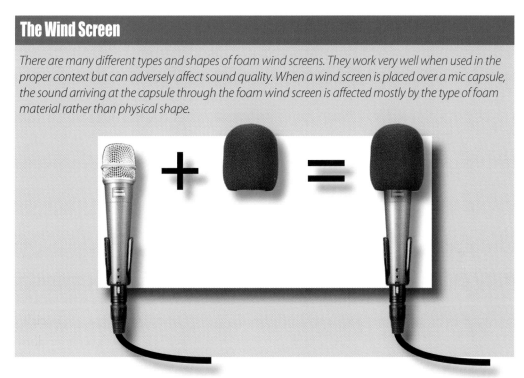

ficiently the mic will work again, but it's frustrating when this happens. If you want the close-miked sound from a condenser mic, use a foam wind screen to diffuse as much air and moisture as possible.

The Room

Most commercial vocal sounds end up in the final mix with reverb and delay added to simulate the interesting and rich sound of a large acoustical environment, such as a concert hall or stadium.

As demonstrated by Audio Examples 6-2 through 6-4, the room plays a key role in the overall recorded sound. Use of reverb and delay effects compounds the importance of your control and understanding of natural room ambience. The acoustical space where the vocal tracks are recorded influences the miked sound and the sound created by any electronic additions or manipulations.

Stylistic Considerations

Usually in commercial popular music it's best to record vocals in a room that's acoustically neutral (doesn't have a long reverberation time) and mike the vocalist from a distance of six to 12 inches. This approach provides the most flexibility during mixdown. You maintain the freedom to use reverberation and other effects to artificially place the vocal in the space that best suits the emotion of the music.

For classically oriented vocal recordings, it's often the technique of choice to find a great-sounding room or concert hall, then mike the singer from a distance that includes the desired amount of room sound. The room sound is all-important to this vocal-recording approach, and it's common for the best classical singers to travel anywhere in the world to sing a piece of music in the concert hall that they feel is best for the music.

Even for commercial pop styles, you should be willing to experiment with different uses of ambience. Mainly, take care that you don't include so much ambience that the vocal loses the close intimacy that sounds good on a lot of popular music.

Wind Screen

A wind screen is used in the studio to keep abundant air caused by hard enunciation from creating loud pops as the microphone capsule is overworked. In an outdoor application, the wind screen is also used to shield the capsule from wind.

Most vocal recordings require the use of a wind screen, also called a *pop filter*. When a singer pronounces words containing hard consonants, such as "p" and "b," there's a lot of air hitting the mic capsule at once. When the air from these hard consonants, called *plosives*, hits the mic capsule, it can actually bottom out the capsule diaphragm. In other words, this "pop" can be the physical sound of the microphone

Embroidery Hoop Wind Screen

This wind screen uses a piece of a nylon stocking stretched over an embroidery hoop and attached to the bottom part of a standard mic clip. Most embroidery hoops fit very nicely in the mic clip that comes with a Shure SM57 or SM58. Mount this device on a separate mic stand and place it front of the mic between the singer and the microphone diaphragm. This design alters the vocal sound less than most other wind screen designs. An added bonus to this screen is its flexibility in positioning. If the sound you need requires the vocalist to stand one foot (or any other specified distance) from the microphone, simply position the wind screen one foot from the mic capsule. The singer is then given a visual reference to gauge distance from the mic and a barrier to keep from moving too close.

These wind screens are also commercially available for those of us who aren't inclined to tackle "do it yourself" projects.

diaphragm actually hitting the end of its normal travel range. On our recorder, we hear this as a loud and obvious pop. Audio Example 6-11 demonstrates the sound of a problem plosive. This pop is usually difficult to get rid of in the mix so it's best to find a way to not record it.

Audio Example 6-11

The Problem Plosive

A wind screen can diffuse the air from the singer before it gets to the mic capsule, therefore eliminating the problem plosive. Wind screens come in many different forms. Moving-coil and ribbon mics often have the wind screen built in. Most condenser mics don't have

Attaching the Wind Screen to the Mic Stand

The embroidery hoop screen can be attached to a regular mic stand with a special clamp—normally used in live applications to hold a guitar mic on the same mic stand as the singer/guitarist's vocal mic.

Mounting the hoop on a long goose neck lets you easily position the screen while eliminating the need for a separate mic stand.

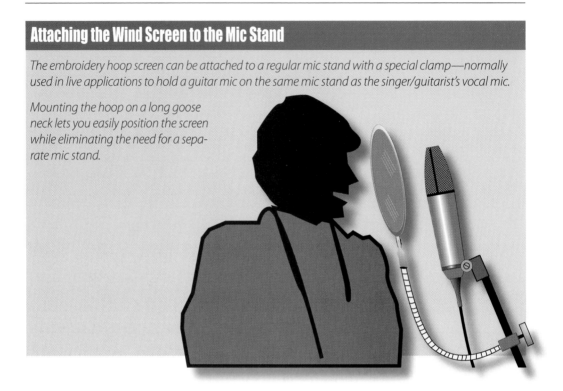

the wind screen built in. Because the condenser microphones sound full from a distance, we can have the singer stand back far enough that plosives aren't much of a problem, and we'll still get a full, natural sound. Depending on the singer and the sound you want, you might not be able to keep the mic far enough away to avoid plosives while still achieving the sound you want.

If a singer has hard enunciation, if you're trying to get a close sound, or if you're outside on a breezy day, try a foam wind screen. They come in different shapes, sizes, and colors, but they're all made from molded, porous foam. Their purpose is to diffuse the air before it reaches the mic capsule. Foam wind screens are the typical choice for outdoor applications because they surround the mic capsule completely and offer the most complete wind diffusion. Purists often reject foam wind screens for

Using a Pencil as a Wind Screen

Here's another type of wind screen that's inexpensive, convenient, and quite effective. Tape a pencil to the microphone so that it lies directly in front of the mic diaphragm—deflecting air that heads straight at it—therefore eliminating unwanted pops. This technique has little effect on vocal sound quality.

The position of the pencil is crucial to the effectiveness of this technique.

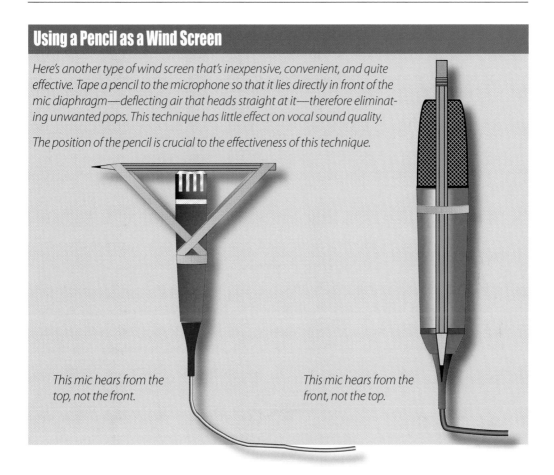

This mic hears from the top, not the front.

This mic hears from the front, not the top.

any use other than outdoor applications because they muffle the sound and attenuate the high frequencies more than the other designs.

Another type of wind screen can be constructed from a piece of old pantyhose, an embroidery hoop, and a mic clip. This design works very well, is inexpensive, and typically sounds much better than a foam wind screen. The nylon, stretched over the hoop and placed between the singer's mouth and the microphone, usually diffuses the air enough to avoid plosives and muffles the sound less than a foam wind screen.

Try taping a pencil to the mic so it goes across the front of the mic capsule. If the pencil is directly in front of the center of the mic capsule, it will diffuse the air enough to eliminate the pops. This technique works best on large capsule mics.

Each of these wind screens can have a different effect on the overall sound quality of the vocal track. These differences might be very noticeable or subtly different. Some listeners might have difficulty hearing the difference in sound quality when comparing one wind screen to the next, especially if they're listening on a marginal monitoring system. However, even if the sonic differences are subtle, we should always strive to record the best sound possible because the final product will benefit.

Listen to Audio Examples 6-12 through 6-15. These four different examples use the same vocalist through the same setup. The only thing that changes is the wind screen.

Audio Example 6-12 uses no wind screen.

Audio Example 6-12

No Wind Screen

Audio Example 6-13 demonstrates the use of a foam wind screen over the mic. Listen for a difference in the high-frequency content.

Audio Example 6-13

Foam Wind Screen

Audio Example 6-14 was recorded using an embroidery hoop with nylon stretched over it. This wind screen has a different and subtle effect on the vocal sound.

Audio Example 6-14

Nylon over an Embroidery Hoop

The vocal in Audio Example 6-15 was recorded with a pencil taped to the mic so that it ran across the center of the mic diaphragm.

Audio Example 6-15

Pencil across the Diaphragm

Repairing a Problem Plosive

Sometimes even using a good wind screen won't eliminate all pops—or you might have opted to keep a take for musical reasons, in spite of a plosive problem. Try the following three techniques along with, or instead of, a wind screen.

1. Move the mic slightly above or below the singer's mouth. This will get the air moving past the diaphragm instead of moving directly at it. There might be a slight sound difference, which could be either detrimental or beneficial, but this is typically a good way to avoid pops.

2. Point the mic at an angle to the vocalist. This position, like the previous suggestion, allows the air to move past the capsule instead of at it.

3. Move the mic very close to the vocalist (closer than two inches). The movement of air doesn't reach its peak energy until it's gone more than an inch or so from the singer's mouth, so you might be able to position the mic at a point before the air achieves maximum flow, therefore avoiding pops. Positioning the vocalist close to the microphone works best on moving-coil microphones. Condenser mics suffer from close proximity to the singer because the moisture from the vocalist has an adverse effect on the sound and operational status of the mic.

Sometimes, if you've tracked the vocals with the bass or drums turned up artificially high in the monitor mix, a plosive problem can go unnoticed until mixdown, when you begin isolating parts. It might be possible to bring the original vocalist back into the studio to repair the track, but you might not get the same sound or emotional impact that you got on the original take.

One simple solution is equalization. The pop that happens as a result of the strong plosive is heavy in bass frequencies, usually below 100 Hz. If you're quick with the EQ controls you can often turn down the lows at the precise word or part of a word where the problem exists. This technique is very effective and especially useful when you only have one or two problem spots to focus on.

Electronic Plosive Repair

Sometimes simply turning down the lows at the problem spot makes the vocals sound thin and unnatural. Or maybe there are too many complex spots to fix. If you're having big problems like these, electronic plosive repair is definitely worth a try. (This technique will also get you used to using processors creatively and efficiently.)

This kind of repair requires the use of an equalizer and a compressor/limiter with external triggering capability. Follow this procedure:

1. Plug the output of the problem vocal track into a mult in the patch bay or use a simple Y cord to split the output of the track.
2. Patch one output of the mult or one side of the Y cord into the input of the compressor/limiter, then patch the output of the compressor/limiter into a line input of your mixer's channel line in, fader in, and so on.
3. Patch another output of the mult or the other side of the Y into the equalizer input. Outboard graphic or parametric equalizers work best for this technique because they typically have the greatest ability to zero in on a problem frequency.

4. Plug the output of the equalizer into the input of the compressor labeled external input, external, key input, or key. We already have the vocal track patched through the main ins and outs of the compressor. In normal operation, the compressor/limiter turns up and down in response to the audio signal coming into the main input. We're setting the compressor up so that it will turn up and down in response to the signal that comes into the external input. When the internal/external switch is on internal, the processor works normally, responding to the signal that comes into the main input. When the internal/external switch is on external, the processor responds to whatever signal is coming into the external or key input.

5. Set the equalizer so that the bass frequencies are boosted. If you can listen to the output of the equalizer, adjust the EQ so the plosives are as obnoxious as they can be.

6. Set the internal/external switch to external or push the key button. By pressing the external or key button, we're telling the processor to respond to the signal we've patched into the external or key input, instead of the signal that's actually running through the main ins and outs. Because the equalized signal has accentuated the plosive problems, we can adjust the processor controls so that the VCA (*voltage controlled amplifier*) only turns down when the plosives occur. This gives us an automatic pop remover.

7. Set the ratio control to about 7:1.

8. Set the attack time to fast.

9. Set the release time to medium-fast.

Play the section of the tune that contains the problem plosive and adjust the threshold control so that gain reduction is indicated on the gain reduction LEDs every time the plosive occurs. We want gain reduction to occur only when the problem plosives happen. This might take some fine adjusting of the threshold, but because the trigger is responding to the external input that contains the equalized version of the track, and the equalized version of the track has highly exagger-

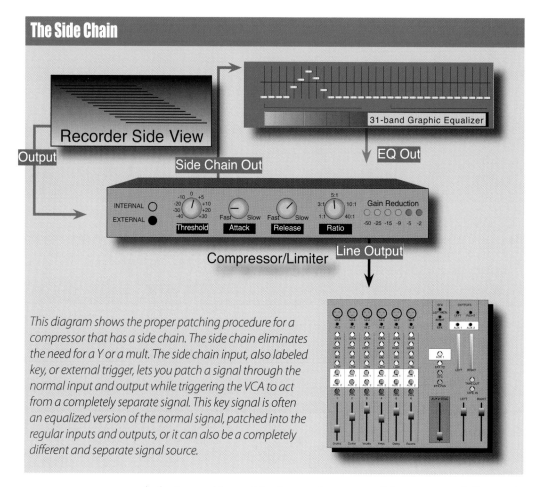

The Side Chain

Recorder Side View

31-band Graphic Equalizer

Output

Side Chain Out

EQ Out

INTERNAL   EXTERNAL
Threshold   Attack   Release   Ratio   Gain Reduction

Compressor/Limiter

Line Output

This diagram shows the proper patching procedure for a compressor that has a side chain. The side chain eliminates the need for a Y or a mult. The side chain input, also labeled key, or external trigger, lets you patch a signal through the normal input and output while triggering the VCA to act from a completely separate signal. This key signal is often an equalized version of the normal signal, patched into the regular inputs and outputs, or it can also be a completely different and separate signal source.

ated plosive problems, it's almost always possible to successfully repair problem plosives using this technique.

If there's a problem, readjust the EQ. Turn more bass up, turn a different bass frequency up, or turn the highs and mids way down. You can get the compressor set so that the only time the gain reduction LEDs show gain reduction is when the plosives occur. When you adjust the equalizer that is patched into the external input, you're not affecting the tone quality of the track. The main input and output of the compressor are not being equalized by this technique.

You're just sending an exaggerated EQ to the VCA to trick the unit into responding when you want it to instead of when it would normally.

Once these adjustments are completed, the compressor should automatically turn the track down every time a problem plosive occurs. The rest of the track should be left unaffected by the processor.

If you own a compressor that has a side chain insert (sends and returns or ins and outs other than the main inputs and outputs), you can de-pop a vocal track with fewer steps. You only need to have an equalizer; it's not necessary to use a mult or a Y chord. The side chain output is a separate send of the signal that's coming into the compressor.

Follow this procedure if your compressor/limiter has a side chain.

1. Plug the output of the problem track into the main input of the compressor.
2. Plug the main output of the compressor into a line input of the mixer. (This is the patch for normal compressor use.)
3. Plug the side chain output (send out) into the input of the equalizer.
4. Plug the output of the equalizer into the side chain input (return) of the compressor.
5. Set the internal/external switch to external or key.
6. Adjust the equalizer that's patched into the side chain to boost the problem frequencies.
7. Adjust the ratio, attack time, and release time to the desired settings (probably about 7:1 ratio with fast attack and medium-fast release).
8. Adjust the threshold so the gain reduction LEDs only indicate gain reduction when the problem plosives happen.

The Proximity Effect

If you're using a condenser mic to record a vocal sound that's very close and intimate-sounding, you might choose to close-mike the vocalist. You'll need to use a condenser mic that has a bass roll-off switch. The bass roll-off is built into most condenser mics and typically turns down the frequencies below 75 or 80 Hz. Any time a singer or narrator moves close to a microphone, the low frequencies get louder in relation to the high frequencies. This can result in a boomy or thick sound, especially if the voice is being recorded through a high-quality condenser mic. The proximity effect describes low frequencies increasing as the mic distance decreases. This effect is the most extreme when using a cardioid pickup pattern.

Bass Roll-Off

Rolling off the lows lets you get a close sound without getting a thick, boomy sound. Some condenser microphones have variable bass roll-offs that will turn the lows down below a couple of different user-selectable frequencies.

Listen to Audio Examples 6-16, 6-17, and 6-18. Notice how the vocal sound changes with the adjustment of the bass roll-off.

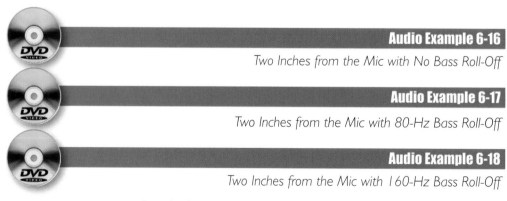

Audio Example 6-16

Two Inches from the Mic with No Bass Roll-Off

Audio Example 6-17

Two Inches from the Mic with 80-Hz Bass Roll-Off

Audio Example 6-18

Two Inches from the Mic with 160-Hz Bass Roll-Off

Often the lead vocal track doesn't need the frequencies below about 80 Hz. In fact, those frequencies can get in the way of the rest of the mix and make things sound muddy. It's common to use the bass roll-off even when miking a vocalist with a high-quality condenser mic from a distance of about a foot.

As we've seen with other instruments, the lows contain a lot of energy. If we roll off the bass on the vocal mic, we'll record more of the usable vocal sound and end up with cleaner vocal recordings. Also, our effective record levels will be hotter because the inaudible low frequencies aren't adding to the signal level.

If you're miking the vocal with a moving-coil or ribbon mic, be aware that these mics very typically roll off naturally in the low frequencies. Not many moving-coil or ribbon mics have bass roll-off switches built in because the roll-off is already happening as a result of the mic

The Bass Roll-Off

Most condenser microphones offer a bass roll-off feature. A switch somewhere on the mic body lets you apply the roll-off. Some mic designs even give you a choice between roll-off frequencies and contain a small switch near the bass of the mic housing that is user-adjustable. You choose between flat (often labeled LINEAR, LIN, Flat, or with a simple flat line) and specific roll-off frequencies (possibly 60, 75, 80, 150, or 175).

A bass roll-off doesn't simply cut a band centered on a specific frequency. Instead, it turns everything below a specific frequency down at a rate indicated in dB per octave.

An 80-Hz bass roll-off typically cuts the frequencies below 80 Hz at a rate of 12 dB per octave. In this case, at 40 Hz (one octave below 80 Hz), a 12-dB decrease in amplitude is realized. At 20 Hz (two octaves below 80 Hz) a 24-dB decrease in amplitude is realized.

Roll-Off at 160 Hz

The graph below represents the frequency response of a microphone set to roll off the lows below 160 Hz. A bass roll-off is also called a high-pass filter because it lets the frequencies above a specific point pass through unaffected.

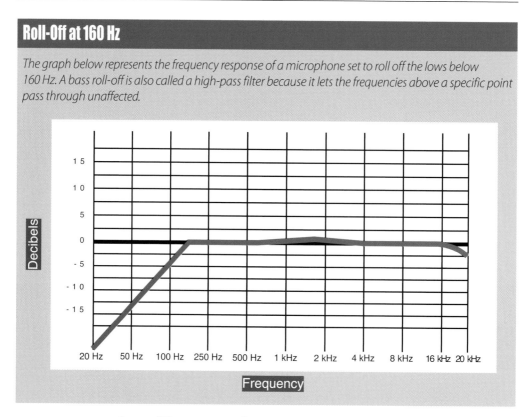

design. This is not really a disadvantage as long as we operate from an educated perspective. If we use each mic according to its strengths and retain the lessons we learn from our experiences, our recordings will continue to improve.

We can take advantage of the proximity effect to fill out the sound of a moving-coil or ribbon mic by choosing these mics for close-miking applications. Live sound reinforcement is a perfect place for using the moving-coil and ribbon mics to capture a full, warm sound from close proximity, which is what they do best.

A studio recording setting is different than live recording because we don't always need or want to close-mike the instruments and voices. Instead we often want to capture room ambience along with the intended sound source. Ambience, in the proper proportion, can add individuality and life to an otherwise bland sound.

Listen to the moving-coil mic in Audio Example 6-19 to hear the characteristic sound of one moving-coil mic. This is the moving-coil microphone from two inches.

Audio Example 6-19

Moving-Coil from Two Inches

Audio Example 6-20 demonstrates the moving-coil mic from about six inches. The sound rapidly thins as the mic distance increases from the singer.

Audio Example 6-20

Moving-Coil from Six Inches

In Audio Example 6-21, the mic is about 15 inches from the singer's mouth. This type of texture might be usable in a small sound reinforcement application when a singer has pulled way back from the mic to nail a high note, because the acoustic vocal sound would probably be fairly dominant. In the studio, however, this sound is typically far too thin and gutless to be usable.

Audio Example 6-21

Moving-Coil from 15 Inches

The Pad

Condenser mics produce the strongest signal of all the mic types. Close-miking especially loud singers with these mics might overdrive the electronic circuitry in the mic or, more likely, the signal might overdrive the input to the console.

Almost all condenser mics have a built-in pad, or attenuator, that makes it easy to compensate for this problem. If the sound you're getting is always distorted no matter what you do with the levels on the console, you probably need to apply the pad on the microphone.

The pads usually reduce the signal by 10 or 20 dB, and some mics give you the option of -10 or -20. This amount of attenuation is almost always sufficient to avoid overdriving the console input. Be sure to use the least amount of pad necessary to clean up the sound. If you attenuate the mic signal further than is necessary, you degrade the signal-to-noise ratio. If you over-attenuate by 10 dB, you'll degrade your signal-to-noise ratio by 10 dB.

Different Sounds of Different Pickup Patterns

Some condenser mics have selectable pickup patterns. In other words, one mic can be switched to cardioid, omni, bidirectional, and sometimes hypercardioid. These are called the microphone's *directional characteristics*.

Each pickup pattern might offer a different sound, and each of these sounds might be useful in different ways. Experiment with variations between pickup patterns and mic distance. Once you find the combination of mic choice, pattern selection, and mic distance that adds life, emotion, and superior natural sound quality to a vocal part, you won't turn back. If you spend a little extra time perfecting your mic technique, you'll gain it back several times over as your music comes together with greater ease, inspiration, and confidence. Good mic technique adds depth to a vocal track that you simply can't get with equalization and other processing.

Cardioid, hypercardioid, and supercardioid pickup patterns are the most commonly used when recording vocals. These patterns include the least amount of acoustic room sound while achieving the closest, warmest sound from a fairly close proximity. Listen to Audio Example 6-22, the sound of a condenser mic with a cardioid pattern from eight inches, no pad and no bass roll-off.

Audio Example 6-22

Cardioid Condenser Mic from Eight Inches

Audio Example 6-23 demonstrates the same mic from the same distance as Audio Example 6-22. This time the pickup pattern is hypercardioid. Notice that the sound is a little more open and roomy.

Audio Example 6-23

Hypercardioid Condenser Mic from Eight Inches

Next, the same mic, again from the same distance, but with the pickup pattern is switched to omnidirectional. This pattern isn't nearly as colored by the proximity effect, and the sound, although still close, has a totally different edge.

Audio Example 6-24

Omnidirectional Condenser Mic from Eight Inches

Finally, let's try the bidirectional pattern. This isn't always the most obvious choice for a solo lead vocal, but I've had some very good results using this technique on some singers in some rooms. Listen to the room sound and the overall sonic clarity of Audio Example 6-25. This approach also provides less coloration from the proximity effect than the cardioid patterns.

Audio Example 6-25

Bidirectional Condenser Mic from Eight Inches

Positioning the Microphone

Some singers have a good, smooth sound; other singers have a nasal quality when they sing. And others tend to have a thin, edgy sound. Where you place the mic in relation to the singer will affect the tonal quality of the vocal sound. If you place the mic directly in front of the singer's mouth (pointing directly at the singer), you'll get a pretty even and natural tonal balance. But if he or she makes much noise while singing, it will come through loud and clear on your recorder. These noises typically include lip smacks, nose sniffs, breaths, and sometimes even the sound of air leaking through the nose while the performance is happening.

If the sound isn't good directly in front of the singer, try moving the mic up about three or four inches above the singer's mouth and pointing it down at the mouth. This usually eliminates a lot of the lip smacks and other noises, plus it cleans up the nasal sound that some singers have a problem with.

If you position the mic four to six inches below the vocalist's mouth and then aim the mic up at the mouth, you might fill out a thin-sounding voice, but you might get more extraneous noises than you care to deal with.

The basic microphone position is a crucial factor. Sometimes a difference of one inch in either direction will dramatically affect the quality and impact of the vocal sound. Each singer offers a different set of variables, so there are no absolute solutions. Keep up the quest for the best possible sound—you'll know when you've hit the right combination.

Dynamic Range

Compression can be the single most important contributor to a vocal recording that's consistently audible and understandable in a mix. Most lead vocals on commercial hit recordings are compressed. So far in this book, we've seen each instrument benefit from compression, and vocals realize much of the same benefit.

Some producers don't like the sound of the compressor's VCA turning up and down so they'll record the vocal tracks without compression. But during mixdown, the engineer still needs to manually ride the vocal level to compensate for the wide vocal dynamic range. The engineer in this case is acting as a manual compressor, substituting for the automatic VCA-controlled compressor.

Dynamic Range

These graphs represent vocal energy (the curve) in relation to the rest of the mix (the shaded area). The top graph (not compressed) shows the volume of some lyrics sinking into the mix, probably being covered up.

The bottom graph indicates the same performance and lyrics after being compressed. This time the lyrics peak at the same level, but after they are compressed, notice that the softer lyrics are turned up so they can be heard above the rest of the mix. Once the compressor/limiter has decreased the dynamic range and levels have been adjusted to attain the proper peak level, your vocals should be consistently understandable—more emotional nuance will be heard and felt.

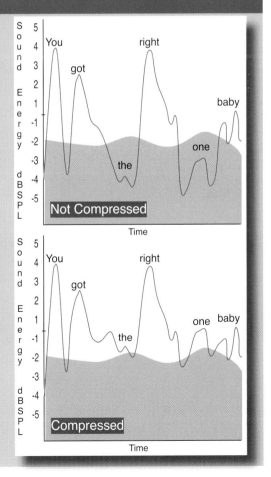

When recording vocal tracks, even with compression, the engineer often rides the record level fader to compensate for the loudest parts of the song. This method works very well if the engineer is familiar with the song and the artist's interpretation, but it also has the potential to cause more problems than it solves. Practice and experience provide the necessary skills to successfully perform this technique.

The benefit of riding the record level fader while recording vocal tracks is the need for less compression. If you can cut 5 or 6 dB off the hottest part of the track by riding the fader, you've decreased the amount of leveling required by the compressor. Less action from the compressor almost always results in a clearer, more natural sound.

Even though the most common vocal recording technique utilizes a compressor/limiter, your choice to include a compressor in your vocal recordings should be based on the vocalist, song, vocal range, dynamic range, emotion, and other musical considerations. Avoid ruts. Evaluate each situation separately. There are many times when a compressor is your best friend when you are recording vocals. There are also many situations in which the compressor sucks the life out of a brilliant performance.

Compressor/Limiter/Gate/Expander

Vocalists almost always use a wide dynamic range during the course of a song. Often they'll sing very tenderly and quietly during one measure and then emotionally blast you with all the volume and energy they can muster up during the next. Most of the time you need a compressor/limiter to avoid overloading your recorder with signal.

As the compressor's VCA (*voltage controlled amplifier*) turns down the signal that passes the threshold, the entire vocal track occupies a narrower dynamic range. When the vocal is in a narrow dynamic range, the loud sounds are easier to record because they aren't out of control, plus the softer sounds can be heard and understood better in the mix.

Vocals are usually compressed using a medium-fast attack time (3 to 5 ms), a medium-long release time (from a half second to a second), and a ratio between 3:1 and 7:1 with about 6 dB of gain reduction at the loudest part of the track.

A vocalist who is used to recording in the studio can make your job much easier. Less compression is needed for singers who use mic technique to compensate for their changes in level. A seasoned professional will back off a bit on the loud notes and move in a bit on the soft notes. This technique on the vocalist's part will help you record the most controlled, understandable, and natural-sounding vocal track. If you set the compressor so it indicates no gain reduction most of the time with 2 to 4 dB of reduction on the loudest notes, and if the vocal is always understandable and smooth-sounding, that's good.

Listen to the vocal track with rhythm accompaniment in Audio Example 6-26. The vocal isn't compressed. Notice how it sometimes disappears in the mix.

Audio Example 6-26

Vocal without Compression

Audio Example 6-27 demonstrates the same vocal, compressed using a ratio of 4:1 with up to about 6 dB of gain reduction. This time the peak level is the same, but listen for the softer notes. They're easier to hear and understand.

Audio Example 6-27

Vocal with 4:1 Compression

Sibilance

Avoid over-compressing the vocals. If the attack time isn't instantaneous or at least nearly instantaneous, it's possible to compress most of the words but not the initial sounds. For instance, a word starting with "s" or "t" might have a very fast attack—an attack too fast to be turned down by the compressor. The initial "s" or "t" will sound unnaturally loud and, like other transient sounds, won't register accurately on a VU meter. These exaggerated attacks are called *sibilant sounds*. When sibilant sounds are recorded too hot, your recordings will have a splatting type of distortion every time sibilance occurs. Sibilance distortion also happens when a sibilant sound occurs in the middle or end of a word.

Each singer has a unique sibilant character. Bone structure, physical alignment of the vocalist's teeth, jaw position, and size all play a part in exactly how the singer produces sibilant sounds. Some vocalists don't produce strong transients; other vocalists produce megatransients. I find that a singer with straight teeth and a perfect bite typically produces a very strong transient on consonants that have a "hiss" sound ("s," "t," "ch," "zh," "sh").

Sibilance problems often slide by when recording to the multitrack (analog or digital), but when cassettes are duplicated you might find a big problem with sibilance distortion. Small tape has less headroom and therefore distorts easier than most multitrack recorders.

The De-Esser

Use a de-esser to help compensate for sibilance problems. A *de-esser* is a fast-acting compressor set to turn down the high frequencies that are present in the sibilant sounds; it is often built into a compressor/limiter. If the de-esser is activated, the VCA responds to the highs instead of all frequencies at once, therefore turning down the exaggerated sibilance. De-essers often have a control that sweeps a range of high frequencies, letting the

Sibilance

These graphs represent the changes in amplitude over time of the word "Sally." The top graph has an average level of about 0 VU, but the "S" is about 3 dB above the remainder of the word "...ally."

If the compressor's attack time is slow enough that the VCA doesn't begin to act until after the "S" and if the remainder of the word is compressed, exaggeration of the initial sibilant sound results.

The bottom graph represents the result of compressing the word "Sally." Notice the difference in level between the "S" and the remainder of the word. This type of compression technique, when used in moderation (1 to 3 dB), can help increase intelligibility and understandability. However, this scenario leads to overexaggerated sibilance that degrades your music, especially in cassette duplication.

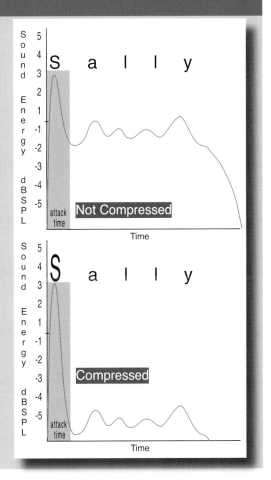

user choose which high frequency will be compressed. The threshold control lets you set the de-esser so it only turns down the high frequencies of the sibilant sounds but leaves the rest of the track alone.

Good compression technique, proper mic choice, and positioning are usually the answers to sibilance problems. But these problems have become particularly problematic with the growth of digital recording. Digital metering helps you record the full range of the transient accurately so any transfer to an analog medium, such as cassette tape, provides an opportunity for sibilance distortion. Through education and the proper use of compression and de-essing you can record vocal tracks that are clean and clear and work well within any musical structure.

Listen to the vocal in Audio Example 6-28; it's over-compressed, exaggerating the sibilance. The compressor in this example is set to a medium-slow attack time, letting the sibilance pass through uncompressed. The ratio is at 7:1 with up to 15 dB of gain reduction.

Audio Example 6-28

Exaggerated Sibilance

Equalization

When tracking vocals to the multitrack, apply equalization only if necessary after positioning the best-sounding microphone for the best possible sound. If you print an extremely equalized vocal to the multitrack, you're making EQ decisions that are best reserved for mixdown. Once the final instrumentation and orchestration choices are made, you can make intelligent decisions based on the final textural support. It's better to work with a good raw sound during mixdown than to fight an EQ problem you created in overaggressive tracking. During mixdown it's often necessary to EQ the vocals to help them stand out in the mix. Frequencies that need to be cut or boosted are dependent on the orchestration of the completed arrangement.

If you're using very few tracks or doing a live stereo recording of an entire group, it might be necessary to boost the presence range on the voice (between 3 and 5 kHz) to increase the understandability of the part. Also, try cutting the lows (below abut 80 Hz) to give the voice a more transparent, clear sound.

Recording Environment

The voice is the most personal of instruments. Most of the magic in a vocal performance comes from the emotional interpretation of the true meaning in a song. We might have all our ducks neatly in a row technically, but if the singer isn't feeling comfortable, secure, and confident, there's a good chance that the vocal recording won't be all that spectacular.

The producer and engineer set the emotional tone for the session. If they're uptight and impatient, guess how the session will go? "Not well" would be a good guess. If the producer and engineer are positive and emotionally supportive, they can usually get an artist to perform beyond everyone's expectations.

Only the most experienced and self-confident singers can walk into an emotionally dead, cluttered, poorly lit, uncomfortably cold, and clammy room and instantly start performing tender and meaningful lyrics with believability.

It's your job as the engineer or producer to see to it that the vocal room is at a comfortable temperature, that the lighting is soft and flattering, and that there isn't a lot of clutter around. Create a mood in the room. Singing is an emotional art. Get the singer into the right emotional frame of mind.

I've done Christmas albums in the middle of summer and had the full array of decorations all over the place to get into the spirit. I've had vocal groups in the back of my van to capture the feeling of four wild and crazy guys singing goofy songs on the way to a gig. I've turned the studio lights up, down, and off. I've used different-colored lights. I've had singers standing outside the studio on a city street singing their hearts out, and I've had singers wailin' away in the bathroom. I've recorded singers who only felt good singing in the biggest room of the best studio in town, and I've recorded singers who really like the down-to-earth feel of a great home studio. In other words, do what it takes to get your vocalist in the mood to sing the songs he or she wants to sing.

When the moment of truth is upon you and the singer's in the mood and singing the best parts ever, check to make sure that he or she doesn't have change rattling in a pocket or that there isn't a noisy bracelet, necklace, or earring that's audible during the recording. These kinds of physical noises can pass by undetected while recording, but when you're boosting highs in the mix for the sake of clarity, these transient sounds might quickly become very apparent. Missing this kind of detail while recording tracks can mean heartache during mixdown and might result in sacrificing the vocal sound or possibly re-recording the vocal. Neither of these options is very fun to deal with.

Physical Aids

Always have plenty of coffee cups, cold water, hot water, coffee, tea, and so on available. It's a sure bet that someone will be looking for something to drink or eat. A studio that is well stocked with food, beverages, and condiments can really set a good tone for the feeling of a session. This detail might seem kind of trivial and irrelevant to creating great music, but it's very relevant to making musicians feel at home, relaxed, and comfortable. These factors are all very important to a successful session.

What a singer eats and drinks has a definite impact on the working of the voice. You should be aware of appropriate and inappropriate food and drink for a studio vocalist. I'm not suggesting that you boldly dictate the artist's eating and drinking habits in a session. In fact, it's probably best to hang back a little at first. But if the singer's having problems in a session, tuck these suggestions away in your memory bank. These foods are good for the voice and will help the vocalist relax the vocal cords:

+ **Warm water**. This can be warmer than lukewarm but not hot. The warm water relaxes the vocal cords just the right amount for singing. Cold water or other iced beverages tighten the vocal cords, and hot water or other hot beverages can actually loosen the vocal cords up too much.

+ **Bananas**. The oil in a banana is soothing to the throat without causing phlegm or other mucous. Have the singer eat the banana slowly to coat the throat.

I see a lot of different singers show up with different things that they like to eat or drink. I'm always on the lookout for another good vocal food aid, but warm water and bananas are the two items that consistently work.

There are some items that might hinder a vocalist's progress. Watch out for these home remedies:

+ **Hot water**. This can make the throat too loose.

+ **Ice-cold beverages**. These tighten all of the vocal muscles.

+ **Alcohol and other drugs**. Some musicians assume that alcohol, drugs, and the studio go together—they don't, especially if you're engineering or producing. Even if it's just a couple of rounds of beers for the band, the first result is usually that everyone starts to lose a little accuracy and, after a half hour or so, you've got a lethargic band on your hands. Performance energy decreases, mistakes increase, tempos slow down, tempers can flare, and so on.

+ **Citrus products**. Oranges, lemons, and so on tend to do more to irritate a throat than they do to help a voice. If your vocalist is a little thrashed already, citrus fruit usually just makes things worse.

- **Caffeine.** Caffeine is a diuretic. Dehydration diminishes laryngeal lubrication, causing wear to take place at a much greater rate than normal.

- **Syrups or other thick liquids.** Many of these liquids cause mucous secretions.

When to Start Recording

Depending on the style, the singer, and the vocal technique, you might only have a very finite window of excellence when working with a singer. The voice is a very physical instrument. If the song demands an aggressive and consuming performance, the amount of setup time you get is minimal. This is when you must know your setup well enough to be fairly close to functional from the first sound emanating from the singer's mouth. We all need some time to fine-tune levels and any processors in the signal path, but if you take too much time, you run the risk of missing something magical.

I'm certainly not trying to understate the importance of experimentation and spending whatever time it takes to get just the right mic set up and patched into just the right stuff—that is very important. However, you can't do that every time you record the lead vocalist throughout the project. You'd never get an album completed.

I have come to the point where, even when I know I'm not completely ready, I press record from the very first take. I've just had to endure too many times when I've said, "Rats, that's probably about as good as that line will ever be, and I wasn't in record!" It hurts nothing to record every take and it just might make you look like the hero. Especially, be sure you record the first complete run through. This is the point at which the singer is fresh and, if you don't tell him or her you're recording, is the most free and uninhibited.

If you're recording to analog tape, you can always record over a bad take. If you're using a digital hard-disk system, save everything anyway! I can't say this strong enough. You might need a single word or phrase from a take you thought was terrible. Or, in a remix/dance mix situation, you'll be looking for little variations to make the mix feel new and fresh.

Punch In Punch Out

Punching in is the process of going into record while the track is playing back, keeping the part of the track before you press record, then recording from that point until you punch out. *Punching out* is the process of going out of record while the recorder continues playing back, keeping the part of the track after the part you've punched in. This is a very common technique. If the vocal track is excellent with the exception of a few out-of-tune notes or awkward interpretations, it doesn't make sense to re-record the whole track. It's common to re-record just the questionable sections or words.

The voice is fairly fragile, and many singers wear out pretty quickly in comparison to instrumentalists. To continually re-record complete takes in order to get the perfect pass isn't practical. Be sure the singers you record understand that punching in is common and that even the best of singers use this advantage of multitrack recording. Sometimes inexperienced singers expect to walk into a session, sing the part once, have everyone ooh and ahh and start collecting the royalties. But singing in a session is hard work and demands a lot of time to perfect each performance. I'm sure you'd like to feel good about your recordings for the next 30 or 40 years, so spend the time to get it right.

Punching in and out is an art that demands focused concentration on the part of the singer and the engineer. Have the singer sing along, leading up to the punch spot so he or she will be in the right groove when the punch happens. Also, have the singer keep singing the song

Punching In/Punching Out

The mistake in the bad take needs to be replaced by punching into record after the word "Paradise," then out of record before "your."

Punching in is typically accomplished by pressing the record button, or both the record and play buttons, while the recorder is playing back. Punching out is typically accomplished by pressing the play button while the track is recording.

The ground rules change dramatically depending on whether you're operating in a digital computer-based environment or recording to analog tape. In the digital domain, it's so easy to feather takes together after the fact that precision and "the art of the punch" are much less important.

Bad Take

...the bird of Paradise life up your nose.

Mistake

Repaired Take

...the bird of Paradise fly up your nose.

New Take

while you punch out at the right time. As soon as the singer knows where you're punching out, you have problems. When vocalists don't keep singing past the spot where the engineer intends to punch out, they tend to hold the last note past the spot where the next note in the song starts. This mistake can ruin the note after the punch point, and you'll need to re-record it. This process can get you leapfrogging through most of a song, fast. It's always best to instruct the singer to sing until the recorder stops. This approach also provides you, the engineer, with a second chance if you happen to miss your intended punch-out zone.

Sometimes you'll have a very small window for punching in. Good engineers develop the knack for timing the punch-in. A good punch combined with a good performance will be so smooth that no one would ever guess the insert wasn't recorded at the same time as the rest of the track. Concentrate and focus on the punch-in. As the engineer (and/or producer), you hold the authority to ask all nonessential personnel to leave the studio while you and others essential to the task at hand complete the job with excellence. It's easy to be distracted when other people are hanging around, and staying focused is necessary. Nobody has ever expressed anything but appreciation when I've asked people to leave for the good of the recording project.

Video Example 6-1

Punching In and Out, in the Computer-Based Digital Domain

Perseverance

Even with great singers, you might need to punch in the same exact spot 10 or 20 times. Believe me, it's not fun if you've performed with mechanical precision on the first 19 takes and you end up ruining the track on the twentieth take. Somehow the rest of the people around the studio never jump up and happily compliment you on the great job you did on the first 19 takes when that happens. Concentrate and take comfort in the fact that no one has ever spent the rest of their life punching in one word until it was right. Sessions always end at one point or another.

If you have enough tracks, it's a good idea to let the singer sing straight through the song once or twice. Record both takes. Often the first take is the best, especially for inexperienced singers. Once I have the mic and wind screen positioned, the compressor patched in, and the headphone mix roughed in, I'll run the tape and have the singer sing the song. I always record this take, even while I'm still tweaking levels and processing. It doesn't hurt anything to record that pass—at worst you've had a pass to get levels set. But if the take is obviously great, you get to hear people say, "You mean you recorded that? Aren't you a swell engineer!" instead of "Boy, I wish we had recorded that one."

If you have a couple of reasonably good takes, the vocalist usually starts to relax a bit because there's a backup. They'll feel free to go for more emotion in the track and to try new and innovative licks. Vocals are mostly mental. If you can provide your singer with a comfortable mental situation, you'll capture better vocal performances.

If you can afford the tracks to keep all vocal takes until mixdown, do it. Often during mixdown you'll hear some unacceptable parts that didn't seem so bad when you recorded them. If you've kept other versions of the lead vocal on other tracks, chances are you'll be able to switch tracks during the mix (if only for a word, a phrase, or a verse), repairing the unacceptable passage. Sometimes the first half of one take works great and the second half of another works great. Together they might make up one great take.

Some singers can't deal with punching in and out, having to continually recapture the moment while singing this or that word a little earlier, later, or more in-tune. If that's the case with the vocalist you're recording, simply print several takes of the complete track. Deal with combining them into one good track during mixdown. Many great recording artists print five to ten full takes and let the producer and engineer piece together an acceptable compilation of the best parts. However, this method requires a lot of tracks, and it makes mixdown a lot more involved than if there's simply one good vocal track.

Affordable digital audio workstations have made it possible to perform audio manipulation at home. Until relatively recently, this type of control over pitch and phrasing was performed on very high-cost equipment reserved for only the biggest and best studios. In fact, much of what you can accomplish at home on your Macintosh or PC couldn't be accomplished with respectable quality at any cost just a few years ago. The tools available to us are getting better all the time.

In this era, I often find myself capturing the life and fire of the first or second take, then digitally manipulating the pitch or phrasing to suit the artistic expectations of the artist, the band, and myself.

Panning

Lead vocals are traditionally panned to the center position. This keeps them the center focal point and, since they're usually very strong in the mix, distributes the vocal energy evenly between the left and right channels. Sometimes certain vocal effects are panned evenly to left and right for a big sound, but no matter what effects we use, the entire lead vocal sound should be evenly balanced between left and right.

Background vocals can be panned left and right depending on how many tracks there are, but the entire backing track should still be spread out evenly between left and right. When I use multiple backing vocal tracks, I like to spread them across the stereo spectrum while keeping them from the center position. This technique lets you place the lead vocal in the center of the stereo mix with little conflict and competition from the backing vocals.

A duet has, essentially, two lead vocalists. I've had good success panning them both to the center position, and I've also had good results panning them slightly apart. When positioned at 11:30 and 12:30, the two parts separate just enough in stereo to play well off each other, but they're not far enough apart to distract the listener by ping-ponging back and forth across the stereo panorama. A very slight panning to either side of center also translates well to mono.

Backing Vocals

When recording background vocals, there are several considerations to keep in mind: Do you want a natural, live sound? Do you want a textured, layered sound? Do you have one singer to do one part? Are you trying to make one background singer sound like several? If you have a group of singers, how good are they at singing parts together? The list of considerations goes on and on. I'd like to present some guidelines that'll help you through some basic backing vocal recording situations.

First of all, use as few mics as possible to get the job done. If you have four singers in one room, the temptation is to set up four separate mics to get a good, controlled blend at the mixer. With this type of setup there's typically so much phase interaction between the four mics that the overall sound of the vocals takes a nose dive and won't sound full and clean, especially when you're recording in a small room.

Try using one good microphone in an omni or bidirectional setting. Move the singers around the mic until you find the blend you need. Once you get a good performance recorded, try recording it again on another track. This live doubling technique produces very big, full-sounding backing vocals. Have the singers change places on the doubled take to capture a slightly different blend, adding to the dimension of the live double.

If you want ultimate control of the vocal blend during mixdown, record the singers at the same time but isolate each singer in separate rooms, using separate mics. Or, record them one at a time to different tracks. This technique eats up tracks quickly but allows you flexibility in the mixdown, plus it gives you the ability to get each part just right, one at a time, instead of trying to get the entire group to sing it right or simultaneously.

If your multitrack has a variable speed control, record two or three tracks of the same part. Each time you record a new track, change the speed of the recorder slightly—this change doesn't need to be drastic. Changes measured in hundredths of a half step or tenths of a cent are typically effective. If you alter the speed of the multitrack between 1 and 7 cents during record mode, then play back at normal speed, you've effectively changed the harmonic content of the vocal track. If you record a few different takes all at different speeds, the backing vocal sound will be much larger as a result. Often the slight timbre changes produced by this technique give your backing vocals an airy, ringing texture that's very difficult to achieve in any other way. Because the timbre changes are constant between the tracks, the resulting group sound takes on the sound of a double occurring an octave above the recorded parts. With a digital audio workstation you can achieve this effect by adjusting the pitch and formants of the different tracks, slightly altering the pitch and timbre until you find the texture that best suits the music.

Use these tips as guidelines to achieve the sound you want, but let the needs of the song rule the procedures you take. Maybe the only way the vocal group can perform their task of emotionally interpreting musical thoughts is to record in one small room, using separate microphones on each singer. If that's the case, you need to make sure everything works out well for the project. As long as you're aware of the potential damage caused by combining multiple mics in a small room, you'll do your best to isolate the vocalists, constantly referencing the sound in mono to verify the sonic integrity of the group vocals.

Recording Vocals in the Digital Domain

Most digital editing and recording packages display audio data in a graphic waveform. This waveform shows exactly what the sound is doing. If it gets louder, the waveform gets bigger; if there's silence, the waveform display is a straight line. Editing becomes nearly as visual as it is aural.

In the waveform view, it's easy to trim off either end to eliminate unwanted data, or even to remove data from anywhere within the waveform. If the recording went on for a few seconds too long, it's very easy to slide the end of the waveform to the left, trimming the excess. Only the portion of the wave that's seen is heard.

Punch-In

The punch-in, when using a hard disk recorder, holds a different level of intensity and precision than when using a tape-based recorder. In the tape-based domain, the punch-in is destructive—one mistake and an entire phrase might be ruined.

There is an art to tape-based punch-ins. The operator learns to punch in and out of record with amazing precision. Replacing a word or portion of a word is common. However, one slip of the finger, one note held a little too long by the performer, and the material before, during, and after the intended record zone is damaged, usually irreparably.

With the advent of computer-based recording, the art form of punching in and out of record is dying. No longer do the recordist and the artist need to work perfectly together in the same "zone" to perform the perfect series of punches repeatedly. Most computer-based systems offer a "fast punch" option, but if you happen to make a mistake, it's no big deal. Simply access the waveform edit window and resize the audio boxes to include whatever you need from the old and new takes. Even if it sounds like you cut off part of the original audio, it can be easily resurrected and positioned to perfection. No problem!

Channels, Tracks, and Takes

A few terms are often used interchangeably, although they refer to different interrelated functions. Tracks, channels, and takes are not all the same. These words need to be differentiated so the concepts can be understood and put into practice.

Channels reside on a mixer. Each of the identical rows of faders, knobs, and buttons is a channel. To say a system has 24 channels refers only to the mixer, not to the multitrack recording capabilities.

Tracks are individual recording zones on a multitrack recorder. A 24-track analog tape recorder has 24 separate portions spread evenly across the width of tape. Audio is recorded separately across the horizontal distance of the tape. A modular digital multitrack operates on the same horizontal track scheme.

The computer-based digital recorder also has tracks. Although there's no tape, a track is still represented on a list, and the onscreen transport operates along a horizontal line like in the tape-based systems.

A track in a digital system typically has provisions for its own level, balance, equalization, and routing control (its own channel) within the software realm, just as it would in a traditional analog setup.

Takes add another dimension to tracks. When a track is created and the instrument is recorded, you're done—in the tape-based domain. The computer setup, on the other hand, provides for multiple takes on each track. Without creating another track, you can record a completely separate take. In this way, the track list remains small and manageable, while the possibilities for creating options for each track are virtually limitless—depending on available disk space.

Comping

Comping is a technique that has been used in the multitrack world for about as long as multitracks have been in existence. The concept is simple—find the best parts from several takes, then compile them into one track that represents the performance in the very best way.

Once you've recorded a good take, record another take, but save the old version. The computer-based system allows for plenty of takes, so let the singer fly a bit. Record several takes straight through the song. Stop as seldom as possible. Only stop to focus on a section that you know hasn't quite made it to the perfection of the previous takes. When you have several takes and you're convinced that each section has been performed to the highest standards, you've succeeded.

The actual comping process involves reevaluating each take. Use a lyric sheet to mark the best take for each lyric. Once you're convinced you know where each chunk of brilliance is located, start compiling all the sections to one new track. Simply copy from the source takes, and then paste to the new comped track.

After all the preferred sections are in place, some adjustments to edit points, level, equalization, or pitch might be necessary. There's usually a way to get the comped track to sound smooth and natural, as if it was the only take of the day. Crossfading between regions serves to smooth out many rough spots.

Tuning

A great-sounding recording that was made prior to the technological boon we're in commands much respect. There are musical problems that we almost routinely repair and perfect today; our predecessors would have toiled for hours to achieve similar results. We take for granted the minute control available to each of us regarding intonation, timing, and all the mix parameters.

Intonation is definitely an attribute that we, as modern recordists, can effectively manipulate. If a note is a little out of tune, we don't need to ruin the singer trying to get it a little closer. We can simply tune it.

With the Auto-Tune software packages available now, it's not even necessary to have a good ear or perfect pitch to ensure that all vocals or instruments are in tune. Simply set the parameters within the software package and process the desired audio; your part will be tuned to your satisfaction. Auto-Tune by Antares provides 19 different scales to reference intonation, along with the facility for detailed graphical manipulation of pitch and vibrato.

Audio Example 6-29

Out-of-Tune Vocal

Audio Example 6-30

Automatic Vocal Retuning

Finding the Groove

Shifting tracks in time is a feature unique to the digital era. In the analog, tape-based domain, a singer or instrumentalist is required to control the performance relative to the groove. Although ideally the musician will produce the very best possible performance, if a portion is a bit out of the pocket (not in time) in the digital domain, it can be easily slid into place.

When vocals are recorded along with a MIDI sequence, finding the groove becomes extremely easy. The MIDI beat grid is typically right there onscreen. With graphic waveforms built along with the sequence, the beginnings of notes and words are simple to spot at a given location. Slide the audio waveform back and forth until the feel is right.

With controls like these available, it becomes increasingly important that the recordist have musical skills, understanding, and opinions. A technical engineer with no basis for making musical judgement calls must rely on the expertise of a skilled and experienced musician to effectively use the features and flexibility available in today's musical tools.

Breaths

One of the worst things to do on any vocal track is to eliminate all breaths. For a track to sound natural, real, and believable, some breaths need to be heard; they make the recording sound alive. However, they shouldn't be so loud that they're distracting to the lead vocals or to the instrumental bed.

With a digital editor, breaths during backing vocals can easily be turned down, left out, or repositioned. The most important consideration is the groove. If the breaths are left in as part of the track's life, they need to be in time with the groove. If they're not, move them, turn them down, or eliminate them. Musical judgment is the key.

Entrances

One of the primary indicators of well sung, cleanly performed backing vocals is the precision of the entrances. If every part starts together, they'll probably stay together, often all the way through the release.

Entrances are easy to place. It's always clear where the waveform begins and, when the backing vocal tracks are lined up vertically, any part that's slightly out of time is instantly detectable. The computer-based digital recording system is laid out perfectly for fine-tuning these details. The previous two illustrations demonstrate how easy it is to see when tracks are out of the groove and how simple it is to slide the segments into place to produce a precise vocal performance.

Releases

Releases are nearly as important as entrances to the polished feel of a song. The most critical releases are *transient releases*. Words that end in s, t, k, sh, and ch sounds are very distracting when the tracks lack precision.

With a digital editor and some patience, these ending sounds can be easily lined up with great precision after the fact. As with breath placement, these sounds should fit together nicely with the groove. Transients act like additional percussion instruments in most cases, so they should be placed with that in mind.

Readjusting Formants

Formants control the timbre of the sound. When you play an analog tape at slow speed, the vocal obviously gets lower and very dark- and deep-sounding. The dark, deep part is the formant change. Often, digital audio software lets you maintain the pitch while changing the formants. You get to keep the pitch while changing the size of the singer's mouth from large to small—from Lurch to Alvin the Chipmunk.

Detuning fattens because it changes the overtone structure of the vocal sound, simulating the effect of a different vocalist or group on the altered track. Because formants control the apparent size of the voices, independent of the pitch, this adjustment can produce some amazing vocal effects. Alter the formants slightly on several layers of the same or a group of backing vocalists for a fat sound.

Recording Vocals to Computer

Separate Mixer

Many soundcards provide line inputs only, so getting a microphone signal in requires some sort of mic preamp. You can use either a dedicated mic preamp, which often comes with compression and EQ built in, or you can simply use a small mixer, sending the line-level outputs into your computer line inputs.

In this domain, you're also confronted with the decision of whether to perform all mixing tasks internally or to include multi-channel outputs patched into an external mixer. You can't beat the convenience and cost in a small studio of simply connecting the stereo output from the soundcard to a simple monitor system. For that fact alone, this is the most appealing setup to some.

The disadvantage to a small setup with no real contributing external mixer is the demand placed on your computer. If you're using plug-ins and virtual instruments, and you're mixing within the computer, you had better have a monster computer, just to keep up with the processing requirements. It's for this very reason that computer manufacturers are providing easy CPU interconnects that simply allow you to add another computer to your system in order to cover additional processing requirements. Multiple computers work together, functioning as one very powerful computer.

If you don't have the luxury of this type of system, it's often well worth the cost to include an interface that provides 16 or more analog or digital outputs that can easily be connected to a digital or analog console. This eases the burden on your CPU, while at the same time providing easy access to outboard processors.

I've found that combining a powerful computer with an excellent small- or large-format recording console provides an environment where I can create a much larger-sounding mix, and where I have easy access to some of my favorite outboard gear that I've collected over the years.

Plug-Ins versus Outboard Processing

There are several excellent plug-ins that provide high-quality compression and equalization. You might be faced with the decision of whether to compress and EQ on the way into the recording system or just record straight in without processing, saving the final processing decisions for mixdown. There is a down side to this concept.

Because the voice is a widely dynamic instrument, you're typically forced to record at unnaturally low levels to avoid overloading the digital levels during recording. Because the vertical waveform resolution in a digital system is finite, recording at low levels really means recording at lower resolution.

There is a good compromise to this dilemma. While tracking voice, or many other instruments, use a high-quality compressor to take advantage of the dynamic control it offers. Be somewhat conservative on the amount of compression you use—this way, you can still fine-tune the sound during mixdown. The strongest argument for external analog compression during tracking takes into consideration that the stronger the record level, the more bits you're actually using.

Conclusion

Recording vocals, more than any other instrument, involves people skills as much as technical skills. Relations between the artist and the engineer or producer are usually key in getting a good take. A great take consists of an excellent recording of an especially emotional interpretation of a song. A good technical recording of a bad lyrical interpretation won't get anyone anywhere in the music business.

Practice these techniques. The more vocalists you record, the better. They'll each have a different set of technical and emotional demands for you. Rise to the occasion. Be accommodating but be diligent. Do your best to get the vocalist to do his or her best, and you can both expect a vocal take that far exceeds the norm.

Master the principles I've presented in this chapter, then use them while you expand on them. I'm always trying new techniques. It doesn't usually take that long to set something up if you already have the visual picture in your mind. Experiment!

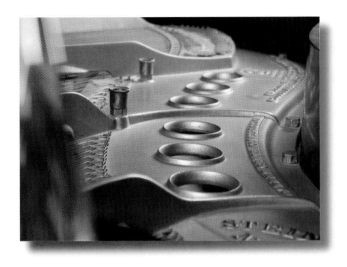

Recording Great Piano and Rhodes Tracks

Piano is popular in almost all commercial styles. Because, practically speaking, piano contains virtually all usable musical pitches and often dominates the musical texture of a song, it's especially important that we study recording techniques for this instrument.

Acoustic piano and the Rhodes-type electric piano typically fulfill the same musical function, but there are differences in the way the sounds are recorded and in the effects that are appropriate for each.

Before you start miking any piano, see that it's in tune and has been serviced to eliminate buzzes, clicks, and thumps. If there are physical noises that occur spontaneously while the piano plays, your job is suddenly much more difficult than it should be. The piano must sound good by itself so that it will meet the high standards you should be setting for your recordings.

Grand Piano

The Basics

Whether you are recording a nine-foot grand piano, a spinet piano, an old-time upright piano, or a sampled piano, it's understood that we're trying to achieve the full, rich sound that only an acoustic piano can provide. A great piano, miked and recorded well, has life, transparency, and openness that's hard to beat.

Most people don't have a full-sized grand piano living in their personal studio, but if there's a decent console or spinet piano around, there are some techniques we can pull out of a hat to simulate the sound of a grand piano. Or, if you have a sampler with some really good piano samples, you're in luck.

Basic Piano Miking

Two condenser mics are aimed at the strings from above the piano with the lid open on the long or short stick.

- *Mic 1 is centered over the treble strings, 6–18" above the strings and 6–18" behind the hammers.*
- *Mic 2 is centered over the bass strings, 6–18" from the strings and 2–4' from the end of the piano, depending on the size of the piano and the desired sound.*

Condenser microphones are the best to use on piano because of their typically excellent frequency response curve and their accurate transient response.

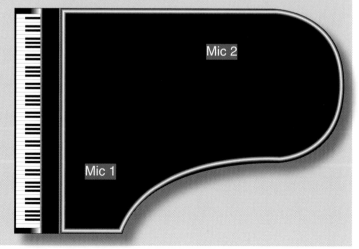

In Audio Example 7-1, listen to a grand piano miked with a couple of good condenser mics for a wide, impressive solo piano sound.

Audio Example 7-1

Stereo Grand Piano

We'll compare the other acoustic piano sounds to the grand, so listen closely to each example. Take notes on the differences in sound. Also, note the subjective differences that you perceive in the "feel" of these different sounds. Some sounds might seem more open or airy while others might seem blocky, chunky, or thick. Use your own terms. Keeping track of these sometimes intangible impressions is valuable, especially when you need to communicate with other people you're recording with. Often our choice of one sound over another is based largely—or totally—on the impression the sound gives us, rather than the technical perfection of the recording.

The method of choice for most engineers when recording grand piano is two good condenser mics aimed at the strings. One mic is placed over the high strings, and the other is placed over the low strings. When these mics are panned across the stereo spectrum, the piano has a very big sound and provides good support for most vocal or instrumental solos. How far apart you pan the highs and lows is dependent on the musical context: If the two mics can be printed to separate tracks of the multitrack, save these pan decisions for mixdown.

In order to get a good transition from lows to highs and a good recording of most of the piano range, it's necessary to keep the mics about a foot or more from the strings. If the mics are placed much closer, the mid notes might get lost in the blend. This can sometimes be at the expense of the very highs and the very lows, but that's okay if you're getting the sound that supports the music or the piano part doesn't use the extreme highs and lows of the keyboard.

Always experiment with the exact mic placement for two specific reasons:

- Different musical parts have different musical ranges for the left and/or the right hand. Musical style and consideration dictate the microphone placement.
- Again, the phase interaction between the two microphones is critical. If the distance between the mics changes a few inches, the sound of the piano changes drastically when heard in mono.

There are quite a few variables involved with piano, so let's look at some of the differences in sound that we can bring about with the various techniques we apply.

Condenser mics are the best choice for achieving the most accurate and natural-sounding recording of any piano because the piano

Mics Close to Piano and Each Other

If mics 1 and 2 are close to the strings, they need to be close to each other to fill in the mid notes. This decreases the punch of the very high and very low notes, but it produces a close sound that's quite good—as long as the musical part doesn't emphasize the extreme highs and lows.

Phase interaction between the mics can be detrimental to a mono track, especially as the mics move closer together. Be sure you check the sound of the two mics summed to mono before you record the piano track.

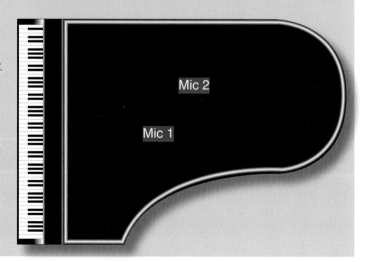

is technically a percussion instrument. The felt hammers hitting the strings produce a transient attack to each note, and as we've found with drums and percussion, condenser mics respond better to transients than other mics.

The intensity of the transient is dependent upon the condition of the felt hammers and the brilliance of the strings. The felt hammers on any piano can be conditioned to produce a sharper attack with a brighter tone or a duller attack with a mellower tone. If you have the felt hammers on your piano conditioned, keep in mind that a brighter sound with more attack stands out in a rhythm section mix very well.

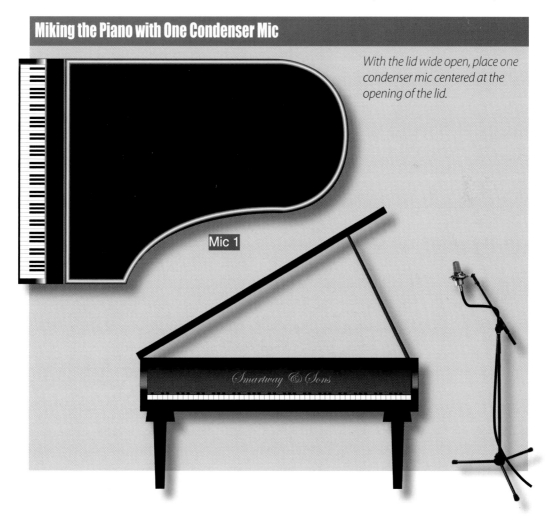

Miking the Piano with One Condenser Mic

With the lid wide open, place one condenser mic centered at the opening of the lid.

Mic 1

Smartway & Sons

On the other hand, solo pianists often prefer a darker, mellower tone. This conditioning is called *voicing the piano*.

The grand piano in Audio Example 7-2 is miked with one condenser mic inside the wide-open lid, from a distance of about three feet. It's necessary to keep the mic back a little to get an even balance between the low notes and the high notes.

Audio Example 7-2

One Condenser Mic from Three Feet

Mic Choice and Technique

Each condenser microphone provides a unique sound on a piano. Even though two mics might have identical specifications, the sounds they produce might be very different. Here are some mics that I've used on grand piano and some of my observations on them. Keep in mind that each room and each piano is a little different. These are just a few of the combinations I've tried; you might find great result with other mics.

+   **AKG 451, AKG 460, Neumann KM84.** I've found these mics and those similar in style and price to be the most accurate mics on piano. They capture a sound that's very true to the natural sound of the instrument. These mics have become my first choice for grand piano.

+   **AKG 414.** This is also a great mic and the first choice piano mic for many engineers. It has a more present high end and low end than the mics in the AKG 451 category, and in some mixes, the added highs and lows might get in the way of the other instruments.

+   **Neumann U87.** This mic is very warm in the lows and mids, but for my taste is a little lacking in presence. Many engineers prefer this mic for piano.

+ **Neumann TLM170.** In the right musical context, this is a fabulous mic, and it sounds good on vocals as well as piano.

+ **Cheaper condenser mics, such as the Sony ECM22P.** These often sound fine on piano. Check the sound of several different mics on your piano; each situation is a little different.

Most of us have a limited number of choices when it comes to mic selection. If all you own is a moving-coil mic such as the SM57, then that's what you'll need to use. But as your engineering skills and

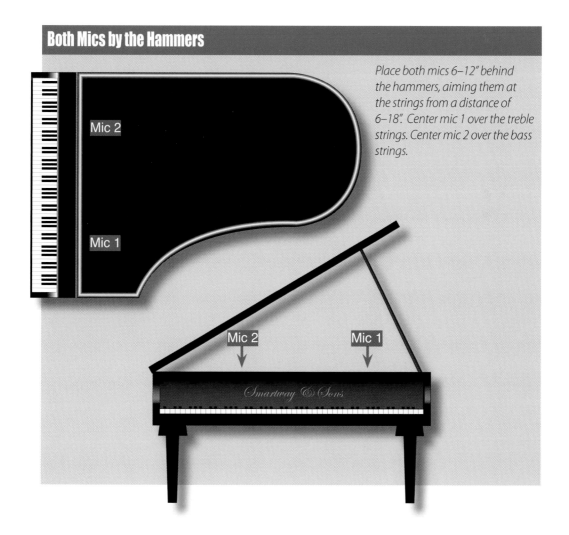

Both Mics by the Hammers

Place both mics 6–12" behind the hammers, aiming them at the strings from a distance of 6–18". Center mic 1 over the treble strings. Center mic 2 over the bass strings.

opportunities increase, try some of these mics—along with anything else you can get your hands on.

If you mike the piano with a moving-coil mic, you usually get a sound with a little more edge and less accuracy in the transient. The piano in Audio Example 7-3 is miked with one moving-coil microphone from about three inches. Listen closely to the attack of each note and notice whether the sound is full or thin.

Audio Example 7-3

One Mic from Three Inches

Moving farther away from the piano provides an interesting texture, depending on the room where the piano is being recorded. It's usually best to mike the grand piano from within four feet of the soundboard. Close-mike technique gives us an intimate sound that we can add space to with reverb if it's needed in the mix.

Room sound is easy to add with a good controllable reverb, but if the piano on tape has too much room sound, it's difficult or impossible to get rid of. The piano in Audio Example 7-4 is miked with a condenser microphone about six feet from the open piano lid. Notice the room sound.

Audio Example 7-4

One Mic Six Feet from the Open Piano Lid

When miking the piano with two mics, move in closer to the strings still enabling balance control between the treble and bass strings. With two mics, we can get as close as six inches from the strings. A distance of eight to 12 inches is usually the best distance for miking the grand piano with two mics.

Listen to the piano in Audio Example 7-5 miked with two condenser mics. First I solo the mic for the bass strings, then I solo the mic for the treble strings. Listen as I blend the two mics for a good even mono sound, then pan the two mics slowly apart for a wider stereo image.

Audio Example 7-5
Two Condenser Mics from about Eight Inches

There are several options for mic placement when miking the grand piano. The mics can either both be placed by the hammers, or they can be positioned with one mic over the treble strings by the hammers and the other over the bass strings, about halfway toward the far end of the piano.

In Audio Example 7-6, the piano is miked with two condenser mics a few inches behind the hammers—one aimed toward the high notes and one aimed toward the low notes. The mics are about a foot apart and about eight inches from the strings.

Audio Example 7-6
Two Condenser Mics by the Hammers

To get a wider stereo image or to gain better control of the lows in relation to the highs, move the mics farther apart. Compare Audio Example 7-7 to the previous example. Notice the difference in treble-to-bass balance with the mics further apart in Audio Example 7-7.

Audio Example 7-7
Two Condenser Mics Farther Apart

Try miking the grand piano with the same kind of coincident stereo miking techniques we've used on other instruments in this book. Set up a coincident stereo X-Y mic configuration with the piano lid up and the mics facing the strings. Audio Example 7-8 demonstrates the sound of a grand piano with two cardioid condenser mics placed at the edge of the open piano facing in and positioned in an X-Y configuration.

Audio Example 7-8

X-Y Configuration

Be sure your mic cables are wired in proper phase; always check the piano in mono. If the left mic and right mic are 180 degrees out of phase, your mix might be in for big trouble if anyone listens to it

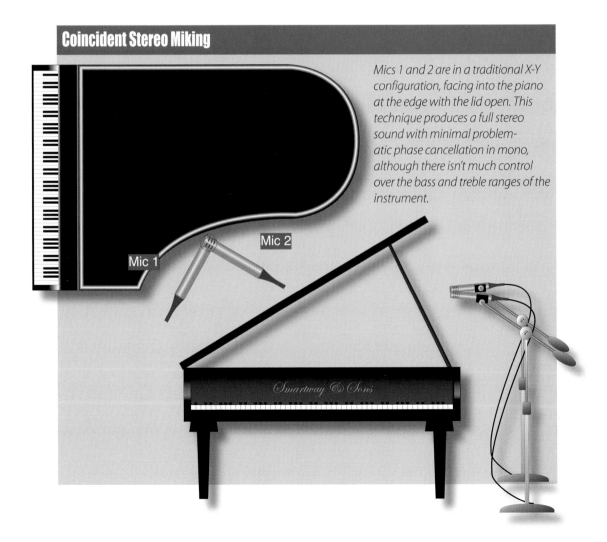

Coincident Stereo Miking

Mics 1 and 2 are in a traditional X-Y configuration, facing into the piano at the edge with the lid open. This technique produces a full stereo sound with minimal problematic phase cancellation in mono, although there isn't much control over the bass and treble ranges of the instrument.

Mic 1

Mic 2

in mono. Audio Example 7-9 demonstrates the stereo sound of a piano with the two mics 180 degrees out of phase.

Audio Example 7-9
Stereo Sound with Two Mics 180 Degrees Out of Phase

Although Audio Example 7-9 sounds fine in stereo, Audio Example 7-10 demonstrates the exact same take, this time combined to mono.

Audio Example 7-10
Mono Sound with Two Mics 180 Degrees Out of Phase

From the previous two Audio Examples, you can hear how crucial it is to test piano in mono, just in case the mono monster is lurking around the stereo corner.

There will probably not be many times when mic placement alone results in two piano mics being exactly 180 degrees out of phase, but there will often be times when the mics are in a phase relationship that ends up sounding thin and weak when summed to mono.

Listen to the three recordings of a piano in Audio Examples 7-11 through 7-13. The mics, the piano, and the player are all the same. On all takes, the mics are in the same general position—only slight position changes are made. You'll hear each track in stereo first, then in mono. Notice the sound change in mono.

Audio Example 7-11
Configuration 1 in Stereo, Then Mono

Audio Example 7-12

Configuration 2 in Stereo, Then Mono

Audio Example 7-13

Configuration 3 in Stereo, Then Mono

Video Example 7-1

Moving the X-Y Closer to and Farther from the Piano

Video Example 7-2

Moving the Mic Together and Apart in the Piano

From these examples, it's clear that checking the piano in mono is an important part of getting a good, usable track.

Stereo or Mono

Even when the piano is miked with two mics, it's not always best to keep the piano stereo in the mix. If the stereo tracks are hard-panned, the sound might be unnatural, with the highs and lows spread far apart in the stereo image. Often the two mics—or tracks—are simply used to get a good balance between the treble, mid, and bass strings. A mono track might sound very natural, and if the sound needs to spread apart in the stereo spectrum, we can use the same kind of delay effect we've used on other instruments to create a stereo sound. Again, be sure to check these delay effects in mono to verify that you have commercially usable tracks.

Audio Example 7-14 demonstrates a piano track recorded with two mics blended to a mono track.

Audio Example 7-14

Two Mics Blended to Mono

Audio Example 5-15 demonstrates the mono track from Audio Example 7-14 panned left, with a doubling delay of about 11 ms panned right.

Audio Example 7-15

Mono Track Panned Left with an 11-ms Delay Panned Right

Chorus, phase shifter, and flanging effects don't produce a natural sound on the acoustic piano and are rarely used. Audio Example 7-16 demonstrates an acoustic piano through a flanger. This unnatural piano sound is used only for special effects.

Audio Example 7-16

Flanged Piano

If the piano remains stereo, the mics might be soft-panned at about 10:00 and 2:00. If the piano is in the same rhythm section with a guitar, the stereo piano tracks often lean to one side—say at about 11:00 and 4:00—and the guitar track or tracks are positioned across the panorama to offset the piano.

Instrument Maintenance

Even if you do everything technically perfect, don't overlook the importance of keeping the piano in tune and properly serviced. Without good conditioning and intonation, there's not much chance of recording an acceptable piano track.

It's sometimes tempting to try tuning or voicing a piano yourself. This is a difficult task that is best left to professionals. It's not uncommon for would-be piano technicians to attempt to brighten the piano sound by putting shellac, fingernail polish, or tacks on the felt hammers. Although these techniques might provide some good and interesting piano sounds, they can also cause a lot of problems if done incorrectly—problems that can cost a substantial amount of money to repair. Be careful! Have the pros service your piano.

Setting the Mood

Creating a comfortable, pleasant atmosphere for the pianist is an important part of a good recording, especially when recording a very emotional solo piece. The room temperature should be comfortable, and your attitude should be positive and supportive.

If these seem like unimportant factors to you, you're wrong. Recording music is an emotional experience for both the artist and the engineer. A negative attitude can destroy the emotion of a session and therefore destroy the interpretation of the music. Too many engineers, producers, and musicians get so into the technical aspects of the recording process that they inhibit the artistic flow of the music. Somewhere between perfected details and totally free interpretation, there's a balance where the technical and emotional sides of the music are as good as they can cumulatively be for a particular moment in time.

Processing Piano Sounds

No Two Pianos Sound Identical

No two pianos sound the same. When you're trying to get the best sound from any instrument, remember to use mic choice and technique before equalizing the sound. Fine-tune the sound quality by changing the mic distance and placement over the strings. Adjust the mic placement for the least problematic phase interaction between the mics.

Listen to the sound changes resulting from these different mic placement combinations. Each Audio Example (7-17 through 7-22) uses the same two condenser mics, panned hard left and hard right, on the same piano through the same console.

Audio Example 7-17 demonstrates a stereo piano mic setup with one mic four inches behind the hammers, centered over the treble

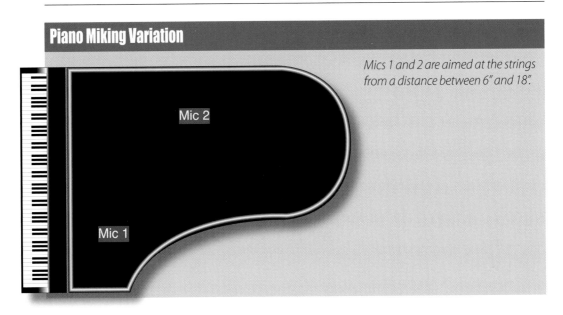

Piano Miking Variation

Mics 1 and 2 are aimed at the strings from a distance between 6" and 18".

Mic 2

Mic 1

strings, and one mic three to four feet behind the hammers, centered over the bass strings. Each mic is about six inches from the strings.

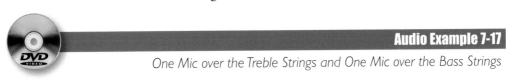

Audio Example 7-17

One Mic over the Treble Strings and One Mic over the Bass Strings

Piano Miking Variation

Both microphones are about 6" behind the hammers and 12" from the strings.

Mic 2

Mic 1

Audio Example 7-18 uses the exact same configuration as the previous example, except the mics are about 18 inches from the strings.

Audio Example 7-18

Mics 18 Inches from the Strings

In Audio Example 7-19, both mics are about six inches behind the hammers and about a foot from the strings. One mic is centered over the treble strings, and the other mic is centered over the bass strings.

Audio Example 7-19

Both Mics Six Inches behind the Hammers

Audio Example 7-20 is the same as the previous example, except the mics are further apart. The treble mic is aimed at a point about 10 inches in from the highest string, and the low mic is aimed at a point about 10 inches in from the lowest string.

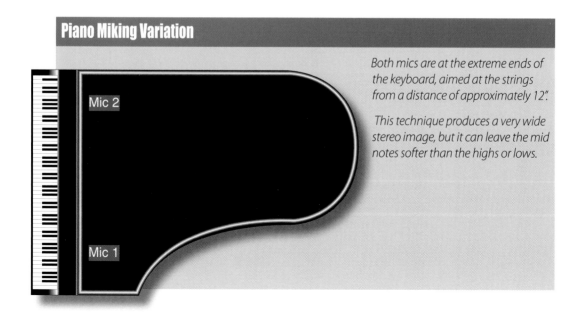

Piano Miking Variation

Both mics are at the extreme ends of the keyboard, aimed at the strings from a distance of approximately 12".

This technique produces a very wide stereo image, but it can leave the mid notes softer than the highs or lows.

Mic 2

Mic 1

Audio Example 7-20

Mics over the Hammers but Farther Apart

In Audio Example 7-21, there's a stereo pair of mics in an X-Y configuration facing into the piano, about one foot inside the piano with the lid up in its highest position.

Audio Example 7-21

Stereo X-Y Configuration Aiming into the Piano

Audio Example 7-22 demonstrates the same configuration as 5-21 but with the piano lid in its lowest position and a packing blanket

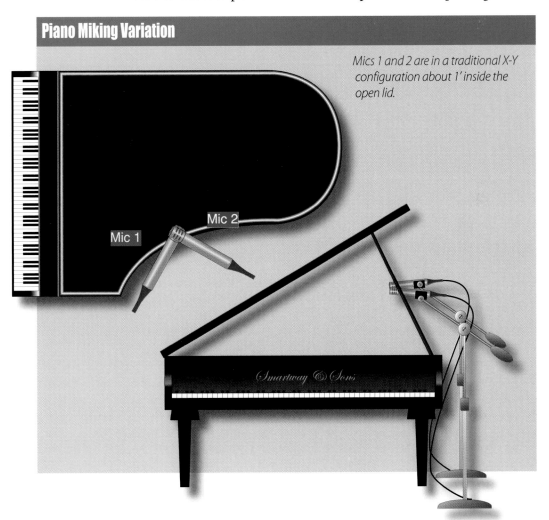

Piano Miking Variation

Mics 1 and 2 are in a traditional X-Y configuration about 1' inside the open lid.

Mic 1   Mic 2

Smartway & Sons

Piano Miking Variation

Place a stereo pair of mics at the opening of the lid, then use a packing blanket over the top for acoustic isolation and separation.

The packing blanket can do a good job of isolating most grand piano recording techniques, but it can also hinder the acoustic life of the piano sound.

covering the opening. This is one of the techniques we might use to help acoustically isolate the piano tracks.

Audio Example 7-22

X-Y with the Lid Lower and a Blanket over the Opening

Listen closely to Audio Examples 7-17 through 7-22. These are valuable comparisons that will help your opinions about sound mature to new levels. We can learn as much by noting configuration changes that don't noticeably change the sound quality as we do by noting configuration changes that do make significant sound changes.

Recording Levels

Suggested recording levels vary from piano to piano, depending on the low-frequency content of the piano sound and the sharpness of each note's attack.

The piano is a percussion instrument—because the hammers hit the strings—and there are transients in the attack of each note. We can only estimate optimum recording levels based on judgment, experience, and knowledge. Our goal is to record at levels that accurately capture the transients while still maintaining hot enough levels to stay away from the noise floor—or, in digital recording, to fully use the digital audio resolution.

As I mentioned earlier in this chapter, pianos are voiced bright and aggressive or warm and smooth to suit the performer's taste. If the sound is bright and aggressive, we must record at lower levels—in the range of -7 to -3 VU—at the hottest part of the track. As a rule of thumb, record at colder levels when the sound contains less low-frequency information.

If the sound is warm and smooth—in other words, it contains more low-frequency information and has a softer attack—you are typically safe to record at hotter levels. Recording levels of about 0 VU at the hottest part of the track should work fine.

These suggested levels refer, primarily, to analog recording. If you're recording directly to any digital storage device, the primary concern is to avoid recording at levels hotter than zero on the machine's meter. In digital recording, it's best to have the strongest part of the track reach zero on the meter. If there isn't one portion of the musical take that reaches zero, you're not using the complete resolution of your digital system. If you record at low levels on a digital system you probably won't have a noise problem, but you probably will have a clarity problem.

If you record piano too hot to analog tape, the first thing you'll lose is definition of the transient attack, and then you'll hear distortion as the levels increase. If you record too cold to analog tape, there will be an unacceptable amount of noise in relation to the piano signal (an unacceptable signal-to-noise ratio).

Practice recording the piano at different levels. Record the same piano part peaking at different levels: -9 VU, -7 VU, -3 VU, 0 VU, +3 VU, +5 VU, and +7 VU. Write down what you notice about the changes in each sound. Notice the variation in clarity of attack, the amount of audible distortion, and the difference in audible noise. This exercise will help you better understand the recording procedure for acoustic piano.

Equalizing the Piano

Most of the time, it's best to print the piano track or tracks to the multitrack without EQ. Using a pair of good condenser mics placed for the best sound and the least detrimental phase interaction should produce tracks that sound good. If EQ is necessary, it'll usually be fairly subtle—and best left for mixdown.

If you're recording live to two-track master or if you're recording and mixing a band live, you might need to EQ the piano while recording.

As I mentioned before, there's a difference between the sound that works best for solo piano and the sound that works best for piano within a complex orchestration. Solo piano should be full and even in the low end, mids, and highs. Essentially, you need to cover the entire frequency spectrum evenly. Audio Example 7-23 is an example of a good, full solo piano sound.

Audio Example 7-23

Solo Piano Sound

Musically, a piano part that works well in a rhythm section is usually percussive. A more aggressive approach to equalization combined with a more percussive musical part usually results in a part that can be heard well in the mix without being in the way of other instruments or voices.

Acoustic piano within the context of a full band orchestration should be somewhat thin in the low end. The kick drum and bass guitar cover the low frequencies quite well; to include an abundance of lows in the piano sound could result in a muddy-sounding mix that's confusing in the low frequencies.

To thin out the lows, try cutting in the range of 60 Hz to about 150 Hz. This is very noticeable to the solo sound, but it won't be noticed in the context of a rhythm section. This will prevent the low frequencies of the piano from conflicting as much with the low frequencies of the bass guitar or kick. Listen to Audio Example 7-24 as I cut 60 Hz, then sweep from 60 Hz up to about 150 Hz.

Audio Example 7-24
Cutting the Lows from 60 Hz to 150 Hz

To give the piano more clarity and an aggressive edge, boost slightly between 3 kHz and 5 kHz. Be careful! Dramatic equalization might sound fine on one monitor system and terrible on another. In Audio Example 7-25, I'll start with the EQ flat, then I'll boost the 4-kHz range slowly until I reach a 7 dB boost.

Audio Example 7-25
Boosting 4 kHz

Compressing the Piano

The dynamic range of the piano can be very wide, depending on the musical part. Most solo pieces contain some very soft passages and some very loud passages. If you're recording to a digital format that will end up being released on CD or other digital format, it's nice to have that wide dynamic range recorded the way it happened from the instrument. If you're recording a piece that will be listened to on a standard cassette or within the context of a rhythm section, your recording might be easier to listen to if you compress the signal.

Try a ratio of about 3:1 with a medium-fast attack time and a medium-slow release time. Adjust the threshold for 3 or 4 dB of gain reduction at the hottest part of the track. This approach will give you natural-sounding compression while letting you record 3 or 4 dB hotter to tape on everything but the peaks. The piano track in Audio Example 7-26 was recorded using this technique.

Audio Example 7-26

Compressing the Piano

Exciting the Piano

An exciter can add clarity to the piano's high end without using normal equalization. Exciters work by boosting specific harmonics rather than simply boosting a range of frequencies. Equalizing and exciting produce similar results, but an exciter often sounds cleaner, which gives the piano a more transparent edge than equalization. Be cautious. Overusing an exciter or equalizer could cause problems if your recording is heard on many different systems. Listen to the piano in Audio Example 7-27. I'll add the exciter after the first few measures.

Audio Example 7-27

Exciting the Piano

Reverberation

If at all possible, save the addition of reverberation for mixdown. Reverberation is very appropriate for acoustic piano in the proper musical context, especially on ballads and solo pieces. A solo piano in a concert hall has a very rich, reverberant sound; a live ensemble performance in a concert hall has the same kind of sound. Ballads with open spaces in the orchestration give the listener the opportunity to hear the sound of the hall. Using a smooth, warm hall reverb with a medium to long predelay and a decay time of two to three seconds usually produces an interesting and very usable piano track.

The solo piano in Audio Example 7-28 uses hall reverberation with a 75-ms predelay and a 2.5-second decay time.

Audio Example 7-28

Hall Reverb, 75-ms Predelay and 2.5-Second Decay Time

On faster songs with busier arrangements, the hall reverb tends to add clutter and can make the mix sound muddy. If you want your mix to sound close, tight, and punchy, a good piano sound with no reverberation works great.

If you want the piano to blend into the mix without sounding like it's at the other end of the hall, try adding a little plate reverb with a short predelay (between 0 and 50 ms) and a short decay time (between .5 seconds and 1 second). This effect adds an interesting ambience while maintaining a feel of closeness. The piano in Audio Example 7-29 has a plate reverb with a 35-ms predelay and a decay time of .6 seconds. The track starts dry, then I slowly add the reverberation.

Audio Example 7-29

Plate Reverb with 35-ms Predelay and 0.6-Second Decay Time

Another reverberation effect that fills out the piano sound and helps it blend with the rest of the mix is *room reverb*. This type of reverberation is designed to give the listener the perception that the sound is being heard in a specific-sized room—typically smaller than a concert hall, gymnasium, or theater. Adding a fairly tight-sounding room to the piano often results in a subtle change that makes the instrument sound more interesting. This sound-shaping technique gives your recordings an interesting edge that is difficult for the listener to consciously hear, but without it there would be a very noticeable loss of character in the sound. The piano in Audio Example 7-30 starts dry, then I add room reverberation.

Audio Example 7-30

Room Reverberation Delay

Using digital delay on piano isn't common, especially from the purist's perspective, but it can produce an interesting effect on some styles in some settings. A floating, emotional, freestyle solo piano might sound great with the right type of delay. Longer delay times that match the tempo of the quarter note or eighth note usually work best. Short delay times, below about 100 ms, usually give an artificial flavor to the acoustic piano sound. The piano track in Audio Example 7-31 has a delay time of 300 ms; the regeneration is set for three or four repeats.

Audio Example 7-31

300-ms Delay

Miking the Vertical Piano

Having a nine-foot grand piano at your disposal is ideal. The first part of this chapter is dedicated to understanding the sound of the grand as a point of reference—a benchmark. But hardly anyone has a nine-foot grand piano in their home studio. Most home recordists are fortunate to have a spinet, console, studio, or upright piano to work with; these all fall under the category of *vertical pianos.*

Realizing that not everyone has a grand piano—or even a decent vertical piano—we need to use what we know about the grand piano as a guideline to help us get the most from any piano. There are a few techniques that can help us get a very usable sound from a vertical piano.

One of the primary and most obvious differences between a high-quality grand piano and a marginal-quality home console piano is the sound of the low notes. A good grand has great richness and depth on all of the low notes. An average console piano loses any resemblance to a full sound about an octave or two above the lowest A on the keyboard.

Try putting a separate mic on the lowest notes; experiment with boosting lows and cutting certain lower mids (around 300 to 700 Hz) to get the console piano to approach the rich sound of the grand.

To get the best sound out of a vertical piano, use two condenser mics placed about six to 12 inches from the strings, pointing at the strings, and three or four inches above the hammers. Center one mic over the treble strings and one mic over the bass strings. Pointing the mics away from each other at a 90-degree angle to each other enhances the stereo image.

If you have a console piano and you want to record parts that sound good and musically enhance the texture of your music, start by devising a musical part that uses the strong range and avoids the weak range of the console piano. In other words, leave the bass range of your orchestration to instruments such as the bass guitar and kick drum. Devise a piano part that doesn't go much more than an octave or so below middle C and stays out of the upper octave. The difference in sound quality between

Miking the Vertical Piano

- *Remove the top and front panels to gain access to the strings.*
- *Use one or two condenser mics on the console, spinet, or upright piano. If you use one mic, point the mic at the front of the piano. Position the mic around middle C, 12–18" inches from the strings.*
- *If you use two mics, center one over the bass strings and one over the treble strings. Point the mic at the strings from a distance of 6–12".*
- *To widen the stereo image, point the mics slightly away from each other.*

the grand and vertical piano can be minimized with the right musical part played within a rhythm section and mixed properly.

If your musical arrangement doesn't include the low notes or the very high notes, center a pair of mics over middle C and use a coincident miking technique, such as the standard X-Y. This will give your recording a good stereo image, along with clarity in the range of notes that sound good on the vertical piano.

If you're trying to make the vertical piano sound good as a solo instrument, patch both channels through separate parametric equalizers.

Miking the Vertical Piano

Angle mics at up to 90° in relation to each other. Angles up to 90° increase the stereo image; angles greater than 90° create negative phase interaction as the mics approach 180° out of phase.

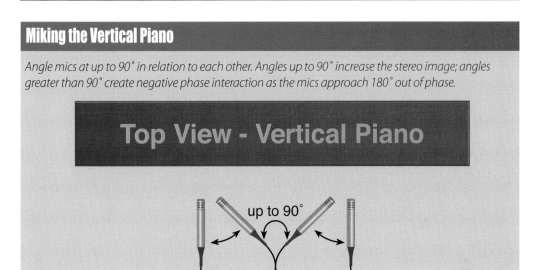

Adjust the mid band to cut at 200 to 300 Hz. Adjust the bandwidth between .5 octaves and 1.5 octaves. Each piano is amazingly different, so you'll really need to focus your listening. This one adjustment should clean up the mids enough to be able to hear the bass and treble ranges better. This is the minimum amount of cut you'll need to clean up the

Miking the Vertical Piano

Try an X-Y configuration aimed at the strings from a distance of about 12". Adjust the mic position toward the bass or treble strings, depending on the musical part. If the highest range on the instrument isn't being used, move the stereo pair of mics toward the bass end of the piano and vice versa.

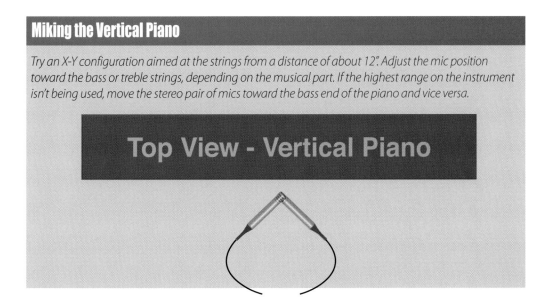

sound, but don't be afraid to use whatever it takes to get the job done; usually a 2- to 6-dB cut should be sufficient.

Adjust the low band to boost between 2 and 6 dB, set the bandwidth between one-half octave and one octave, and sweep the frequency selector from 120 Hz to 60 Hz to find the sweet spot that produces a strong, solid low end. Give the piano as much punch as possible without creating an obviously boomy sound.

Finally, set up a 2- to 6-dB boost in the high band. Set the bandwidth between one and two octaves and sweep the frequency selector between 3.5 kHz and 7 kHz to achieve clarity and attack in the treble strings.

After the musical part is composed to enhance the good sounds and avoid the not-so-good sounds, and after the raw sound of the vertical piano is miked for the sound you need, use dynamics and effects processing and adjust the levels in the same way you would for the grand piano.

If your reverb has controls to adjust equalization, boost the low frequencies to get a full, warm solo piano sound.

Sampled Piano Sounds

If you own or have access to a sampler, you can get some really great piano sounds. The advantage of a sampled piano is that, in most cases, you reap the benefit of someone else's work. Somebody records a very good piano with very good microphones through very good preamps in a studio that sounds good, and you get to use it in your recordings—what a deal!

The disadvantage to a sampled piano is that you don't always get the full benefit of the natural harmonics that occur on every string in the piano. The real acoustic piano might have a smoother, more natural sound throughout the range of the instrument than the sampled piano. On the other hand, many piano parts in many songs don't require the full benefit of a real acoustic piano, so the subtle differences between the real and sampled piano might be totally insignificant.

These differences in quality between the real and sampled grand piano live in the gray zone that isn't always noticeable or obvious; the practical differences are totally dependent on the musical context.

The method of choice for recording sampled piano or any other electronic keyboard is directly into the console, either through a direct box or plugged into line in.

There are some really good samples available that give the player access to some incredible instruments that only the best players or studios have. For most home recordists, the question usually comes down to this: Is it better to get the best possible recording of a vertical piano to keep the pure harmonics present in the instrument or it is better to use a sample of an incredible instrument that's been recorded in a world-class studio?

I've had the opportunity to work with several great-sounding nine-foot grand pianos, and it's tough to beat a good stereo recording of an instrument like that—period. There will always be a difference, but at least the margin is shrinking.

If you don't have access to a grand piano, try the sampled pianos that are available to you. For a fairly reasonable cost—often less than a good vertical piano—a good 16- to 24-bit sampler gives you access not only to great piano sounds, but to any other acoustic or synthesized sound you can imagine.

Rhodes-Type Sounds

The musical function of the piano part is almost always to provide a predominant harmonic and rhythmic bed for the rest of the orchestration, and this role is very important to the feel of a song. That's why it's important to learn as much as possible about recording a good piano track and then practicing until the piano sounds you're getting are comparable to pianos you hear on other recordings.

Actively compare your piano recordings to recordings you hear on your favorite CDs or tapes. At this you should be capable of listening critically and analyzing a sound with respect to its overall quality.

The other instrument that fulfills the same function as the acoustic piano is the Rhodes, or electric piano. The Fender Rhodes piano came on strong, especially in the early '70s, because it was portable, stayed in tune when moved, and had a rich, full sound quality. Like the grand piano, it provides an interesting musical texture over which to lay the rest of an arrangement. Although the Rhodes itself isn't as common as it was in the '70s, its sound has been cloned, copied, modified, and sampled into almost every keyboard available today.

The original Suitcase Rhodes had stereo outputs that plugged into the speaker cabinet it sat on. The stereo effect was an auto pan back and forth between the 12-inch speakers in the cabinet. When these first came out, this was the epitome of high-tech, leading-edge, fun listening—technology has come quite a long way since the introduction of the Fender Rhodes.

The Rhodes is texturally different from the acoustic piano, even though its musical function is the same. The method of choice for recording electric piano, or any other electronic keyboard, is directly into the console, either through a direct box or plugged into line in.

Rhodes Effects

To get a simulation of the original suitcase Rhodes stereo-panning sound, use an auto panner; many current multi-effects processors have auto panners built in. This effect simply takes the input signal and pans it from left to right according to how you set the processor. Of course, the output from the processor needs to be stereo, but you probably won't need the piano to pan hard left and right in the mix; the extreme panning sounds unnatural and might be distracting to the rest of the arrangement. Adjust the speed of the panner to work with the tempo of the song.

The original stock Rhodes sound was fairly mellow. Listen to the Rhodes sound in Audio Example 7-32. It is similar to the original sound. After a few measures I'll include the auto panner.

Audio Example 7-32

The Rhodes and the Auto Panner

The ideal recording level for Rhodes electric piano sounds is 0 VU. All the effects that sound good on acoustic piano also sound good on Rhodes. Reverb, delay, and compression are common on this instrument.

The Rhodes piano sound in Audio Example 7-33 has hall reverb with a 2.5-second decay time and a 125-ms predelay.

Audio Example 7-33

Rhodes with Hall Reverb

As the Rhodes grew in popularity and players experimented with the different types of sounds that could be found in the instrument, it became popular to include more of the sound of the actual tines in the piano being hit. To us, that translates into boosting the upper harmonics of the sound at the attack of the note.

Audio Example 7-34 demonstrates the original Rhodes sound.

Audio Example 7-34
The Original Rhodes

Audio Example 7-35 demonstrates the tine sound that became—and still is—very popular.

Audio Example 7-35
The Tine Sound

The tine sound became popular because the attack clearly defined the sound in a way that didn't interfere with the rest of the musical texture; the upper harmonics made the reverb and other effects sound even better and more interesting than they did without the tine sound.

Chorus, flanging, and phase shifting are also very common—and sound great—on electric piano. Because the electric piano is simpler in its harmonic content, the richness and fullness that these effects add enhances rather than clutters the original sound.

It's best if you can keep the original sound clean and dry on the multitrack or within the sequence, and then fine-tune the exact effect you'll need during mixdown. Chorus sounds can be an integral part of the piano sound; if you must print the chorus effect with the piano because of a lack of tracks or limited outboard equipment for mixdown, it will probably sound all right. Still, try to save the addition of reverberation until the mix.

Listen to the smooth, sweeping sound as I add the phase shifter to the electric piano in Audio Example 7-36.

Audio Example 7-36

Electric Piano with Phase Shifter

For a little more complex sweep, try adding a flanger like the one in Audio Example 7-37.

Audio Example 7-37

Flanged Electric Piano

And for less of a sweep sound and a more interesting blend of changing harmonics and overtones, add a chorus to the electric piano, like the one in Audio Example 7-38

Audio Example 7-38

Chorused Electric Piano

Another possibility, although not common, is the use of distortion on a simple and pure Rhodes sound. In the earlier Rhodes days, players used guitar pedal distortion on Rhodes occasionally to mimic the sound and effect of electric guitar. This technique doesn't totally fill the shoes of a guitar, but it's worth keeping in your bag of tricks for that one session for which this sound is the only right choice.

Audio Example 7-39 is the sound of distorted electric piano. If the musical part is appropriate, this sound has the potential to be very effective.

Audio Example 7-39

Distorted Electric Piano

Equalizing the Rhodes

Equalize the piano sound according to the needs of the particular musical piece. For solo electric piano, the sound should be full and smooth in the low end. Often no EQ is needed in this case, because the Rhodes sound is typically full and smooth in the lows and low mids. Audio Example 7-40 demonstrates an electric piano sound that might work well in a solo piece or exposed, open orchestration.

Audio Example 7-40

Solo Rhodes Sound

If the arrangement is full and contains other active rhythm section instruments, such as guitars, synthesizers, and possibly strings or brass, it's not necessary for the electric piano to fill out the texture in the lows and low mids. In this case, roll off the lows between about 60 and 120 Hz to clean up the low end. Turning the lows down on the piano results in a low end that's easier to understand and conflicts less with the other low-frequency instruments. Also, try boosting between 2.5 and 5 kHz to accentuate the clear edge of the tine sound. Audio Example 7-41 starts flat, then I turn the lows down and sweep between 60 and 120 Hz. Next, I boost the highs and sweep between 2.5 kHz and 5 kHz.

Audio Example 7-41

Cut the Lows, Boost the Highs

The actual frequencies that you select to boost or cut are totally dependent on the needs of the musical arrangement. If another instrument in the song is accentuated at 2.5 kHz, you might need to cut 2.5 kHz on the electric piano but boost 5 kHz to accentuate the tine sound.

An exciter on the electric piano can accentuate the upper harmonics of the tine sound and help the piano cut through the rest of the orchestration without an abrasive edge to the sound. Listen to the high end in Audio Example 7-42 to hear the effect of the exciter on the Rhodes-type sound.

Audio Example 7-42

Excited Rhodes

An effect we really haven't covered so far is the harmonizer, which is capable of changing the pitch of the incoming signal. Typically, the pitch can be altered in half-step increments above or below the incoming signal. The pitch is typically adjustable within a range of 12 half steps in either direction, or in one-cent increments above or below the incoming signal—usually with a range of 99 cents in either direction. (One cent is 1/100th of a half step.)

The harmonizer can be used for special effect by setting the pitch change to a certain number of half steps. Many harmonizers can even produce two separate pitch changes simultaneously so you can create a chord from a single note on the keyboard or any other instrument, as in Audio Example 7-43.

Audio Example 7-43

Harmonizer on the Rhodes

A much more common use for the harmonizer, with respect to the electric piano, involves using the fine-tune control and adjusting the two pitch shifters almost imperceptibly above and below the incoming signal. Set one pitch change between one and eight cents above the original pitch, and set the other pitch change between one and eight cents below the original pitch. These pitch changes don't really sound out of tune, but the interaction between the original incoming signal and the affected outputs adds harmonic depth and richness to most sounds. Pan the two shifted outputs hard left and hard right, keeping the original panned center for a very full and interesting sound. This sound can also be used on any other instrument to get a full, wide sound. Try this technique on guitars, voices, synth sounds, or even on some brass and string tracks.

Listen to the electric piano in Audio Example 7-44. After the first few bars I'll add the harmonizer, set eight cents sharp on the left and eight cents flat on the right.

Audio Example 7-44

Subtle Harmonizer on the Rhodes

If you have a harmonizer that only produces one pitch change at a time, try panning the original track hard left and the harmonized output hard right.

On exposed and open musical pieces, it's common to use multiple effects on an instrument such as the electric piano. Using delay, reverb, chorus, harmonizer, EQ, and compression together can produce a great sound when you use them in the right amounts. The key is that you need to understand what each effect is doing and combine them using a controlled, deliberate approach. Try to hear the sound in your head, then use your equipment efficiently to set it up. Avoid the random-knob-turning syndrome.

Modern technology gives you unbelievable control over effects. Practice each of the processing techniques that we've covered. Be sure you're familiar with all of the controllable parameters. Know your equipment, then start building sounds.

The electric piano sound in Audio Example 7-45 has been equalized to accentuate the tine sound. It has a room reverb, a hall reverb, and a slight flange; the harmonizer is six cents sharp on the left and six cents flat on the right. Some of the effects might be very subtle, but each effect works together to build the overall sound.

 Audio Example 7-45

The Rhodes with EQ, Room, Hall, Flanger, and Harmonizer

Conclusion

Acoustic piano and electric piano provide the framework for many songs. Often the orchestration can sound full even if you strip away all of the instruments except the piano. It's important that we practice recording these instruments and that we always use processing that enhances the music being made on the instrument. If we go too far out of the boundaries, it can be distracting to the rest of the song; but on that one occasion when it suddenly becomes appropriate to go outside normal limits, you should be prepared to do so.

Practice! Set up normal sounds and abnormal sounds. I'm sure you've noticed that it's often easier to recall the essence of a sound you got two or three months ago than it is to recall the way you set it up, so keep a log of how you set different sounds up—including all settings and a verbal description of the sound.

If you don't have immediate access to a piano, check around with friends, schools, churches, or the local musicians' union hall until you find a good piano to practice on, and then practice recording it. If you're serious about recording, there will be a time when the experience of actually trying these techniques on a real piano will pay off.

We've covered a lot of ground in this book. It's important that you continue to review all of the previous chapters. Experiment with each technique in the situation that it's presented in, and then try each technique in other situations that make musical sense to you.

Special thanks to Robbie Ott for his assistance in performing the grand piano examples in this chapter. Robbie is an excellent musician, songwriter, and vocalist, and he's involved heavily in Christian Music Ministry.

Index

3-1 rule, 105

A

absorption, 2
  absorption coefficients, 16-18
  acoustics, 4, 11
absorption coefficients, 16-18
acoustic bass
  compressors, 181
  equalization, 181
  microphones, 179-181
  overview, 178-180
  rooms, 179-180
acoustic guitars
  amplifiers, 75-77
  arpeggios, 91
  Audio Examples
    compressors, 88
    direct input, 76
    double tracks, 90-91
    equalization, 93-94
    microphones, 76, 78, 81-82
    picks, 73
    reverberation, 94
    rooms, 77, 82
    Studio Traps, 26
    tuning, 74
  compressors, 88-90
  direct input, 75-77
  double tracks, 90-91
  equalization, 92-94
  frequencies, 75-77
  microphones, 75-77
    frequencies, 78-86
    mono, 78-83
    positions, 78-86
    stereo, 83-86
    types, 77-78
  mixing, 75-77
  overview, 71-72
  picks, 73
  reverberation, 94-95
  rooms, 77
  single lines, 92
  solos, 92
  strings, 72-73, 87-88, 95-96
  strum patterns, 91-92
  tone, 74-75
  tuning, 73-74, 87-88
  types, 95-96
  Video Examples
    equalization, 77
    microphones, 78, 82, 86
  vocals, 86-87
  woods, 74-75
acoustics
  absorption, 4, 11
  angles
    concave, 14-15
    convex, 15, 19
    overview, 13-14
  dead acoustics. *See* absorption
  designing, 2-3, 16
    absorption coefficients, 16-18
    bass traps, 20-21
    convex ceilings, 19
    diagrams, 22-24
    diffusion panels, 18
    engineers, 22
    Fletcher-Munson curve, 26
    hearing range, 26
    Live End Dead End, 23-24
    mixing, 26-30
    monitors, 22, 26-30
    planning, 22-24
    positions, 22
    Primacoustic Studio Acoustics, 28
    speakers, 22
    Studio Traps, 25-26
    Studio X, 27
    volume, 26-30
  diffusion, 4, 11, 18
  dimensions, 13